THROUGH THE SOUTH SEAS
WITH JACK LONDON

MARTIN JOHNSON AND A PATHE MOTION-PICTURE OPERATOR ON A HUNT IN THE SOLOMONS

Through the South Seas With Jack London

BY
MARTIN JOHNSON

With an Introduction and a Postscript
BY
RALPH D. HARRISON

Numerous Illustrations

WOLF HOUSE BOOKS
Cedar Springs, Michigan
1972

Copyright, 1913
By DODD, MEAD & COMPANY
Published, November, 1913

DU
22
J6
1972

WOLF HOUSE BOOKS
Box 181
Cedar Springs, Michigan 49319

CONTENTS

		PAGE
INTRODUCTION		ix

CHAPTER

I	ON THE TRAIL OF ADVENTURE	1
II	THE BUILDING OF THE "SNARK"	13
III	ON THE HIGH SEAS	49
IV	A PACIFIC PARADISE	84
V	MOLOKAI, THE LEPER ISLAND	117
VI	THE LONG TRAVERSE	137
VII	IN THE MARQUESAS	158
VIII	THE SOCIETY ISLANDS	180
IX	SOME SOUTH SEA ROYALTY	200
X	THE SAMOAN GROUP	242
XI	LOST IN THE FIJI ISLANDS	260
XII	SOUTH SEA CANNIBALS	268
XIII	OCEANIC CRUISING	309
XIV	THE END OF THE VOYAGE	334
POSTSCRIPT		368

ILLUSTRATIONS

Martin Johnson and a Pathe motion-picture operator on a hunt in the Solomons . . . . . . *Frontispiece*

FACING PAGE

Snark at Honolulu	8
Complement of the *Snark* in Solomon Islands	8
A Solomon Island Army	20
On the Ballassona River, Solomon Group	32
A Te Motu Round House, Santa Cruz Group	44
"War and Peace"— Foate Cannibals in Mission Boat. Artificial Islands off Malaita, Solomon Group	56
War Canoes in Their Shelter	68
Manufactured Islet, with Shrine of a Native Chief — Solomon Group	80
A Man of Roas. Solomon Group, Island of Malaita	92
Chief of Florida Island, Solomon Group	92
Group of Roas Women, Solomon Islands	100
A Mission School, teacher and members of class	112
Molokai, the Leper Settlement, Hawaiian Islands	122
Leper band at Molokai, the leper island of the Hawaiian Group	132
Santa Cruz natives in catamaran canoes	146
Canoe House in Solomon Islands	154
Marquesas Islanders	166
The Old Home of Robert Louis Stevenson, Marquesas Islands	176
The Price of a Wife — feather money	184

Illustrations

	FACING PAGE
A Study in Ornaments	196
Mission Schooner trading among the Islands	210
The Haunt of the Crocodile, Solomon Islands	224
Houses on Outrigger Canoes, Solomon Islands	238
Types of Solomon Islanders	246
At Otivi Village, Santa Cruz Croup	256
The Landing Place at Namu, Santa Cruz Group	264
Mrs. Godden and her School people, New Hebrides Islands	278
Cannibal Village, Foate, Solomon Group	292
Artificial Island, off Malaita, Solomon Group	312
"Penduffryn," the largest cocoanut plantation in the world. Island of Guadalcanar, Solomon Islands	322
Making copra at "Penduffryn," Solomon Islands	330
A Florida canoe — Solomons	342
Trading station, Langakauld-Ugi — Solomons	354

INTRODUCTION

Accounts of dare-devil exploits have always been read with deep interest. One of the salient features of human nature is curiosity, a desire to know what is being said and done outside the narrow limits of one's individual experience, or, in other words, to learn the modes of life of persons whose environment and problems are different from one's own environment and problems. To this natural curiosity, the book of travel is particularly gratifying.

But when we add to the fact that such a narrative treats of races and conditions almost unknown to the inhabitants of civilised countries the consideration that those voyageurs to whom the adventures fell are men and women already prominently before the public, and so deserving of that public's special confidence, the interest and value of such a work will be seen to be extraordinarily enhanced.

The cruise of Jack London's forty-five-foot ketch *Snark* was followed eagerly by the press of several continents. The *Snark* alone was enough to compel attention, but the *Snark* sailed by Jack London, a writer of world-wide celebrity, was irresistible. The venture caught the world's fancy. Periodicals devoted columns to a discussion of the *Snark* and her builder, and to the daring crew who sailed the tiny craft for two years through the South Seas.

When it became known that such a voyage was in contemplation, hundreds of persons wrote to Mr. London, begging that he allow them to accompany him. On the other extreme, they were legion who threw up their hands in horror at the mere suggestion. The belief was widespread, and was, indeed, almost universally expressed, that the famous writer and his fellows were setting out on a cruise from which there would be no return. As an instance of the capriciousness of things maritime and the fallibility of human judgment, it is interesting to reflect that the *Snark*, a ten-ton yacht, the stanchness of which was greatly doubted, travelled her watery miles without mishap, and is still afloat, while the *Titanic*, the most wonderful craft that ever put out to sea, the last word in shipbuilding, declared unsinkable, bore over a thousand of her passengers to death, and lies to-day, a twisted mass of wreckage, irrecoverably lost in the depths of the Atlantic.

Hardships there were a-plenty for the little yacht's crew, of which seasickness was not the least. The *Snark* was not a " painted ship upon a painted ocean." Even a seasoned sailor would find it difficult to accustom himself to the pitch and toss of so small a boat. The effect upon the *Snark's* complement, composed mainly of " landlubbers," may easily be imagined.

Introduction

Mr. Martin Johnson, who started in as cook, soon became the close friend and chief companion of Mr. London. He was thus enabled to make studies of the South Sea natives, many of whom are unquestionably the strangest creatures in existence. His photograhic records — over seven thousand different negatives — are the finest in the world: they are absolutely unique. We have read of some few of the little-known places visited by the voyageurs, in Mr. London's " Cruise of the *Snark*"; but the present work, being much more detailed and complete, gives the first real insight into life aboard the yacht and among the myriad islands of the South Pacific. The illustrations are from photographs made by Mr. Johnson, with a few from prints by Mr. J. W. Beattie, of Tasmania.

After reading such a narrative, we seem to lose our wonder at the voyages of vessels like the *Half Moon*, the *Pinta*, and the *Santa Maria*. Surely the playing of sea-pranks can go no further. The conclusion seems justifiable that if men are to outdo the exploits of the past, they will only succeed by forsaking the water and mastering the air.

RALPH D. HARRISON.

Indianapolis, U. S. A., April 5, 1913.

THROUGH THE SOUTH SEAS
WITH JACK LONDON

CHAPTER I

ON THE TRAIL OF ADVENTURE

THROUGH all my twenty years of life I had been in pursuit of Adventure. But Adventure eluded me. Many and many a time, when I thought that at last the prize was mine, she turned, and by some trickery slipped from my grasp. The twenty years were passed, and still there she was — Adventure! — in the road ahead of me, and I, unwearied by our many skirmishes, still following. The lure was always golden. I could not give it up. Somewhere, sometime, I knew that the advantage would incline my way, and that I should close down my two hands firmly upon her, and hold her fast. Adventure would be mine!

I thought, when I made it across the Atlantic on a cattle-boat, and trod the soil of several alien countries of the Old World, that I had won. But it was not so. It was but the golden reflection of Adventure that I had caught up with, and not the glorious thing itself. She was still there, ahead of me, and I still must needs pursue.

In my native Independence, Kansas, I sat long hours in my father's jewellry store, and dreamed as I worked. I ranged in vision over all the broad spaces of a world-chart. In this dream-realm, there were no impediments to my journeying. Through long ice-reaches, across frozen rivers, over snow-piled mountains, I forced my way to the Poles. I skimmed over boundless tracts of ocean. Giant continents beckoned me from coast to coast. Here was an island, rearing its grassy back out of the great Pacific. My fancy invaded it. Or here was a lofty mountain-chain, over whose snow-capped summits I roamed at pleasure, communing with the sky. Then there were the valley-deeps; dropping down the steep descents on my mount, I explored their sheltered wonders with unceasing delight. Nothing was inaccessible. I walked in lands where queer people, in costumes unfamiliar, lived out their lives in ways which puzzled me, yet fascinated; my way led often amid strange trees and grasses and shrubs — their names unguessable. To the farthest limits of East and West I sallied, and North and South, knew no barriers but the Poles. I breathed strange airs; I engaged in remarkable pursuits; by night, unfamiliar stars and constellations glittered in the sky. It is so easy, travelling — on the map. There are no rigid limitations. Probabilities do not bother. Latitude and longitude are things unnoticed.

But all these dreams were presaging a reality. How it came about I hardly know. I must have tired out that glorious thing, Adventure, with my long pursuit; or else she grew kind to me, and fluttered into my clasp. One evening, during the fall of 1906, while passing away an hour with my favourite magazine, my attention was attracted to an article describing a proposed trip round the world on a little forty-five-foot boat, by Jack London and a party of five. Instantly, I was all aglow with enthusiasm, and before I had finished the article I had mapped out a plan of action. If that boat made a trip such as described, I was going to be on the boat. It is needless to say that the letter I immediately wrote to Mr. Jack London was as strong as I could make it.

I did my best to convince Mr. London that I was the man he needed. I told him all I could do, and some things I couldn't do, laying special stress on the fact that I had at one time made a trip from Chicago to Liverpool, London, and Brussels, returning by way of New York with twenty-five cents of the original five dollars and a half with which I had started. There were other things in that letter, though just what they were I cannot now remember, nor does it matter. My impatience was great as I awaited Mr. London's reply. Yet I dared not believe anything would come of it. That would be impossible. Why, I knew that my letter was one of a host of letters; I knew that among those who had applied must be many who could push far stronger claims than mine; and so, hoping against odds, I looked to the outcome with no particular optimism.

Then, four days later, when hope had about dwindled away, the impossible happened. I was standing in my father's jewellry store after supper on the evening of Monday, November 12, 1906, when a messenger boy came in and handed me a telegram. The instant I saw the little yellow envelope, something told me that this was the turning-point in my life. With trembling hands I tore it open, my heart beating wildly with excitement. It was Jack London's reply, the fateful slip of paper that was to dictate my acts for several years to come.

The telegram was dated from Oakland, California, a few hours earlier in the day. "Can you cook?" it asked. And I had no sooner read it than I had framed the reply. A little later it was burning over the wires in the direction of California. Could I cook? "Sure. Try me," I replied, with the bold audacity of youth — and then settled myself down to another wait.

The interval was brief. I spent it in learning how to cook. One of my local friends gave me temporary employment in his restaurant; and when, on Friday, the 23rd, the first letter came from Jack London, I had already been through the cook-book from cover to cover, learning the secrets of the cuisine: bread-baking and cake-making, the preparing of sauces and puddings and omelets, fruit, game, and fowl — in short, the "chemistry of the kitchen"; and what of my practical experience in the restaurant, I had even served up two or three experimental messes that seemed to me fairly creditable for a beginner.

The letter was long and detailed. It spoke of the

ship, of the crew, of the plans — to use Mr. London's own words, it let me know just what I was in for.

There were to be six aboard, all-told. There were Jack and Mrs. London; Captain Roscoe Eames, who is Mrs. London's uncle; Paul H. Tochigi, a Jap cabinboy; Herbert Stolz, an all-around athlete, fresh from Stanford University; and lastly, there was to be myself, the cook. We were to sail southern seas and northern seas, bays and inland rivers, lakes and creeks — anything navigable. And we were not to stop until we had circled the planet. We were to visit the principal countries of the world, spending from three to six months in every port. It was planned that we should not be home for at least seven years.

"It is the strongest boat ever built in San Francisco," ran the letter. "We could go through a typhoon that would wreck a 15,000-ton steamer. . . . Practically, for every week that we are on the ocean, we will be a month in port. For instance, we expect that it will take us three weeks to sail from here to Hawaii, where we expect to remain three months — of course, in various portions of the Islands.

"Now as to the crew: All of us will be the crew. There is my wife, and myself. We will stand our watches and do our trick at the wheel. . . . When it comes to doing the trick at the wheel, I want to explain that this will not be arduous as it may appear at first. It is our intention, by sail-trimming, to make the boat largely sail herself, without steering. Next, in bad weather, there will be no steering, for then we will be hove-to. But watches, or rather lookouts, must be kept at night, when we are sailing. Suppose we divide day and night into twelve hours each. There are six of us all-told on the boat. Each will take a two-hour turn on deck.

"Of course, when it comes to moments of danger, or to doing something ticklish, or to making port, etc., the whole six of us will then become the crew. I will not be a writer, but a sailor. The same with my wife. The cabin-boy will be a sailor, and so also, the cook. In fact, when it's a case for all hands, all hands it will be.

"From the present outlook, we shall sail out of San Francisco Bay on December 15. So you see, if you accompany us, you will miss your Christmas at home. . . . Incidentally, if you like boxing, I may tell you that all of us box, and we'll have the gloves along. You'll have the advantage of us on reach. Also, I may say that we should all of us have lots of good times together, swimming, fishing, adventuring, doing a thousand-and-one things.

"Now, about clothes. Remember that the boat is small, also that we are going into hot weather and shall be in hot weather all the time. So bring a small outfit, and one for use in warm weather."

Thereafter, my days and nights were more golden than ever with dreams. The days flew by swiftly, but their heels seemed heavy to the anxious wight who spent his hours grubbing in a restaurant. It appeared to me that the time for my departure would never come. I shudder as I think of what weird messes I may have served up to my friend's customers in the moments of my abstraction. Meanwhile, a letter from Mrs. London dropped in, telling me how to get my passport. At last the day came for my going. A letter was pressed into my hands by one of my local friends, who was an Elk, even as I. When I opened it, I found it to be an introduction for me wherever I might find myself. Surely here was goodwill and loyalty of which to be proud; and doubly proud was I when I found that the letter was endorsed by the Grand Exalted Ruler of the Elks. As I was later to find, this little slip of paper would open many a door which otherwise had remained shut to me.

With only a small satchel of clothing and a camera, I boarded a Santa Fé train, said the last good-byes, and sped westward toward California. The dreams did not cease as I passed through the several states that intervened. Whether by day or by night, they persisted. That glorious will-o'-the-wisp, Adventure, was still before me, though now much nearer and more tantalising. But the advantage was mine. Mounted on that monster of steam and iron, the modern train, I felt that Adventure would be hard put for speed in a race with me. And yet, that train seemed to me the slowest thing that ever ran on two rails.

My thoughts kept constantly turning upon the man whom I was journeying to meet. What sort of being was he, that had compelled the attention of the world by the magic of his pen, and by the daring of his exploits? One thing I knew. The places I had roamed in fancy, his foot had trod in reality. And he had sailed over the seas. In '97, he was a gold-seeker in the far North. He had been a sailor and a tramp, an oyster-pirate, a Socialist agitator, and a member of the San Francisco Bay fish-patrol. His voyages up to this time had carried him far over the earth, and his experiences would overlap the experiences of an ordinary man a score of times and more. Above all, he was a student, and a writer of worldwide celebrity. Wherever civilised men congregated, wherever books were read, the name of Jack London was familiar.

Why he was making this trip in so tiny a craft? That question he answered shortly afterward, when he wrote: " Life that lives is life successful, and success is the breath of its nostrils. The achievement of a difficult feat is successful adjustment to a sternly exacting environment. The more difficult the feat, the greater the satisfaction at its accomplishment. That is why I am building the *Snark*. I am so made. The trip around the world means big moments of living. Bear with me a moment and look at it. Here am I, a little animal called a man — a bit of vitalised matter, one hundred and sixty-five pounds of meat and blood,

SNARK AT HONOLULU
COMPLEMENT OF THE SNARK IN SOLOMON ISLANDS:
MRS. JACK LONDON, MR. JACK LONDON AND
MARTIN JOHNSON IN THE CENTRE

nerve, sinew, bones and brain — all of it soft and tender, susceptible to hurt, fallible and frail. I strike a light back-handed blow on the nose of an obstreperous horse, and a bone in my hand is broken. I put my head under the water for five minutes, and I am drowned. I fall twenty feet through the air, and I am smashed. I am a creature of temperature. A few degrees one way, and my fingers and ears and toes blacken and drop off. A few degrees the other way, and my skin blisters and shrivels away from the raw, quivering flesh. A few additional degrees either way, and the light and life in me go out. A drop of poison injected into my body from a snake, and I cease to move — forever I cease to move. A splinter of lead from a rifle enters my head, and I am wrapped around in the eternal blackness.

"Fallible and frail, a bit of pulsating, jelly-like life — it is all I am. About me are the great natural forces — colossal menaces, Titans of destruction, unsentimental monsters that have less concern for me than I have for the grain of sand I crush under my foot. They have no concern for me at all. They do not know me. They are unconscious, unmerciful, and unmoral. They are the cyclones and tornadoes, lightning flashes and cloudbursts, tide-rips and tidal waves, undertows and waterspouts, great whirls and sucks and eddies, earthquakes and volcanoes, surfs that thunder on rock-ribbed coasts, and seas that leap aboard the largest crafts that float, crushing humans to pulp or licking them off into the sea and to death — and these insensate monsters do not know that tiny sensitive creature, all nerves and weaknesses, whom men call Jack London, and who himself thinks he is all right and quite a superior being.

"In the maze and chaos of the conflict of these vast and draughty Titans, it is for me to thread my precarious way. The bit of life that is I will exult over them."

And again:

"Being alive, I want to see, and all the world is a bigger thing to see than one small town or valley. We have done little outlining of the voyage. Only one thing is definite, and that is that our first port of call will be Honolulu. Beyond a few general ideas, we have no thought of our next port after Hawaii. We shall make up our minds as we get nearer. In a general way, we know that we shall wander through the South Seas, take in Samoa, New Zealand, Tasmania, Australia, New Guinea, Borneo, and Sumatra, and go on up through the Philippines to Japan. Then will come Korea, China, India, the Red Sea, and the Mediterranean. After that the voyage becomes too vague to describe, though we know a number of things we shall surely do, and we expect to spend from one to several months in every country in Europe."

The article in the magazine, which had first drawn my attention to the proposed trip, had given me little knowledge of the man with whom in all probability

I was to spend the next seven years of my life. The nearer I came to Oakland, the California city in which the Londons were then living, the more intense grew my curiosity. Worst of all, I was haunted by a fear that if I didn't hustle and get there, Jack London would have changed his mind, and I should be obliged to come back in humiliation to Independence.

It was about nine o'clock in the evening when I arrived in Oakland. As soon as I was off the train, I hunted a telephone and called up Jack London. It was London himself who came to the 'phone. When I told him who I was, I heard a pleasant voice say: " Hello, boy; come right along up," and then followed instructions as to how to find the house.

They lived in a splendid section of the town. I had no difficulty in finding them. When I rapped at the door, a neat little woman opened it, and grabbing my hand, almost wrung it off.

" Come right in," cried Mrs. London. " Jack's waiting for you."

At that moment a striking young man of thirty, with very broad shoulders, a mass of wavy auburn hair, and a general atmosphere of boyishness, appeared at the doorway, and shot a quick, inquisitive look at me from his wide grey eyes. Inside, I could see all manner of oars, odd assortments of clothing, books, papers, charts, guns, cameras, and folding canoes, piled in great stacks upon the floor.

" Hello, Martin," he said, stretching out his hand.

"Hello, Jack," I answered. We gripped.

And that is how I met Jack London, traveller, novelist, and social reformer; and that is how, for the first time, I really ran shoulder to shoulder with Adventure, which I had been pursuing all my days.

CHAPTER II

THE BUILDING OF THE " SNARK "

THE morning after my arrival in Oakland, I met the other members of the *Snark* crew — the *Snarkites,* as Mrs. London called them. Stolz certainly lived up to his description. He was then about twenty-one years of age, and a stronger fellow for his years I have never see anywhere, nor one so possessed of energy. Paul H. Tochigi, the Japanese cabin-boy, was a manly little fellow of twenty, who had only been in America one year. Captain Eames was a fine, kindly old man, the architect and superintendent of construction of the *Snark,* and was booked to be her navigator.

At the time of my coming to California, the *Snark* had already been several months in the building. And her growth promised to be a slow one. Everything went wrong. More than once, Jack shook his head and sighed: " She was born unfortunately."

Planned to cost seven thousand dollars, by the time she was finished she cost thirty thousand. To a ship-wise man, this will seem an impossible amount to spend on so small a craft. But everything was of the highest quality on the *Snark;* labour and materials the very best that money could buy. I really believe she was the strongest boat ever built.

The idea of the trip had first come to Jack and

Captain Eames up at Jack's ranch near Glen Ellen. While in the swimming pool one day, their conversation turned to boats. Jack cited the case of Captain Joshua Slocum, who left Boston one fair day in a little thirty-foot boat, *Spray,* went round the world, by himself, and came back on another fair day, three years later, and made fast to the identical post from which he had cast loose on the day of his start. This led to some speculation; and out of it all, the idea of a forty-foot yacht emerged. Later, of course, the idea took on tangible dimensions, and a few more feet, evolving at last into the *Snark*. At one time, Jack had thought of calling the yacht the *Wolf* — a nickname applied to him by his friends — but afterward found the name *Snark* in one of Lewis Carroll's nonsense books, and forthwith adopted it.

The start had originally been planned for October 1, 1906. But she did not sail on October 1, because she was not yet finished. She was promised on November 1; again she was delayed — because not finished. It was then deemed advisable to postpone sailing until November 15; but when that date rolled around and the *Snark* was still in the process of construction, December 1 was decided on as the auspicious time for a start. And still the *Snark* grew and grew, and was never ready. In his letter to me, Jack had set December 15 as the sailing-date; but on December 15 we did not sail.

During the next three months, I lived at the Lon-

The Building of the "Snark"

don home, and my principal occupation was watching the building of the *Snark* at Anderson's Ways, in San Francisco, right across the bay from Oakland. Anderson's Ways was about one mile from the Union Iron Works, where the big battleships for the American navy are built. There were several reasons for the trouble experienced in getting the *Snark* ready for her long sea-bath. To begin with, San Francisco was just beginning to rise anew from wreck and ashes, and the demand for workmen was urgent. Wages soared skyward; it was almost impossible to hire carpenters, or workmen of any sort. And things that Jack ordinarily could have bought in San Francisco, he was obliged to order from New York. Then, too, so many freight-cars were heading for the ruined city that a terrible tangle resulted, and it was difficult to find the consignments of goods needed for the *Snark*. One freight-car, containing oak ribs for the boat, had arrived the day after the earthquake, but it had taken a full month to find it. Nothing went right. To cap matters, the big strike closed down the shipbuilding plants that furnished us with supplies. The *Snark* seemed indeed born into trouble!

All this time, Jack was toiling continually at his desk, earning money; and all this time Roscoe Eames was spending money freely to make the *Snark* come up to their idea of what a boat should be. Jack was obliged to borrow in the neighbourhood of ten thousand dollars, for the *Snark's* bills came pouring in faster than he could earn money to pay them. He was determined to make of the *Snark* a thing of beauty and strength — something unique in the history of ocean-going vessels.

Some hundreds of persons wrote to Jack, begging him to let them go with him on the cruise. Every mail contained such letters. They continued to pour in almost up to the day we sailed out of the Golden Gate. Most of these letters Jack showed to me. Here was a chef in a big hotel in Philadelphia, a man getting over two hundred dollars a month, who offered his services free. A college professor volunteered to do any kind of work, and give one thousand dollars for the privilege. Another man, the son of a millionaire, offered five hundred dollars to go along. Still another declared that he would put up any amount of money if Jack would allow his son to be one of the crew. And there were offers and solicitations from schoolteachers, draftsmen, authors, photographers, secretaries, stenographers, physicians, surgeons, civil engineers, cooks, typists, dentists, compositors, reporters, adventurers, sailors, valets, " lady companions " for Mrs. London, stewards, machinists, engineers, highschool and university students, electricians — men and women of every imaginable trade, profession or inclination. I began to have misgivings when I thought of the fine chefs who had applied. I contrasted their skilled ability with the little that I had learned from the cook-book! It was just such things as these that

The Building of the "Snark"

made me feel how lucky I was to be a member of the crew of the *Snark*.

There was much protest from the Londons' friends. Many freely expressed the sentiment that they could not see how sensible people would even think of such a trip. And they all knew, with profound certitude, that we were to be drowned. But we paid very little attention to their ominous head-shakings and pessimistic predictions. We who were setting out in search of Adventure were not to be balked by mere words. Also, a number of Jack's Socialist friends wrote letters, urging him to abandon what they evidently considered folly. On every side of us, the conviction was openly aired that we were on our way to the bottom of the sea.

Jack was still spending long hours at his desk. Just then, he was writing his story, " Goliah." One day he read me the first part of it, in which he destroyed the Japanese navy.

" And to-day I destroy the American navy," he told me, gleefully. " Oh, I haven't a bit of conscience when my imagination gets to working."

" Well, I guess you are rather destructive," I ventured, laughing.

" Now I may write a story with you and Bert for heroes," he went on, whimsically; and when I assured him that would be fine —

" But of course I'd have to kill you off at the end; and how would you like that? "

January 12 was Jack's thirty-first birthday. It was also one of our numerous sailing dates, but despite the best of intentions, we were obliged to celebrate it on land. During my long stay in Oakland, I had ample opportunity to get intimately acquainted with both Jack and Mrs. London; indeed, we were all like one big happy family. Fame and popularity have not spoiled them. Jack is just like a big schoolboy, good-natured, frank, generous, and Mrs. London is just a grown-up schoolgirl. They are good comrades, always helping each other in their work. Mrs. London I found to be as full of grit as any of us — as we were later to discover, there was hardly a thing on board that any of the men could do that she couldn't do; and she was a practised swimmer, and could ride on horseback with grace — a gift not vouchsafed all women. And they were both amiable Bohemians. Often, when Jack was not busy, he and I compared notes on England. We found that we had snooped around much the same places in the East End of London. Immediately, I took up his "People of the Abyss," which read almost like a passage out of my own life. For seven days, I had been one of those wretched people who are forever on the move in the slums of this great city, eternally searching for a scrap of food and for sufficient ground-space on which to lay down their weary frames in sleep. All was vividly described in the book. But while the men and women of the abyss spend their whole lives in this torment, I was there only until I could get to Liverpool and take a cattle-boat back to the States.

Once, after reading "The Sea Wolf," I told Jack that I had always been under the impression that the Scandinavians were of a peaceable disposition. But he assured me that most of the events of "The Sea Wolf" were from his own experiences — Wolf Larsen drawn largely from life. He told me that while up North, he had run across some of the most bloodthirsty people he had ever seen, and they were Scandinavians.

Also, I got better acquainted with Tochigi and Bert and Captain Eames. The captain was a stately old man, grey of hair and grey of beard; and what he didn't know about yachts was really hardly worth knowing. In fact, the *Snark* was built according to his plans. Captain Eames' room was next to the galley, a place that would be almost unbearably hot in the tropics; but of course, we planned to sleep on deck, once we got into the real South Seas.

Tochigi taught me a smattering of Japanese during the wait. True, I never mastered the language, but I did become proficient enough to distinguish some of the words he used when in conversation with his Jap friends. Tochigi was a fine fellow, his manners were the most perfect I have ever seen, and he was clever and quick to learn. His English was limited, but every word he did use was the right one. And he always talked in such a low, well-modulated voice that it was a pleasure to listen to him. We took a great liking to each other.

Stolz was away quite a bit. Jack explained to me that he was working his way through Stanford University. If sheer strength counts for anything, Stolz is a fellow who will never want for much. He was always the best swimmer at the swimming pools we went to; he could always dive from higher and turn more somersaults in the air than anyone; and Jack found, by experience, that Bert knew every trick in boxing. He was really more than I expected by Jack's description of him — an "all-around athlete."

Hardly a day went by without someone's rapping at the door and asking if the *Snark's* complement was secured, and if there was not room for just one more. Over at the boat, I was constantly beset by cranks, with all sorts of schemes and ideas and inventions; and there were other people who came simply out of curiosity, wanting to be shown over the boat. Some of their contrivances were very ingenious. There were "old schoolmates of Mr. London," and "girlhood chums of Mrs. London," and there were "distant relatives of the Londons"; some even claimed to be special correspondents of magazines or newspapers. But no one got aboard the *Snark* unless he had written permission from Jack. Interest was widespread; and shortly after, Jack increased it by delivering a lecture on Socialism to over fifteen thousand people in Berkeley.

A SOLOMON ISLAND ARMY

The Building of the "Snark"

Since the destruction of San Francisco, Chinatown had moved to Oakland. On several occasions we went to its theatres, and to the Chinese social gatherings. Early in January the Chinese celebrate their New Year. It was my good luck to see such a celebration. On every side of me, Chinks of every age, men, women and children, shot off fire-crackers, and flung up packs of multi-coloured papers, perforated quite thickly with various-shaped holes. It is their belief that the devil has to come through all these holes before he can get to sinners; and to stave off the enemy and render his progress tortuous, they make the holes small and numerous. Again, I visited secret opium dens, and saw pasty-coloured Chinks lie for hours under the influence of the drug. Much of the deviltry of Chinatown, however, had come to an end with the destruction of San Francisco, as many of the yellow rascals saw in that wholesale catastrophe the workings of an outraged deity.

As for Frisco itself, it looked hopeless. Hundreds of tons of the wreckage had been cleared away, but hundreds of tons still remained. Some few buildings had already been erected. Most of them were stores, little wooden affairs, knocked together until better could be built. The fire and quake had ruined the pavements, and the streets were nothing but great pools of water and mud. A man was actually drowned in one of these pools while walking down Market street. There were constant deaths by accidents;

walls, frail and fissured, had a trick of collapsing and letting down their bushels of brick and stone on the heads of such as were in the streets; the street-car service was badly muddled, and several persons were killed while riding the precarious conveyances. As I have said, wages were sky-high; yet workmen still complained and struck for more. At the time I was there, the bricklayers, who were getting ten dollars a day, struck for twelve dollars and a half. Each of the ten men working on the *Snark* received five dollars a day, and only worked until half-past four in the afternoon.

Having been practically raised in a jewellry store, I was pretty efficient at engraving, and I employed my talent in adding to the decorations of the *Snark*. Just over the companionway was a big piece of finest brass. On it I drew the word " SNARK " in Old English charactery, and the carpenters filled it in with brass-headed nails. Mrs. London was so pleased that she later had me engrave the capstan-head. After that, Captain Eames and I oversaw the painters while they spread a preliminary coat of white paint over the *Snark's* hull and picked out the name " SNARK " in gold.

On rainy days, I stayed at the London home, reading books and magazines. The manuscript of " The Iron Heel," Jack's Socialistic novel, had not yet been sent to the publishers, and I spent some exciting hours poring over it. Jack had evidently let his imagina-

The Building of the "Snark"

tion have full rein in this story, for he had gone far beyond the destruction of a mere navy, as in " Goliah," and had put an end to the entire city of Chicago, and allotted to her inhabitants the most gory deaths imaginable. But the story was one of the most impressive I have ever read; and like Jack's Socialistic speech before the students of a great Eastern university, it later created a sensation.

And still we planned to go, and yet did not go. We set sailing-dates and cancelled them. The time was not yet. Puzzled by the delay, editors and publishers with whom Jack had contracts began to write him for explanations, but Jack could only shake his head and wonder how he was to explain to them when he couldn't even explain to himself. When questioned, Captain Eames would do his best to cheer Jack up by solemnly engaging to have the *Snark* ready for sailing within two weeks from the date of promising, but always the time had to be extended.

The *Snark* was a trim little yacht, forty-five feet on the water-line, fifty-five over all, with a width of fourteen feet eight inches. Her draft was seven feet eight inches. She was of ketch-rig, which means that she was a two-master, with the largest sail on the forward mast — just the reverse of a schooner-rig. Jack had seen boats of a similar design extensively used in the Northern Seas and also on the Dogger Bank in England; as he explained, the ketch-rig was a compromise between the yawl and the schooner, which, while retaining the cruising virtues of the one, embraced some of the sailing virtues of the other.

Never was there another such boat! Despite the delays and the other troubles, not one of the *Snarkites* had lost his enthusiasm. Even with all their vexations and the ruinous expense, Mrs. London and Jack were always smiling and happy. Often the crew would go over the Bay and gather on the *Snark's* deck to discuss possible improvements and to anticipate some of the delights of the voyage that lay ahead of us.

And still the *Snark* was in the building. Her lines were marvels of strength and beauty. As an indication of the way she was built, I need only enumerate a few particulars as to specifications of material. Her iron keel weighed five tons. Her greatest beam was fifteen feet, with tumble-home sides. Her planking was specially ordered Oregon Pine, without butts; men were actually sent to search the Oregon pines to select natural elbows — in other words, timbers grown by nature in the exact form required to fit the angles of the boat, and thus give the maximum strength of each fibre of the wood. The planking was two and one-half inches thick under the water-line, two inches thick above the water-line. The ribs were of specially ordered Indiana Oak, and were set ten inches apart. Angle irons, the full length of the boat, connected the ribs with the keel; these were of the best galvanised iron, each made according to pattern. The *Snark's*

The Building of the "Snark" 25

copper was the finest man-o'-war copper; its cost was over five hundred dollars, to say nothing of the cost of having it put on. For that matter, the boat was copper-fastened throughout; not a nail or screw that was not copper. The only iron used in the *Snark* was the best galvanised iron; all other metal was brass and bronze. She was crown-decked and flush-decked, and had six feet of head-room below. Three watertight bulkheads divided her length into four watertight compartments.

"If we stove in one compartment," Jack explained to me, "we can still bear up with the other three compartments. I just think we'll fool some of the birds of ill omen, after all. The *Snark* is dependable. She's built to sail all seas, face all storms, and to go around the world."

The *Snark* was intended from the first to be a sailing vessel. But because it was felt that cases of sudden emergency might arise, where speed was an absolute necessity, a gasolene engine, seventy-horsepower, was installed. Had Jack adhered to his original idea of a forty-foot boat, there would have been no room for such an appurtenance; but forty-five feet gave plenty of space for both it and a small bath-room. This latter was carefully fitted up with levers and pumps and sea-valves, some of them of Jack's own invention. After the engine, a dynamo was put in; and then Jack decided to light the boat with electricity, and to have a searchlight which would give sharp detail at a half-mile distance. But we did not trust entirely to electrical apparatus for illumination, for if it should break down, it might cost us our lives. For the binnacle light, the anchor light, and the sidelights, which were indispensable, we supplied kerosene lamps. Nor was the use of the engine yet exhausted. We finally planned a giant windlass to be placed on deck, by means of which the anchor could be hoisted without trouble.

The *Snark* had neither house nor hold. The deck was unbroken except for the hatchway forward, and two companionways. The cockpit, large and high-railed, so built as to be self-bailing, made a comfortable place in which to sit, whether in fair weather or foul. The rail, companionways, hatches, skylights, and other finishings were of finest teak; the deck-knees, deck-timbers, etc., of the best oak. There were two bronze propellers; a patent steering-gear; one hundred and five fathoms of extra heavy best galvanised chain; two patent galvanised anchors, and one galvanised kedge-anchor. The *Snark* carried flying-jib, jib, fore-staysail, mainsail, mizzen and spinnaker, also extra storm-jibs, and gaff-headed trysails. Her garboard strake was three inches thick. In the last compartment, in the stern of the boat, were tanks for over a thousand gallons of gasolene. Because of the tightness of the bulkhead which marked off this compartment, we felt reasonably certain that none of this very dangerous fluid could escape; and to reassure us

The Building of the "Snark"

doubly, we were informed that the tanks themselves were non-leakable.

After a time, we added more accessories to the *Snark*. Jack ordered a five-horse-power engine, for running pumps and dynamo; accumulators, electric light globes, and electric fans. Then came the consideration of navigation instruments. These consisted of a Steering Compass, a best Standard Compass, a best Sextant, a best Octant, a best Pelorus, a best Barometer, a best ship's clock; and their cost was five hundred dollars. At the last, Jack added to our equipment what no prudent man would go to sea without — life-boats. These were a fourteen-foot very seaworthy launch, with gasolene engine, and an eighteen-foot life-boat, with air-tanks and other appliances.

During all my stay in Oakland, I enjoyed myself immensely. Jack was continually inviting me out to theatres, prize-fights, and social gatherings. One of the most amusing fights I ever saw took place in Oakland, when a Chinaman and a negro entered the ropes and began to bang and biff each other. The difference in make-up between the two types was considerable, and their methods of fighting were entirely dissimilar. All rules of the game seemed suspended. It was give and take, give and take; but the Chink was getting the worst of it. Both the combatants indulged in lip-fighting, the Chinaman execrating his dusky opponent in strange pigeon-English, and the negro responding with deep, throaty epithets well calculated to stir the ire of even an equable celestial. The fight went some rounds, with the Chink getting the worst of it all the time. But in the end he amazed us. Venting a perfect torrent of abuse upon the negro, he managed to deliver almost simultaneously a blow that must have echoed inside the coon's thick head, and a sweeping punch in the abdomen. Both these little reminders did the work. The negro doubled up and fell senseless to the floor, and when the referee called ten he was still lying there; and the Chinaman, with chest thrown out and head erect, was strutting about the ropes exulting over the conquest. I never could un-understand it — it was such a big negro, and he went down like a stick of wood!

Often, on bright days, I would take one of my cameras — I now had four — and go over to San Francisco to photograph streets where new buildings were going up. Then there was the Bay — it furnished endless material for good photographic studies, as all manner of queer crafts were forever coming and going. And then, the *Snarkites* would take pictures of one another, and of the boat. Jack used to have fun telling me that when we got to the cannibal islands, I could take my camera and go ashore to get pictures, and that would be Exhibit A; then, if some of the omnivorous natives came and made a meal of me, he would take pictures of the feast — and that would be Exhibit B.

But not all my time was devoted to recreation.

That cooking proposition was lying heavy on my mind. I couldn't forget all those fine chefs who had applied. Going over to Frisco on the ferry, I buried my nose assiduously in the cook-book again, searching for details which might have escaped my previous study, and doing my best to memorise every recipe in the book. It was now the rainy season, and of evenings Jack and Mrs. London and I would play cards. Sometimes George Sterling, the poet, who lived at Carmel-by-the-Sea, and who was a frequent caller at the London home, would join us. Oftentimes, Jack and I would wrangle and argue as to which of us was the better player at hearts; but the truth of the matter was that he and I always won and lost about the same number of games. But though Jack and I had these disputes, there was never any doubt as to where poor Mrs. London stood. When it came to playing hearts, she had undisputed title to being the most unfortunate. A good deal of her time, however, was spent at the typewriter; she has typed all of Jack's manuscripts since their marriage; and just now, both were toiling double tides, that they might have a little work on hand. They knew that once on the ocean, they would have a spell of seasickness during which they could not even think of writing or typing.

The Oakland Elks also helped to make my stay in their city pleasant. Before I left, they gave me a letter to put with the one the Independence Elks had given me, so that now I felt doubly armed with credentials. Old Mammy Jenny, Jack's negro nurse, gave me much valuable instruction in cooking, telling me things that no cook-book in the world could have told me. Jack had predicted a diet largely of fish, when once we should be on the ocean. Mammy Jenny told me all she knew about fish. I was considerably relieved, too, when I discovered that most of our provisions would be tinned, and would need little more than warming up to make them suitable for the table. I found great consolation in this thought. It thinned the clouds for me. I took new lease on life.

The weeks were passing, and still the *Snark* was in the building! Jack began to grow impatient. Roscoe Eames made promises. The old captain meant well, but alas! his good intentions were just like all the other good intentions. He tried his best to hurry things along, but nothing could be induced to turn out right. Besides, even good intentions won't build a boat. There were times when Jack vowed he'd sail the shell of her to Honolulu, and finish building her there. Soon Jack's friends began to make bets, some even wagering that the *Snark* would never sail at all. Every time he set a sailing-date, they would bet against it. Everybody was betting. And everybody had quit the head-shaking and the making of evil predictions. We were not going to the bottom of the sea now, because we would never be on the sea. Even the newspapers began a gentle ridicule,

The Building of the "Snark"

giving wide publicity to a poem written by Kelly, the Sailor-Poet, in which the *Snark* was described as setting out on her long voyage — not yet, but soon — and meeting with all sorts of strange adventures on the deep — not yet, but soon; and it recounted somewhat of the things that befell the voyageurs in the various countries they landed at — not yet, but soon. And more letters came from editors and publishers, demanding explanations. A big New York magazine, for which Jack had contracted to write thirty-five thousand words descriptive of the trip, flamboyantly announced that it was sending Jack London, the well-known writer, round the world, especially for itself. This article was so worded that a reader would suppose the magazine was paying for everything, even for the building of the *Snark*. Immediately, everyone who had dealings with Jack began to charge him outrageously, explaining that the magazine had plenty of money and that it might as well pay for its fun. Naturally, after putting a small fortune into the boat, and being at almost incredible trouble to plan and outfit her, Jack was incensed. Such an article gave to the whole thing the colour of being a cheap advertising scheme. Even now, most people believe that the magazine paid for everything, and that Jack received liberal prices for the things he wrote. But such was not the case. Jack built the boat and paid for her; the plan was all his own, and the magazine mentioned had nothing to do with it. For that matter, Jack saw to it that they got no more articles from him descriptive of the cruise of the *Snark*. He played the free-lance, sending his " copy " wherever he chose.

At the beginning of March, 1907, things looked more desperate than ever. Jack declared it was plain the boat could never be completed in San Francisco. " She's breaking down faster than she can be repaired," he said one day. " That's what comes of taking a year for building. I'll sail her as she is, and finish her up in Honolulu. If we don't go now, we'll never go."

But immediately the *Snark* sprang a leak, and had to be repaired before she could be moved from Anderson's Ways. This was finally accomplished, and Jack ordered the boat brought across the Bay to Oakland. On a bright Saturday morning in the middle of March, Captain Eames and Bert and I went over to Anderson's Ways, and got aboard. At nine o'clock Captain Eames yelled, " Let her go! " and the *Snark* slid off her ways as easily as could be desired, and took to the Bay with the grace of a wild water-fowl. There was not so much as a tremble. We created a great excitement as we were towing across the Bay to what is known as the Oakland estuary. All the larger vessels dipped their flags, and the smaller ones saluted by giving three toots of the whistle. We lay anchored in the estuary three weeks, while electricians did the wiring and a crew of riggers and a crew of ship's carpenters worked on the deck and the rigging. Dur-

On the Ballassona River, Solomon Group. No white man has ever been to the head waters of this river

The Building of the "Snark"

ing this time, Bert and I took turns living on board, he sleeping aboard one night and I the next. Meanwhile, Tochigi made himself useful at the London home, and Mr. and Mrs. London continued to turn out reading matter. Jack was writing his famous tramp-stories, the ones now republished in the volume called " The Road." Often, I sat on one side of the table at his house, writing a letter, and he sat on the other side, writing his stories. And as he finished them, he read them to us; and one and all voted him thanks for the entertainment.

I shall never forget the day when the sails were unfurled for the first time. For remember, up to this time I had never seen a real, sea-going ship under sail, and the whole thing was mysterious to me. I did not even know one sail from another, but I was so proud of the little *Snark* that I got in the dingy and made photographs of her from every conceivable position, not caring if the canvas did hang loose and wrinkled enough to make a sailor's heart sore. A few days before the decks were finished, we drew up alongside the wharf, and filled the gasolene tanks. Next day, all hands were down early for the first trial trip. The *Snark's* crew was aboard, and also little Johnny London, Jack's nephew. On the trial trip we went twelve miles out, and met as heavy a sea as will be encountered on an ocean voyage, owing to a heavy ground-swell coming into the Golden Gate. And we were seasick — oh! we were seasick! Everyone aboard was seasick except little Johnny London, and he was not supposed to be a sailor at all.

But Mr. and Mrs. London declared they were not seasick, not the least bit sick. They were just rolled up on the deck enjoying themselves! And poor little Tochigi said nothing, because he had nothing to say. He did his best to smile, but force as he would, the smile wouldn't come. I asked Jack for the honour of bringing the *Snark* into the Golden Gate, and he granted the request, but I noticed that he sat close by and kept watch on me to see that I didn't run into the Cliff House. As we came back to the starting-point, we saw, in the mouth of the Oakland River, a mass of freakish yellow, green and other coloured lights, something on the order of Japanese lanterns hung out on the lawn during a summer church-festival. We made port that night, satisfied that we had seen something, we knew not what. Next day, we found that the Chinese battleship, the *Whang-Ho,* had anchored in the harbour, and I went with Jack and Mrs. London on board this most interesting craft. The *Whang-Ho* was over two hundred years old, and carried wooden cannons and torture implements of various kinds, that had been used on captives of war in the centuries gone by — such as a bird-cage and a back tickler.

During the short time that elapsed between the trial trip and the real voyage, many interesting things occurred. When it was my turn to sleep aboard, I would sit for hours on the *Snark's* deck, looking out over the

The Building of the "Snark" 35

Bay; when tired of that, I would go below, and lying in my bunk, with a good-sized light over my head, would write letters home, or read and smoke. It seemed strange to feel the *Snark* tumbling and rolling with the wash of the sea. Sometimes it seemed as if she were tugging at her moorings, longing to be off on the long, long cruise. Because of her smallness, she responded to the heave and lunge of the ocean much more freely than would the ordinary ship. Even a tug-boat, passing many feet away, would jostle the *Snark* with its wash. Lying in my bunk, I could look up through a skylight and see the masts, and, higher yet, the scintillating stars. At last, after all my hopes and fears, after all the vexatious troubles and delays, the dream was coming true! The time was near at hand, when we should really shake the dust of California from our feet, and ride the little *Snark* round and about the earth!

And then, crash! bump! bump! the dream was rudely shattered. The noise was on every side of me. Two large lumber-scows had dragged their anchors and laid up against the sides of the *Snark,* nearly making a sandwich of our little boat. Nothing could be done. They bumped away at the *Snark* all night long, and when morning came the rail was flattened two inches on one side and bulged out rather more than two inches on the other side; and wherever she is, the *Snark* is lop-sided to this day.

On another night, when I was alone on board, I

went to my bunk early and fell asleep. About three in the morning I was awakened by the sound of the anchor-chain paying out of the hawsepipes, and I rushed up on deck to see what was happening. A terrible storm was raging, and the boat was just like a cork, bobbing and rolling on the waves. I made fast the chains and went back to bed. At four-thirty I again started up from my bunk. Something told me that all was not well with the *Snark*. When I went on deck, I found the boat was within a hundred yards of a pile wharf, heading straight for it, and travelling fast. I knew the anchor had slipped, and if the boat got on the piles it would be good-bye to our cruise. It was blowing a gale, and the rain was coming down in sheets. I lowered the kedge-anchor and stopped the boat for the time being, but knew she would not hold long. I ran below to start the engine, but could not do so because one of the machinists had taken it apart in one place to clean it, and so put it out of commission. I worked for half an hour, with desperate haste, to put the engine into running order; then started her, and went on deck. The kedge-anchor was now slipping, and again we started for the piles. Running to the cockpit, I turned on the propeller, and away went the boat out into the Bay, with the anchors dragging. When I stopped her, she started drifting back; and so I had it, back and forth, toward the piles and then out into the Bay, all the rest of the night, until eight o'clock brought the workmen in a rowboat.

The Building of the "Snark"

The fight for life had continued nearly four terrible hours, but it had been worth it. About twenty-five vessels, many of them larger than the *Snark*, had been wrecked in that storm. Mr. London's remarks to me that morning were quite gratifying, and I felt I had made up for my mistake in letting the lumber-scows bump the *Snark* lop-sided.

There were always so many water-thieves around the Bay that it was necessary to keep a sharp lookout. One night when I was in my bunk I heard a noise, and crept up in my stocking feet to the deck, armed with a big 38-calibre revolver. But I could find no cause for alarm. The night was dark. Far over the Bay was San Francisco, from which the busy ferry-boats were plying, back and forth; and every few minutes, a revolving light from a lighthouse stationed on a nearby rock flooded the deck, making everything bright as day. As a rule, there were a number of large vessels, from various ports, within a short distance of the *Snark*, and I could see their lights, and hear their sailors singing as they worked. During the day, I would go aboard these ships and engage the sailors in conversation, as I was always desirous of hearing something about the places which later I would see.

The galley was now very nearly finished, and many hours I spent in it practising cooking. I made bread and cakes and pies, and fed them to the workmen. These products were of varying degrees of excellence, but the workmen seemed to be able to get away with them, and so I baked all they could eat. I don't believe the men's digestions were very seriously deranged, either. Jack bought a bread-mixing machine a few days later, and then I was able to do in about thirty minutes what before I could only do in several hours. Before the buying was finished, there were few luxuries or facilities we did not have aboard the *Snark*.

Once when I was in the galley, the boat was invaded by the Famous Fraternity. The Famous Fraternity was a group of celebrated authors and artists, all hailing from California and most of them resident there. Among those who came were George Sterling, the man whom the Londons had pronounced one of the greatest of living poets, Martinez, the artist, Dick Partington, another artist, Johannes Reimers, writer, and Jimmie Hopper, famous first as a football hero and then as a writer of short stories, and others, whose names I have now forgotten. I did my very best to prepare them a good dinner; and if their expressions of satisfaction were any indication, I succeeded. I served up a whole gunny-sack full of steamed mussels, and some of my bread, which one and all declared the finest they had ever tasted. They almost beat the workmen eating. I began to think more than ever of my prowess as a cook. In such a glow of pride as possessed me, my misgivings disappeared utterly.

Now let me skim lightly over the troubles that followed up to the very day of our sailing. I don't want this narrative to shape itself as a mere record of mishaps and vexations, for such a record would not reflect things truly. Taken all in all, our troubles were as nothing at all to our delights. But truth compels me to say that in the month preceding our departure, things that before had gone casually and desultorily wrong seemed to take on fresh energy in ill-doing, and to go systematically and diabolically wrong. Had a malevolent intelligence been directing events, they could not have been more discomfiting to the impatient crew of the *Snark*. When the boat was nearly ready for our sailing, she was placed upon the ways for a final overhauling. The ways spread, and the *Snark* fell stern-first into the mud. In the crash, the bed-plate of the big engine splintered, and the engine, in falling, smashed some of its connections. When the windlass was tried out, its gears ground each other flat, and the castings which connected it with the engine broke into fragments. It took two steam-tugs a week, pulling on the *Snark* every high tide night and day, to get her out of the mud and into the water alongside the Oakland City Wharf. We gave up all hope of both engine and windlass until we should have reached Honolulu; and we packed away the broken parts as best we could, and lashed the engine tight to its foundations.

April 18 was now set for the sailing. We began provisioning and buying all kinds of photographic supplies, done up in tropical form — that is, with the film wrapped in tin-foil and sealed in tins, and the paper triple-wrapped and protected with foil. There were a thousand and one things bought toward the last, which it is needless to enumerate here. We bought clothing, and we bought fishing tackle, and harpoons, and guns, and pistols, and we bought paper, paper for Jack's writing, and paper for the typewriter, hundreds of reams of it. I spent a whole day packing this paper behind sliding panels in the two staterooms forward, which were set aside for Jack and Mrs. London. We spent money like water; it took dray after dray to bring down to the wharf the things we purchased. Then there were dray-loads of the things brought from the London home, wood and coal, provisions, vegetables, blankets, other things, and still other things, and above all, books — five hundred of them, on every conceivable topic, selected from Jack's library of ten thousand volumes. The *Snark* was fairly ballasted with books. Mrs. London busied herself in directing the work, and showed a knowledge of stevedoring that astonished us. At last, after hours of toil and sweat, everything was safely aboard. But so much still had to be done that we decided to put off leaving until Sunday, April 21.

And then came one of the worst blows of all. It was Saturday afternoon, and Jack and Bert and I were on the *Snark,* packing things away. All about us, on the wharf, were reporters and photographers and sightseers. Jack had brought his checque-book and several thousand dollars in paper money and gold, and was wishing Roscoe would hurry and come with the accounts of the various firms to which he was indebted, that he might make payment. Without any warning whatever, a United States marshal stepped aboard and pasted a little five-by-seven slip of paper to one of the masts. It was an attachment, issued from the office of the Marshal of the United States, of the Northern District of California, and stated that any person who removed or attempted to move the schooner-yacht, *Snark,* without the written permission of the marshal, would be prosecuted to the full extent of the law.

We were all astounded. What could it mean? Jack hastened over to San Francisco to investigate. We had planned to sail at eleven o'clock on the morrow, so haste was imperative. After several hours Jack came back, accompanied by Mrs. London, and told us what had happened.

It seemed that a man named L. H. Sellers, of San Francisco, who was a ship-chandler, had placed the attachment on the *Snark.* Jack owed him something like two hundred and fifty dollars, and Sellers' account was one of those Jack had intended to close that very day.

"It is just a petty trick of a tradesman in a panic," Jack declared, as he gazed at the writ of attachment pasted on the mast of the *Snark.* "But it will not delay me one minute in getting away on the trip I have planned. If the bill were one thousand dollars, I would pay it and feel the same way about it. I have done several thousands of dollars' worth of business with this L. H. Sellers, and with other firms, and this is the first time I have ever been attached. I do not dispute the bill of Sellers. I owe the claim, and intended to pay it. I never received a bill for the amount of the attachment, and suppose that when L. H. Sellers learned that I was about to sail, he became panic-stricken at the thought of not receiving what was due him. I have been endeavouring to communicate with some officer of the United States district court and settle the matter as soon as possible."

But the matter was not so easily to be settled. Someone had spread the word around that Jack London and his crew were preparing to sneak out of the Bay that night, leaving the statute of limitations to cancel all debts. Representatives of three other big firms, with claims aggregating nearly three thousand dollars, descended upon the *Snark,* and Jack promptly paid them. After that came a drove of smaller tradesmen — "All in a panic," Jack said — and each and every one received his money without delay.

Jack sent agents and lawyers all over San Francisco and Oakland, but the United States marshal could not be found. Then a search was made for the United States judge, but he, too, had disappeared; and after all hope was given up of discovering them, Jack set out

The Building of the "Snark"

to find Mr. L. H. Sellers, but Mr. L. H. Sellers was nowhere to be found, nor Mr. Sellers' attorney. It was plain that the embargo could not be lifted that night.

A little old man, a deputy United States marshal, had been left in charge; and never did miser guard his treasure as that little old man guarded the *Snark*. He stayed on her constantly, to see that Jack London did not whisk her out of the Bay and start on the trip. Of course, we did not sail Sunday, April 21, as planned. The little old man would not allow it. The funny part of it was that Jack was obliged to pay this deputy marshal three dollars a day for his zealous custodianship of the *Snark*. But the old man earned it. He stuck to the boat like glue, even going without meals that the vigil might not be interrupted.

Saturday night all the *Snarkites* walked out on an opposite pier to take a look at the *Snark* and to make plans. Jack and Mrs. London were still smiling. It seemed impossible to dash their spirits.

From where we stood, the *Snark* showed up bravely. She was a little floating palace. Jack could not refrain from bragging to Mrs. London about her bow.

"Isn't it a beauty?" he asked again and again. "That bow was made to punch storms with! It laughs at the sea! Not a drop can come over her! We'll be as dry and comfortable as any craft afloat, with such a bow as that!" And Mrs. London would laugh her assent, and find new virtues in the boat and in that bow.

"Well," I said at last. "We'll get away Tuesday, anyway."

"Yes, we'll get away Tuesday. Think of that!" Mrs. London cried in response. "It will be worth all the trouble, and all the expense. Once we're out on the ocean, we'll forget all our little worries, the accidents, and the Sellerses, and all the rest. Glorious? Glorious doesn't express it."

"And think of what we can do when we get the engine to running again," Jack went on. "Think of the inland work. With such an engine, there isn't a river in the world with current stiff enough to baffle us. We can see so much more by inland voyaging than we could by merely hanging around ports. Think of the people, and the natural scenery! The things we won't know about the various countries through which we pass won't be worth knowing."

"That reminds me," I broke in. "What do you think you'll write about?"

He smiled.

"Well, if we're boarded by pirates and fight it out until our deck becomes a shambles, I don't think I'll write about it. And if we're wrecked at sea, and are driven by starvation into eating one another, I'll keep it quiet for the sake of our relatives. And if we're killed and eaten by cannibals, of course I shan't let the American public get an inkling of it."

A TE MOTU ROUND HOUSE. SANTA CRUZ GROUP

"You won't starve," I assured him. "Think of all the food we have aboard — over three months' supply. And think of your cook! No, you will never starve aboard the *Snark*."

"The thing that's worrying me," Bert here broke in, "is how we're going to find room to get around on the boat. Since that windlass was set up, and the launch and life-boat lashed on deck, there is hardly room to turn around in." And Tochigi, who was always very quiet, said nothing at all.

For days, Jack and Captain Eames had been engaged in one of the most laughable arguments I have ever heard. Roscoe Eames stoutly maintained that the earth is concave of surface, and that we would all sail round on the inside of a hollow sphere; while Jack, who was willing to stick to orthodox cosmology, just as stoutly maintained that Roscoe was mistaken, and that we would sail round on the outside. Each had a number of proofs, which he adduced in the argument; and neither was to be shaken in his confidence. To this day, I think they hold divergent opinions on the subject. Captain Eames was also a vegetarian; and it was this fact that made me wonder how he was to get along satisfactorily on the *Snark*.

Though Jack had answered my question jestingly, I knew that he contemplated writing an extended series of articles on the home-life of the various peoples among whom we were to sojourn. He would treat of their domestic problems; social structures; problems of living; cost of living as compared with the cost in the United States; education; opportunities for advancement; general tone of peoples; culture; morals; religion; how they amuse themselves; marriage and divorce problems; housekeeping, and a hundred other topics.

When we left the wharf that night, we felt more cheerful than ever. Mrs. London was right. That boat was well worth all the trouble and expense. " Barring wreck and worms," said Jack, " she'll be sailing the seas a hundred years from now."

All day Monday we worked on the *Snark*, besieged constantly by reporters and photographers. Jack paid Mr. L. H. Sellers his two hundred and fifty dollars, and lifted the embargo. In the afternoon we were towed out in the Bay, and an expert adjusted our compasses and other instruments for us. It was essential that these be in proper trim, the more so as not one of us knew anything about navigation except Captain Eames, and even his knowledge was of the experimental sort. Jack declared that the rest of us could learn after we were afloat. Thousands of people visited the wharf that day to take a look at us; and the photographers were busy taking snap-shots of the boat. Out in the Bay, we had with us a reporter for the Hearst papers. When he left, he took with him my last message ashore, a telegram to be sent to Independence announcing the imminence of our

The Building of the "Snark"

departure. We worked all that night, stowing and packing, and getting things shipshape for our cruise to Hawaii. At high tide the next morning we were to up-anchor and away.

Daylight broke at last. That 23rd of April, 1907, I shall never forget. Thousands came down to the wharf to bid us good-bye and to wish us a pleasant and successful voyage. Photographers from a popular western magazine took what they announced would be the last views of the *Snark* and her crew. Among the dozens of telegrams I received was one from an Independence friend, which read: "Good-bye. Hope I may see you again." Surrounded by hundreds of people who were prophesying that we would never reach Honolulu, this telegram had a rather gruesome sound to me. Strangely enough, I never did see this friend again. I did not meet my death in the water, but he did. He drowned in one of the rivers near Independence.

Among those who came down to say the farewells were many members of the Bohemian Club of San Francisco, to which Jack belonged. There were writers and artists and newspaper men. George Sterling and James Hopper were on hand, as was also Martinez, the artist. Mrs. London's friends came in a body. Then there were Oakland Elks, and San Francisco Elks, and friends of Tochigi, and Bert's friends, and all the friends of the Eames', and others who came merely out of curiosity to see the world-famous author and his crew sail off in one of the most unique little boats that ever rode the waves.

It was a beautiful, bright, sunshiny day when we passed out of the Golden Gate, with hundreds of whistles tooting us a farewell salute, passed the Seal Rocks, and turned her bow to the westward. My duties on the smallest boat, with only one or two exceptions, that ever crossed the Pacific Ocean, had begun; but instead of getting busy cooking meals, I sat in the stern looking gloomily toward the land, which was the last I would see of good old American soil for nearly three years. I was thinking of the friends and the home I was leaving, and wondering if we were really bound for the bottom of the sea as so many had foretold; and I could not altogether down a feeling that I would just a little rather be on the full-rigged ship that passed us on her way into the harbour. But on the *Snark* I was and on the *Snark* I must remain. Gloomy dreams soon ended, and we settled down to life on the high seas.

So it was that we put forth into the wide Pacific, in a mere cork of a boat, without a navigator, with no engineer, no sailors, and, for that matter, no cook. This lack of a cook did not bother much just then, however, for soon we were all too seasick to care to eat.

When night came, land was out of sight, darkness wrapped us about on every side, and the *Snark* rose and fell rhythmically, the sport of every wave.

CHAPTER III

ON THE HIGH SEAS

AFTER we passed out of the Golden Gate and headed seaward on our voyage, there followed twenty-seven days that are almost beyond description. One cannot describe them by comparing them with anything else, for probably since the world began there has never been anything quite like them. Suffice it to say that these twenty-seven days were the most wild and chaotic that human beings ever experienced.

We headed south, hoping to pick up with the northeast trades. The port for which we were making lay approximately twenty-one hundred miles away, in a straight line. But while we ignored the straight line, and were in no particular hurry, we nevertheless fairly raced over the water. We couldn't help ourselves. The *Snark* tore along before the wind despite all handicaps.

"I wish some of the crack sailors of the Bohemian Club could see us now!" Jack exclaimed, exultantly. "They said the *Snark* could not run — that her lines wouldn't permit it. Well, here's something to make them sit up and revise their criticism — but unfortunately they can't see!"

The water began to get rough. A queer sensation kept asserting itself right in the region of my stomach, and I knew only too well what it portended. As the moments went by, this feeling recurred more frequently, each attack a little more aggravated than the one before it. The sea grew boisterous. It began to lash itself into crested waves.

The galley or kitchen of the *Snark* was tucked away to one side, and was not large enough for two small men to enter, close the door, and then turn around. As a matter of fact, if I was handling a dish of any size, I had to back out of the door to turn around, myself. For the first meal, I decided that I would try some fried onions, a nice roast with dressing, some vegetables, and some pudding; so I got out about a half-peck of onions, and by the time I had finished peeling those onions in that little galley, I decided that onions were all that was needed for that meal. Did you ever peel onions in a kitchen cupboard? That is practically what I was doing. My eyes were watering so that I couldn't see, and my nostrils and throat were burning so that I couldn't talk. The entire crew was kind enough to say that they liked onions, anyway.

Tochigi served the dinner, and we all ate. Then I made for my bunk, feeling, as Captain Eames put it, "rather white around the gills." As soon as Tochigi had served the dinner, he got out his flute, played the most mournful piece I have ever heard, and as the last note died away, rushed precipitately up on deck and relieved his deathly sickness at the rail.

Mrs. London speedily joined him. But Jack and Bert and Captain Eames were as yet unaffected.

The boat was leaking like a sieve. Yes, the *Snark,* the famous *Snark,* that had cost thirty thousand dollars, that had been built by expert shipbuilders, and that was declared to be the tightest craft afloat, leaked! The sides leaked, the bottom leaked; we were flooded. Even the self-bailing cockpit quickly filled with water that could find no outlet. Our gasolene, stored in non-leakable tanks and sealed behind an air-tight bulkhead, began to filter out, so that we hardly dared to strike a match. The air was full of the smell of it. I got up from my bunk, staggering sick. Bert started the five-horse-power engine, which controlled the pumps, and by this means managed to get some of the sea out of our quarters below.

At intervals, I was obliged to spend some necessary moments at the rail. The rail was only a foot high; one was obliged to crouch down on deck, clinging tightly, and lean far out, confronted ever by the stern face of the waves. The unutterable, blind sickness of such moments it is beyond the province of words to portray.

Never had I known anything like it! My head ached, my stomach ached, every muscle in my body ached. There were times when it seemed impossible that I should live. When the sickness was at its height, I was blind, deaf, and — need I say it? — dumb. All stabilities were shattered. The universe itself was rocking and plunging through the cold depths of space. And then, for a brief instant, the sickness would subside, and sight and speech and hearing return, and I knew I was on the *Snark,* the plaything of the waves, and that I, the most desperate of living creatures, was gurgling and babbling my troubles to the uncaring sea. Later, it was laughable, but ye gods! at the time laughter was a stranger to my soul.

It did not ease matters much to discover that the water pouring into the boat had ruined the tools in the engine room, and spoiled a good part of our three months' provisions in the galley. Our box of oranges had been frozen; our box of apples was mostly spoiled; the carrots tasted of kerosene; the turnips and beets were worthless; and last, but not least, our crate of cabbages was so far gone in decay that it had to be thrown overboard. As for our coal, it had been delivered in rotten potato-sacks, and in the swinging and thrashing of the ship had escaped, and was washing through the scuppers into the ocean. We found that the engine in the launch was out of order, and that our cherished life-boat leaked as badly as did the *Snark.* In one respect, however, I was especially marked out for discomfort. I had the misfortune to be somewhat taller than any of the rest; and so low was the ceiling of the galley and the staterooms downstairs that I could never stand upright, but was obliged to stoop. The only place where I could be really comfortable was on deck, and even here things were so tightly packed that there never was room for a promenade.

We didn't discover all our handicaps at once. It took about a week for us to see all there was to see, and to get acquainted with our little floating home. One of our greatest drawbacks was the fact that never for a moment could we let go of one hold unless we were assured of another. To have let go would have meant being jerked off our feet and thrown sprawling until we fetched up against something stout enough to check the fall. Circus gymnastics is as nothing compared with it. I have seen many acrobatic feats, but nothing resembling in mad abandon the double handspring Mrs. London turned one day when her hand missed its hold and she landed down the companionway in the middle of the table, on top of a dinner which I had just cooked, and which Tochigi was serving.

Toward evening of the first day, we passed a steamer, but could not make her out. The air grew chilly as night set in, and the flying spray in the air made it worse. Our dynamo would not work, so we had nothing but the kerosene lamps to depend on for light. After considerable difficulty, we got the mizzen mainstay and jibsails set, and such of us as were not on watch turned in. Mrs. London's watch was from eight till ten; then I relieved her from ten till twelve, and was in turn relieved by Tochigi.

Bert and Tochigi and I occupied one cabin. **Mine**

was an upper bunk; Tochigi's bunk was beneath mine, and Bert slept across the room. Captain Eames had a room of his own, but just now he was unable to sleep in it, for the water and gasolene drove him out. (Captain Eames waxed facetious, and always referred to his room as "the gasolene chamber.") Each bunk had upholstered springs and mattresses and was fitted with an electric light globe and a fan. Such of the crew as were sleeping had to be packed tight in their bunks with pillows to prevent their being tossed across the room.

On the morning of the second day, Jack awoke me at six-thirty, and I got breakfast. He was the only one who could eat. Not much wind was stirring, but a big swell was running. The *Snark* was still racing.

"I gave no thought to speed in building the *Snark*," Jack said that morning. "Only safety and comfort were considered. But if the *Snark* has fallen below our expectations in some things, she has certainly exceeded them in that."

I hazarded a guess. "At this rate, we will compress seven years' travelling into a few months."

"Oh, we'll find a means to stop her," he was confident, and went upstairs to the wheel.

And now occurred another remarkable thing. Jack started to heave-to, in other words, to place the *Snark* bow-on to the wind. The first gust of a gale had started, and the *Snark,* with flying-jib, jib and mizzen taken in, and reefs in the big mainsail and the fore-staysail, was rolling in the trough, the most dangerous position in which a ship can be placed. As Jack put the wheel down to heave-to, the flying jib-boom poked its nose into the water, and broke clean off. Jack put the wheel hard down, and the *Snark* never responded, but remained in the trough. The ship alternately buried her rails in the stiff sea. The mainsail was flattened down, but without avail. Then Bert tried slacking it off, but that had no effect whatever. Hoping to bring her bow up to the wind, they took in all canvas but the storm trysail on the mizzen, but still the *Snark* rolled in the trough. Jack declared he had never heard of such a thing before.

"And we must even lose faith in the *Snark's* wonderful bow," he said, regretfully. "It won't heave-to."

Meanwhile, I had gone back to my bunk, sicker than ever. Tochigi lay prostrate, seeing and hearing nothing. He had not moved since yesterday. Mrs. London and Bert and Captain Eames were able to stay on deck, but even they had occasional tremors and sudden rushes of sickness. Once, in the afternoon, I tried to fool my stomach by eating a cracker, but it was no go. By this time, the floors of stateroom and galley were slushy with water, and all the time more was seeping in. Bert had pumped it out yesterday, but already it was up to our knees. My sickness increased whenever I heard it swashing around on the floor.

Night was coming on, a night of storm and wind. The *Snark* was creaking and groaning, and still in that most dangerous of all positions, the trough. Jack got out his patent sea-anchor, warranted not to dive, and trailed it out a few yards into the sea, then made fast. Almost the minute the line drew taut, the anchor dived. The *Snark* still raced. Then Jack drew the anchor in, and tied a big timber to it. This time it floated, but it had no deterrent effect at all. The *Snark* continued to race. Do what they would, the little boat went right ahead, and remained in the trough of the sea, all the while pitching like a cork.

On Thursday, I prepared only two meals. Bert and Captain Eames and Jack ate. Tochigi lay motionless in his bunk, looking like one dead, and I made for my bunk at the first opportunity. Mrs. London was taken desperately sick, and we saw little of her that day. We were still heading south. Before leaving the Golden Gate, Jack had told us of the flying fish that we were sure to pick up with as soon as we got out to sea, and of the dolphin and porpoises and bonita, to say nothing of sharks. But despite his prediction, we saw nothing at all. The *Snark* headed farther and farther south, the days grew warmer and warmer, but never a shark nor porpoise nor even a flying fish showed up. On Sunday, April 28, we made one hundred and ten miles. The galley floor burst from the pressure of water, and we had a hard time repairing it. For days I wore thigh-boots in cooking,

"WAR AND PEACE."—FOATE CANNIBALS IN MISSION BOAT. ARTIFICIAL ISLANDS OFF MALAITA, SOLOMON GROUP

On the High Seas

and we kept the five-horse-power engine busy with the pumps. On April 30, one week after leaving Frisco, things looked worse than ever, and we were still sick. There were times when only Jack or Captain Eames could eat anything.

We all tried to keep one another cheered up as much as possible. Anyone who has been seasick can in some measure appreciate our predicament. There is something amusing about seasickness — when somebody else is afflicted. At first, you fear you will die; then, after it has a good hold on you, you fear you won't die; and you feel that you are all stomach, and that that stomach is emptying itself faster than it could possibly be filled. The person who is not actually in the throes of seasickness can have no sympathy with the person who is so afflicted. I used to go up to Mrs. London when she was at the wheel, and ask her if I should not prepare for her dinner a nice piece of fat pork with a string tied to it. The effect was magical. Immediately, she would clap her hands over her mouth and make for the rail. There is something infectious about seasickness. I would have to go join her myself, and sometimes Jack would come with us.

On one occasion, I almost gave up, and expressed to Jack the wish that I could see land. He replied: " Never mind, Martin, we are not over two miles from land now; " and when I asked him which way, he said: " Straight down, Martin, straight down."

One whole day I slept, or tried to sleep, in the life-boat. But the life-boat was a joke. By this time we realised that if a really severe storm should strike us, the life-boat would be the first thing to go, and our only resource in case of foundering would be the launch, which is to say, that had the *Snark* gone down, we would have gone down with it. So our only hope was in fair weather and the pumps.

The bath-room had long since gone out of commission. The first day out, the big iron levers that controlled the sea-valves and the bath-pumps broke into splinters. Jack's heart was sore at this, for he had planned that bath-room carefully, and had been to much expense in fitting it up. Another thing that would have dashed most skippers' spirits was the fact that the specially ordered planking from Puget Sound, warranted to have no butts, was literally crowded with butts. But Jack did not let any of these things trouble him much; he merely commented on them, and then set himself to make the best of the voyage. Luckily, we were not becalmed. Had this misfortune been added to the rest, it might have taken us sixty days or more to reach Honolulu.

A little over a week out, a gale struck us, and carried away the jib and staysail. Everybody worked; the boat was creaking and groaning, water spouting in everywhere, and the cockpit filled with water. The engine wouldn't work, and nothing else worked. This gale was a wonderful experience for me. The little boat would go down in the trough of the wave, and

I would gaze up and see the water coming in a massive cone, a million tons of water, looking a hundred feet high. It seemed to overtop our mainmast several times and more. I felt absolutely certain that when that mass of water hit us, we would be gone; but each time our stout little craft would climb the side of the wave until we reached the top, and then would start down the opposite side so rapidly that it produced that peculiar feeling one experiences when going down a Shoot-the-Chutes or the steep incline of a Roller-Coaster. In fact, seasickness is nothing more than this sensation aggravated to a point where it is painful. We were pitched around with great violence — sometimes we would be away over on one side until the water came pouring in the scuppers; and again, the boat would rush downward at such a rate of speed that I just knew we were making for that bottom Mr. London had spoken of; then we would go up again, each time to my surprise, because I was satisfied that we were as good as dead at least twice to each wave we rode. During this storm, the thought came to me that just a year before, on May 1, I was on a big cattle-steamer, going east on the Atlantic; and here I was, a year later, on a fish-bobber, in the middle of the Pacific, going — where? But the sea was not in existence that could swamp us. When the storm broke away the next day, and the sun arose bright and clear, everyone seemed to feel better and to take renewed interest in life.

We had not been long out of port before we became convinced that we had no navigator aboard. Captain Eames was supposed to be the navigator, but the navigation of a small boat is difficult and Jack had to assist him in the work. On certain days we made splendid headway and seemed to have covered considerable distance but our observations and markings on the chart showed that we had not done nearly as well as we supposed. On the other hand, there were days when it had been practically calm, and our records would show that we had fairly whirled over the water. The principles of navigation are fairly simple — and misunderstood by most people. Before we had reached Honolulu, everyone in the boat was navigating, except Tochigi. Of course, most of our mistakes had their roots in the fact that the boat's tossing threw our observations out of line, and our eyes were rather too near to the water. Of course, too, our record of time on board was sadly perturbed, despite our turning the ship's clock back about ten minutes each day.

And still we saw no fish of any sort. Jack could not understand it. He had been in these latitudes before, and always had seen porpoises and dolphins and flying fish, as well as sharks and bonita. But the ocean was absolutely bare in every direction. We were in a watery desert. It was not until we got to latitude 19° that we saw the first flying fish, and he was all by himself.

On Thursday, May 2, we felt that we were certainly

in the trade winds. We went dead ahead of the breeze, with all the sails set except the mizzen, and doing what old sailors, men of forty years on the sea, declare cannot be done — racing along with no one at the wheel. We simply set the wheel over to suit the wind, without even lashing it; and then all went below to supper, and to play cribbage. By this time I had learned a number of new dishes. Tochigi showed me the Japanese way of preparing rice, and it beat anything I had yet cooked. All were feeling in high spirits. The sickness had left us, and the boat looked tidier than at any time since leaving Frisco, for we had spent the day in scrubbing the floors, and generally cleaning things up.

When it came to the actual test, we found that the provisions of the *Snark* were not exactly adapted to that kind of trip. The duty of provisioning the boat had been left to Mrs. London and myself, and I fear that in the buying we lost all sense of proportion. We had bought an enormous crate of cabbages (which, as I have said, speedily found its way into the sea), and a whole case of lemons; and I had made out the list of spices and seasonings, all of which were purchased, enough to run the Delmonico for a year. The amount of pepper we had aboard would last a good-sized family through several lifetimes. When we completed the voyage, we had pepper to throw overboard, and I'll bet the fish in that vicinity have been coughing and sneezing ever since.

But the cooking was a reasonably easy proposition, because most of the time over half the crew didn't care for anything to eat, and the others were kind enough to say that they particularly liked my method of preparing only one dish at a meal, and depending on the can-opener for the rest. And observe the security of my position — they could not fire me and hire a new cook, so they had to like it or do without eating.

The galley had a Primus kerosene stove, which burned without odour. On the galley shelves were all sorts of pots and pans, bottles, tins, and utensils. For each and every separate thing, a hole had been made in the shelves, of just the right size and shape, so that nothing could topple out. On the stove, there were racks to hold the skillets and pots and pans while I cooked; but the pots and pans had a trick of jumping out of their racks and banging down into the bilge-water on the floor. And what didn't leap off the stove slopped and splashed all over the galley and the cook. As for myself, I was flung back and forth from one side of the galley to the other, until my back was a mass of bruises from bumping against the bulkhead.

A few extracts from the diary I kept during this cruise to Hawaii will throw an interesting light on how we lived aboard the *Snark*. The entries in this diary reflect my feelings better than I could recollect them after the lapse of several years.

May 2, 1907.— I feel much better to-day. Am trying to clean up galley. It is getting warmer. No wind scarcely — making about two knots. I've changed watches with Bert, so now I have from four to six in the morning. Mrs. London is certainly a brick — weighs only one hundred and ten pounds, but bears up wonderfully, and is everywhere at once. The last few days I've cooked with my boots on. Mrs. L. helps. Floor of galley only about two feet above inside bottom of *Snark*. Down below, water moves freely from one air-tight compartment to the other. Will we ever reach Honolulu alive?

Evening.— I feel fine. So do all. Even Tochigi is smiling again, and that's nuff said. It's the prettiest evening I've seen in a long time. Bert, who is engineer, finds the dynamo won't work, so he is filling the oil lamps again. Just think of it — we have 19 big electric lights on the boat, and a searchlight, and not one of them working! Jack and Mrs. London are playing cribbage in the cockpit. Tochigi washing clothes over the rail. Ocean calm, except for the swell that is always felt. We had a fine time at supper, telling stories, and joking with one another. Well, I'm going to turn in. My bunk is five feet five inches long, two feet wide, and one foot six inches from the ceiling, but I feel as good in it as on feathers.

Queer that we have seen no fish. Jack can't account for it. Mr. Eames has gone back to his room — he was run out a few days ago by gasolene leaking under his bunk. Water still spouting in. Pumps

64 Through the South Seas with Jack London

needed. Many of Tochigi's books are ruined by being water-soaked. Mrs. London has bad headache, and so have I, but a little sleep will cure that. So here's for the bunk.

Friday, May 3, 1907.— Big sea to-day. Tochigi again seasick. I'm not feeling so well; neither is Mrs. London. At dinner no one could stay at the table, the boat rocked so. Jack and Mrs. London were thrown clear across the cabin. All my dishes swimming around the floor — nothing will stay on the stove I just slid across cabin and ran into Mrs. London coming head-first down companionway. Not badly hurt. We are averaging 5½ knots.

Saturday, May 4, 1907.— Last night we had some hard luck; at five o'clock the gooseneck, the piece of iron that holds the main gaff to the barrel on the main boom, broke, and let down the gaff. We took the gooseneck off the gaff of the storm trysail and replaced the one that had broken; and went below to supper. Just as we sat down the blamed thing came crashing down again, so we had to lash it with ropes, and let it go until we reach Honolulu — if we ever get there. But these goosenecks breaking looks bad. Both were of wrought iron; on the second one we would have depended in time of storm. Jack says it is just like macaroni, the way it snapped. Wind pretty stiff, and a suggestion of rain in the air. Feeling rather sick.

Sunday, May 5, 1907.— Fine day, and everybody

feeling well. I've just now begun to enjoy this trip. Wonder what's going on in the world, anyway! I've come to the point where I've forgotten what the world was like. The past is all like some dream. Our world is a big, blue expanse of water, reaching in an eternal circle to the horizon; a blue, clear-looking sky overhead, in which journeys the hot, glowing sun; and a tiny boat, a speck in the immensity of things, pursuing its solitary way across the deep. Loafed on deck most of to-day. We are far south of the regular track of steamers. Bert and Tochigi and I are all writing on our diaries this evening. The Londons have retired. Captain Eames is at the wheel, singing some sea-song — seems to be happy. Course south by west.

Monday, May 6, 1907.—Baked bread and made biscuits to-day; had fine success. Fourteen days out of Frisco. Bert and Captain Eames took a bath in the ocean to-day — got clear down on the stays, and let the motion of the boat do the rest. Bert keeps declaring that he will let go and have a decent swim, but Jack warns him that if he does the sharks will get him. But Bert says the sharks are all with the dolphins and porpoises and bonita — in other words, that there aren't any. Changed our course to southwest by west. I think we are a little over half-way. To-night, we are going to start a game of whist and play it up until the moment we land. Everybody is making fun of my whiskers. Of course, I haven't shaved since we left, and I have an awful growth of beard, which I shan't scrape off until we reach port. Bert is the same way; there are times when he looks like a pirate. A queer bird hove in sight to-day. It's circling around us. It's white, with a long tail, sharp as a needle, and a long bill. Jack says he never heard of any like it before. I have my washing out. We just tie ropes on our clothes and tow them overboard all night, and in the morning they are clean; all we have to do is hang them up to dry. We crossed the line last night and are now in the tropics, or torrid zone. Have not seen a ship for over a week. Well, Jack's idea was to get away from the crowd, and certainly he has nothing to complain of in that respect. No mail, no telephones, no telegraph messengers, no cranks, nothing at all to bother him. He writes every day, and then does his trick at the wheel, or helps with the sailorising. Tochigi is at the wheel, reading a Japanese novel up-side down and from the back — or so it looks. Last night at supper he took the wheel, and played some weird music on his bamboo flute. We all stopped eating to listen. It is hard to realise that it is over a thousand miles to land in any direction.

Tuesday, May 7, 1907.— Played whist last night, and had a fine time. Jack and Mrs. London won both games. Captain Eames looked on until a lamp fell on his head, and after that he seemed to lose interest. Tochigi had the wheel. When I am feeling sick, my early-morning watch seems terribly long; but if I am

On the High Seas

well, it is really enjoyable. We are taking a good many pictures now-a-days. I develop and print my own pictures, and all the others'. Jack requires a good many as illustrations to his magazine articles. To-day, Bert and Captain Eames set the spinnaker sail. Bert went out on the boom and got a good ducking, but the water is fine and warm, so it wasn't disagreeable. As I write, I have to hold on to the companionway with one hand. Lat. 22°—44′—24″, Long. 136°—4′. We figure that another ten days will put us in Honolulu. Captain has just hung the map with our course, and it's the most zigzagged route I ever saw. Yesterday we actually went out of our way fourteen miles. Everyone is feeling good, even if we are rolling some. I realise now, that, joking aside, this is as perilous a voyage as ever human beings voluntarily ventured on. We could never weather a hard storm. For the boat won't heave-to. And no one aboard knows how to make her heave-to. A fine warm evening, and the most beautiful sunset. It's queer we see no fish, for by all the books we have on fish, this is where they should be found. Jack throws out his trolling line every day, but catches nothing. Our course to-night is west-southwest.

Wednesday, May 8, 1907.— My pay-day — but what's the use? I can't spend any money here. It may be two weeks before we reach Honolulu. Had fair wind to-day — changed course to south by west.

At meals, Mr. and Mrs. London and Mr. Eames eat, Tochigi waits table, and Bert takes wheel; then we three eat. We are having lots of Portuguese men-of-war these days; they are a kind of jelly-fish that move in schools and have a sail in the middle of their backs. Jack and Mrs. London are playing pedro, and Bert is putting out the sidelights. It is getting awfully monotonous, always swaying up and down on these big waves — now away in the valley formed by two big swells, then on top of one of them. We are all over our seasickness, and feeling pretty good. Bert is certainly just right for this trip. He is robust and strong — a young Hercules. We are all discarding our shirts and wearing white trousers and canvas shoes. Fortunately, the breeze keeps the air from getting oppressively warm. Bert takes his daily bath from the stays.

Thursday, May 9, 1907. — Jack and Mrs. London swear they saw three flying fish to-day; we think they are mistaken. Jack has had a spoon-hook out ever since we left, but has not even had a nibble. Tochigi washed out some clothing to-day — I made a picture of him at it. Lat. 21°— 42'— 14", Long. 139°— 22' 15". If only I could get some sleep! But the sea is so rough that I just roll from one side of the bunk to the other. We have all kinds of music. Jack has a big talking-machine, with over five hundred records; some of them are of the finest opera music, vocal and instrumental. How strange it would be, if one could stand off a hundred yards and watch the little *Snark*

WAR CANOES IN THEIR SHELTER

go by on the crested waves, while the voice of Caruso, say, sang from our companionway. I think one would rub his eyes, and think it something visionary, unreal. We have awnings on deck which help to keep off the heat of the sun. And oh, yes, besides the talking-machine and the musical records, we have an Edison language-machine, with Italian, German, Spanish, and French records, and a text-book for each language.

Friday, May 10, 1907.— Sea rough to-day. Everybody needing sleep. Saw some flying fish, but couldn't catch any. Been threatening rain; wind from northeast, course southwest. It's mighty hard to cook, for nothing will stay on the stove. What does slops out. I am thrown around all the time. Water still sopping around in galley. It is a good thing we are prepared for the wet — we have rubber hip-boots, oil-skin coats, rubber sou'-westers. Then, for work, there are blue flannel shirts, blue calico shirts; and for dress, silk shirts. We have also brought pajamas, for use in very warm weather. How the boat rocks and pitches! What wouldn't I give to stand still for only a minute? Tochigi is relapsing into seasickness again.

. . . .

The next day found us in a fierce sea. We were all soaked with water. Indeed, it was impossible to step on deck without getting wet. Great waves, many times higher than the *Snark*, kept sweeping down as if to swamp us, but always we slid along the top of them, seeing for miles around; then would come the dive down into the slough, where everything was blotted from view but a wild swirl of waters. It was next to impossible to cook. Dishes defied all laws of gravitation, and skimmed like birds through the air; and the stove was a sight, what of the things that slopped over it. We were covered with bruises from being thrown up against the vessel. Mrs. London made another aerial descent of the companionway that night, but was only slightly bruised. Captain Eames scraped the skin off his head in the course of one tumble. I got my punishment in burns from the stove. Far above, in the tropic sky, the lightning flashed and the thunder rolled. Lightning had an awful significance to the crew of the *Snark*. We were far out at sea; the copper and other metals would tend to draw the current, and had a spark ever reached us, and ignited the eleven hundred gallons of gasolene on board, there wouldn't have been a splinter left to tell the tale.

Like all sailors, we did not love the sea. It was the eternal menace. Looking upon its placid surface in moments of calm, we could almost forget that it was forever yawning, and that into its maw had gone many a brave ship, of greater tonnage than ours. But in raging storms, with the lightning shooting in fiery lines across the sky, and the artillery of heaven rumbling and banging overhead and echoing on the storm-lashed waves, we came to appreciate the true meaning of things, and to assign to earth and sky and sea the proper values. At such moments, I repeat, we did not love the sea; but we did love the *Snark*. Its ten tons of wood and metal stood between us and destruction. It made life possible to us. It was in such reflections as these, miles and miles from any land, that the words of Jack London rang again in my ears: "Life that lives is life successful. The achievement of a difficult feat is successful adjustment to a sternly exacting environment." Well, we strove to accomplish, and our environment was savage. Supreme courage and unwavering vigilance alone could enable us to adjust ourselves, and come alive out of the welter of foam and frothing waves that assailed the little *Snark* the greater part of her perilous voyage to Hawaii.

Even out in the ocean, several kinds of birds follow in the wake of ships to pick up the leavings. With a piece of meat tied on a string, we succeeded in catching a guny. These gunys are a species of albatross, and they live, sleep, and find their food entirely on the face of the great deep. When these birds are swimming on the surface of the water and wish to rise into the air, they cannot make the ascent as most birds do, simply by flapping their wings. They must start swimming rapidly, with wings extended, until their speed becomes sufficient to enable them gradually to rise into the air. Before they start to fly, they are literally walking on the water. The meat of the guny is not palatable, and looks something like the meat of an ordinary crow.

Every day, Jack wrote two hours. Just two hours, no more, no less. He would get up in the morning and take his trick at the wheel, have breakfast, and then shut himself in his stateroom for just two hours and write. He always laughed at what he called the tomfoolery of waiting for inspiration to come. He doesn't believe there is any such thing as inspiration — he himself can write just as well at one time as at another. It is plain work, he says, and the only way he can do it is to go ahead and do it. Incidentally, I may mention that Jack London never rewrites a story. He writes it just once, and never goes over it to change it. He writes with a fountain pen, and nobody can read his writing but Mrs. London. He turns his manuscript over to her, and she types it and gets it ready for the publishers.

In addition to their writing and typing, both the Londons did their trick at the wheel, and even helped Bert at the sailorising. When the weather was calm and we had gotten over our sickness, we would all gather on deck and talk, and tell each other of our experiences before chance grouped us together on the *Snark*. Of course, Jack had lived more of life than any of us. He spent hours recounting to us tales of the Klondike, and other faraway places he had visited. One of the most interesting things he told us was of how he came to write. Since his days in the grade schools of Oakland, he had nursed the secret wish to become a writer. He spent long hours poring over

On the High Seas

books of history, travel, and fiction. But everything seemed against him. His father, a veteran of the Civil War, was slowly dying, and it became necessary for Jack to turn to and help support the family. He worked at everything and anything. Now he was a sailor, now a San Francisco Bay oyster-pirate, now a member of the Bay Fish Patrol. He mowed lawns and washed windows, and cleaned carpets, and worked in canneries and other factories. Through all this experience, his Socialistic tendencies were strengthened, and he ardently espoused the cause of revolution, and clings to it still. He wrote evenings after he came home from work, but all his manuscripts were returned to him. At last, however, came the day. He had been to the Klondike, and had returned penniless and stricken with scurvy. He could do little work. Between odd jobs, he wrote. One night, coming home, he conceived the idea of turning some of his Arctic experiences into stories. That evening he sat down and produced the great story that made him famous, and that has been read round the world, " The White Silence." It was written from things he knew. It was a bit of life, " cut from the raw, and woven round with words." A big western magazine promptly published it, paying him the scanty sum of five dollars. But his next story, published in an eastern short-story magazine, brought him better monetary return, so that he was enabled to go ahead and write. And we all know that he succeeded.

Another rather amusing thing Jack told us was of an experience in Manchuria, during the Russo-Japanese War. He had been sent as war correspondent by a big American newspaper syndicate, and besides his scratch-pad, he was provided with a camera. One day he started to take some pictures, and was promptly arrested and haled before the military authorities. A fat and rather deaf old Jap officer began to question him.

" Why do you take pictures? "

" Because I wish to."

" And why do you wish to? "

" Because I desire to."

And so it went for half an hour, question and answer, attack and rebuff. Other correspondents who had been rounded up with cameras in their possession followed the same plan. At last, the Jap officer gave up in disgust, and allowed them all to depart, though warning them of what might happen to them in time of war.

During this period, there was strict censorship of all letters and telegrams, both coming and going. The war correspondents were in a quandary. They desired to keep their papers posted on the latest developments, but were unable to get a line of information beyond the frontier. They tried cipher-codes and various freak methods of writing, but without avail. These messages were destroyed as being of a suspicious character. At last, however, one of the enterprising correspondents hit upon a plan. He wrote plain English to his paper. Just at the time, an important military manœuvre was in progress. By building a bridge over a certain river, the Japs would be enabled to transport their supplies, and to gain control of an important position. So the war correspondent wrote to his paper a rather rambling personal letter, of no consequence whatever, but at the end casually mentioned that the Japanese troops were on the bank of the river, with timber and big wooden beams and posts. " I'm not allowed to tell you what they're doing, but you can bet they're not digging a well." Fortunately, the editor was a man of acumen; out of all the chaff he sifted the grain of wheat, and his paper had an enviable beat, that great delight of the editorial heart.

When we all got to navigating in good shape, we found that we were able to produce a widely different set of figures. Of course, each could prove the correctness of his points. I well remember the day that my figures showed we were in the Atlantic Ocean instead of the Pacific. As I think back, I wonder more and more that we ever got anywhere, what of our brilliant navigation. But luck was with us. We did eventually get to port, though not without stress and storm.

Monday, May 13, 1907.— We have had all kinds of excitement to-day. This morning, about eleven, I lay asleep in the bow, when Tochigi awoke me and pointed just ahead on our port side, and there were thirty or forty whales; not very big, but they certainly looked big. I guess they would average twenty or twenty-five feet, and had an enormous fin in the centre of their backs. They were playing, now darting our way, now the other way. They looked very lazy floating on the waves. In half an hour they had disappeared. Jack calls them fin-backs, and says they are very rare. While they were here, the air and water seemed alive with flying fish. These flying fish are of the four-winged kind, about a foot long. Bert and I have been sitting on the deck practising different kinds of knots. It's getting awfully hot. We are all discarding as much clothing as we can. Captain Eames says we will sight Mauna Kea and Mauna Loa next Friday morning, and make Pearl Harbor, on the island of Oahu, Sunday. I hope so, but I'm sceptical. Don't think anyone knows our bearings within a hundred miles or so. Bert and I went in bathing to-day. Got out on the bobstay, under the bowsprit, and every time the boat would dip we would go under, and the speed of the boat made it hard for us to hang on. If ever we let go, it would be all up with us. It's dangerous, anyway, for sharks are supposed to be thick here. Getting hotter every day. Now registers 90°; we are not making much speed at present. My bread was a failure to-day, so I've got to do it again or we'll starve. Great excitement just now: Mrs. London has discovered the Southern Cross, a cluster of stars that sailors use for reckoning after they get too far south to use the North Star. It's directly south, and never changes position. Bert and I shaved to-day, and put on our lightest clothes.

Wednesday, May 15, 1907.— We are making fine time. Best yet — and all sails drawing. Weather perfect. At noon, registered 88°, but since then about 80°. We have things closely packed aboard the *Snark*. Not an inch of wall- or ceiling-space but is utilised. Even the "leaves" of the dining-table close down over a chest-of-drawers that contains all the table-linen. In the two little staterooms forward, devoted to Jack and Mrs. London, there are all sorts of cubby-holes. Closets, large and small, honeycomb the sides and ceilings. Mrs. London can hang her dresses full length, and she has even a hat-box. Then, too, Jack has his tobacco-stores — plenty of tobacco. This evening, the new moon and the stars are brighter than I ever saw them, and there are many new stars, unfamiliar to me. We expect to sight Hawaii to-morrow, that is, if, as Bert says, " we are where we are." Bert has been telling me about his father, who was shot by a desperate leper in these islands. He was sheriff, and was trying to take the leper to Molokai, the Leper Island. I made some good pictures of Mrs. London to-day — she dresses simply these days, bare-headed, blue sailor waist, plain short skirt. Only a few more dog-watches, and then I'll get a good long sleep. This getting up at four in the morning, and steering till six, is no joke. During that time I have to put out the sidelights and binnacles, and stow the sidelights in the bos'ns locker, then call Jack. We turn the clock back about ten minutes each day.

Thursday, May 16, 1907.— This morning at four it was raining when I went on watch, so I put on my oilskins. The wind died out in a little while, and I don't think we have moved over ten knots all day. The surface of the ocean is as calm as San Francisco Bay. Very warm. It is fine these nights, to lie in one's bunk without any bedclothes, and with no flies or mosquitoes to bother. Jack and Bert and I went in bathing on the bowsprit in the afternoon, and Bert let go and swam with the ship. If a shark had put in an appearance, or if a puff of wind had sent the boat ahead, it would have been all up with him. We dressed, and then took pictures of each other. Captain Eames and Mrs. London were at the cockpit, and Tochigi was below making candy. Suddenly Bert yelled, " Look at that fin," and we were all excitement at once. We ran to the stern, and there was a real, live shark, about seven feet long. Jack threw over a shark-hook, attached to a ninethread. The hook was a big thing, weighing over a pound, and a foot long; and the ninethread is a little thicker than one's finger. We baited the hook with a piece of fat pork, and the shark made a dive for it, but did not swallow it. However, we coaxed him up within a few feet of the boat, where we could get a good look at him. He was about the shape and colour of an enormous cat-fish,

On the High Seas

except that he was of slimmer build and his fin and gills were larger. The ugliest head, with little, mean-looking eyes! Just ahead of his fin was the pilot fish, occasionally darting ahead to inspect the boat, or so it seemed. The pilot was a pretty fish, ten inches long, and striped like a zebra. They stayed with us all of two hours. Now and again, the shark would turn over, belly upward, and make a rush for the hook, but never did he get it. The water was so clear that we could see him easily. I brought up a cold lunch, and we never took our eyes off the fish. Tochigi could hardly break away long enough to take the dishes below. About six o'clock we saw the pilot fish take its position back of the shark's head. They swam up close to the side of the boat, then glided off to the north and disappeared. We are moving scarcely at all now. No motion to the boat. With about twenty hours of fair wind, we could sight the islands.

Friday, May 17, 1907.— Great excitement again. We think we've sighted land. If our conjectures are correct, the island of Hawaii is to our port bow, and Maui dead ahead. They were discovered by Mr. and Mrs. London, while they were playing cribbage in the cockpit and watching one of these perfect tropical sunsets. Both spots of land loom up like high mountains, and look about fifty or sixty miles distant. Jack has given orders that all on watch to-night go forward every five minutes and take a lookout. It got dark so early, or rather we sighted the supposed land so late, that we got only about a half-hour's light to watch them; but on my watch in the morning I ought to get a good look at them, or at least at Maui, for we have changed our course to west-northwest, and will draw off from Hawaii by morning if the wind does not die down. It is now only about two knots strong. Previous to our discovery, we had been in low spirits, for Bert discovered that out of three observations, none agreed, and all varied about sixty miles. We suspected that our chronometer had gone wrong; and we feared that we might flounder around for weeks and never find the islands. Jack had given orders to be saving on food and water, and to wash in salt water, but he has countermanded that order now. Jack is poring over his maps, on the cabin table.

Saturday, May 18, 1907.— Marvel of marvels! We have really found the islands. They are in exactly the place the reckonings put us, but it seems strange to be coming in from the south. This morning on my watch the clouds were so dense on the horizon that I could not make out land. Jack came on deck at five o'clock, and we searched the horizon for an hour, and finally gave up and decided that it was clouds we saw last night. But just then Mrs. London came on deck and cried, " Oh! " and then, " Isn't that lovely! " and sure enough, the clouds had parted, and disclosed the snow-peaked active volcano of Mauna Loa on the island of Hawaii, only about twenty miles to port. It was a fine sight — Mauna Loa, over thirteen thousand

Manufactured Islet, with Shrine of a Native Chief—Solomon Group

feet high, the largest active volcano in the world! Well, we kept off her until noon, when we sighted Maui, reaching over ten thousand feet into the air. This evening Molokai is off our port bow, Molokai, the island where hundreds of poor wretches afflicted with leprosy are isolated. We are headed direct for her, and will round her in the morning and sight Oahu. Expect to be in Pearl Harbor to-morrow night. We have a fine breeze; making almost six knots. To-night the watches will be doubled — one person forward and one at the wheel: Mrs. London and Tochigi from eight till twelve, Mr. Eames and Bert until four, and Jack and I until eight. To-day, Tochigi found a flying fish on deck, that had flown aboard and fallen helpless.

Sunday, May 19, 1907.— This morning Jack took the lookout, and I took the wheel. Until daylight we could not make out our position. Molokai gradually came in view to our port, and as the light grew stronger we could make out the rocks that the steamer *Manchuria* ran into on Oahu. About that time, the wind played out, and all day we have remained in almost the same spot. It's awfully exasperating to be within sight of Honolulu, or nearly so, and not be able to get there. It is a fine day. This evening the wind freshened a bit, so that we got about twenty-five miles closer — that is, within twenty-five miles of Honolulu — but the wind didn't last long. I can hear the sails jibbing back and forth, and the booms are cracking around in a way I don't like. A calm is often far more dangerous to the rigging of a small vessel than is a storm. Worst of all, the currents are carrying us toward Molokai; and if we are wrecked on its rocky coast, we will never be allowed to leave. But we will surely make Pearl Harbor in the morning. This afternoon we baited a hook with pork and caught a guny. He was a large one — measured over six feet from tip of one wing to tip of other wing. They are said to get seasick when caught, but this one didn't. When we let him overboard, he gave one disgusted look at us, and swam away. He tried to fly, but think his wings were too full of water from struggling to get free. The ocean is now alive with life. Flying fish are everywhere. There are fish of every sort, and schools of porpoises. Late this evening, we sighted a steamer, and a couple of sloops are away off on our port horizon.

. . . .

The next morning, twenty-seven days out of Frisco, we were near to Honolulu. We were met by the customs tug, from the deck of which papers were thrown to us. One of the papers had pictures of the *Snark*, and a long story, telling that, considering the twenty-seven days out of San Francisco, all hope had been given up of the *Snark's* ever reaching port — that she had evidently gone down with all hands. When the customs tug volunteered to tow us into Pearl Harbor, eighteen miles from Honolulu, Jack jumped at the chance. The *Kamehameha* and the *Kalaohkun,* of

On the High Seas

the Hawaiian Yacht Club, came out to meet us, and escorted us into Pearl Harbor. We passed several Japanese *sampans,* the first I had ever seen, queer little flat boats used by the Jap fishermen. Once a monstrous turtle, said to be the largest ever seen in these parts, swam near us, and lifted his ungainly head to gaze at us. We took his presence as an omen of good luck.

Pearl Harbor has a small mouth like a river, which is called Pearl Locks. Inside, the harbour is deep and large. It was then being fitted up as a base of supplies and repairs for the American navy, by Captain Curtis Otwell, who was in charge of the entire construction work. A little later, we dropped anchor in Pearl Harbor, and furled the sails. I cannot begin to tell how good it was to be on solid ground again, after twenty-seven days of pitching and rolling on the sea. It seemed too good to be true. We called the harbour " Dream Harbour." It seemed to suit better than any other name — for was this not all a dream? We were met by a throng of reporters, camera fiends, Kanakas, and a general mixture of nationalities, and one and all gave us a hearty welcome to their island.

CHAPTER IV

A PACIFIC PARADISE

LAND at last! It seemed like Paradise. When we saw the rich, soft grass, we felt like getting down and rolling on it, it looked so good. Commodore Hoborn, of the Hawaiian Yacht Club, had tendered the use of his bungalow to Jack and Mrs. London, an offer that was gratefully accepted. The bungalow was only a few yards from our anchorage, so that the *Snark* family remained within easy hailing distance. We unlashed our boats, covered the sails, and threw out the spinnaker-boom; and then the Londons went ashore with the commodore, while we remained for the time on the *Snark,* besieged by reporters and photographers.

When the customs inspector's tug offered to tow us into Pearl Harbor, Jack had been quick to accept the kindness; but I had kept looking toward Honolulu, where I knew there was fresh meat and fruit, to say nothing of the varied life of the city. But I soon thought differently. Along the coast for several hundred feet out the water was white with breakers. After we got nearer to the mouth of Pearl Harbor, we could see palms along the shore, and other tropical trees, while in the water plied busy Chinese junk-fishers and Japanese *sampans* and native sloops, the occupants in a state closely approaching nudity. The air was warm and balmy. We all gaped with wonder — all except Jack, who had been here before.

It was two o'clock that afternoon when we got shore-leave. We could hardly walk. The land tilted and heaved, even as the *Snark* had tilted and heaved. I caught myself spreading my feet apart to prevent my falling, just as we did on the boat. A train ran every hour to Pearl City, so we made haste to catch it. It was one of the queerest trains imaginable, a little yellow car and a miniature engine, loaded down with Chinamen and Japs dressed in their native costumes, and the reporters who were returning to Pearl City after interviewing the crew of the *Snark*. Pearl City, which was only a mile away, consisted of a depot and a few Japanese and Chinese stores. We ate our lunch in a roadside hotel, where girls played guitars and danced and sang all through the meal.

All the next day we packed things back and forth from the boat to the bungalow, and put up hammocks and mosquito netting. It was a one-storey building, with low, protruding roof. There were four rooms, but even this seemed commodious after nearly a month on the *Snark,* where space in every direction was rigidly economised. One continuous window let in the sunshine on all four sides of the bungalow; and the yard was filled with little forests of cocoanut palms, and a profusion of bananas, figs, papaias, guava palms, and other tropical trees. The grass was large and blue, and, fortunately, sheltered no chigoes — or, as they are often called, chiggers — to drive us mad with their biting. Along the shore was the sea-wall and a long boat-landing; here the water was so clear that one could see to the bottom in ten feet of it, to where the coral lies in wonderful patterns, and shells nestle down almost out of sight, and fish of every colour swim back and forth.

The weather was perfect. It is always perfect. The temperature never varies over ten degrees — from about 75° to 85°. There was always plenty of food, growing right to one's hand; no tropical diseases to be seen, at least not yet; no dirt, no smoke; everything so pleasing and satisfying as to be beyond description. The only thing that really kept us on the jump was the mosquitoes. Sitting in our main room, in pajamas, reading, talking or writing, we were obliged to burn mosquito powder all the time, and even that did little to rid us of the pests. Mark Twain had a bungalow near here a few years ago, and the story is told that he had netting put all around his bed, alow and aloft, that he might sleep without losing any of his blood; but the mosquitoes got in anyway, and nearly tormented the life out of him. At last, however, he made the discovery that when the mosquitoes once got inside the netting, they could not find their way out, so he used to lie there as a bait until all were safely ensnared, then crawl out and sleep upon the floor.

A Pacific Paradise

In the next few days, we were continually finding new things to do and to see. We swam in the crystal-clear water, despite the natives' warnings about sharks. For my part I had plenty of leisure. After an heroic silence of days, the crew finally broke out in protest against my cooking; they simply could stand no more of it. When on the sea, it had been eat it or starve; but now that they were ashore, there was greater latitude of choice. After that, we all boarded with different white families in the vicinity, and the poor harassed crew forgot its troubles in the delight of eating once more the things that humans eat, cooked as humans would cook them.

The people of Oahu were very accommodating, always bringing us fruit and looking after our wishes with a care unknown in the States. The conductor on the mile-long railroad-run to Pearl City brought us various fruits gathered along the way; and when we were riding and saw anything we wanted, he would stop the train to get it. Coming from Honolulu one night, the main train switched, and took me direct to our bungalow, carrying along four other coaches of Japs and Chinese. The conductor was an American. He said that he didn't care whether " the cattle "— referring to my fellow-passengers — got anywhere or not.

Much of our time, however, was spent on the *Snark*, where we were constantly receiving visitors. I met a great number of American and English people, and many natives. As for the population of the islands, the Japanese greatly predominate. I think, in figures, it runs about as follows: sixty-one thousand Japanese, forty-five thousand Chinese, twenty-three thousand British, twenty-five thousand Americans, twelve thousand five hundred natives (Kanakas), four hundred and fifty South Sea Islanders, and six hundred and fifty Portuguese; and as nearly all these people dress in their native costumes, the whole has a decidedly cosmopolitan look. As for Honolulu, it consists mostly of stores run by Japs and Chinese — many call it Little Japan. There are many half-castes and quarter-castes on the islands. I knew one man who could trace through his ancestry connection with every one of the principal divisions of the human family.

On June 3 occurred the first split in the *Snark* crew. Captain Eames decided that he had had enough yachting, and departed on the steamship *Sierra* for California. Shortly after, word came from Bert's mother, asking him to return and continue his course at Stanford University. Bert considered a while over this, but in the end decided to do as she had asked. He formally resigned from the crew, and went to Honolulu to stay until he could work his way back to California. It seemed as if the newspapers could never get through inventing falsehoods about Jack and the rest of us. When Bert left, they reported that Jack was a big, bullyragging brute, and had beaten all of us into a pulp. As a matter of fact, there was never so much as a quarrel among us.

Jack and Mrs. London had gone to Honolulu, and were staying at the Seaside Hotel. Every day, Jack would send me his exposed films and I would develop them and send prints by the next train. Never was there so obliging a person as Tony, conductor of the mile-long railroad I have mentioned, and which, because of its nature, we called the Unlimited. Tony was not only conductor, but he was also engineer, fireman, brakeman and porter. If he could help us at the house, he would bank the fire in the engine, and leave his train for half a day. Once, while watching me at my photographing, he found that he was five minutes late for the run to Pearl City, so he decided not to make the trip. As he explained, nothing but Japs and Kanakas (Hawaiians), and Chinamen rode on it, and he didn't care anything about them. As for us, when we rode he absolutely refused to collect any fare. When I had made Jack's prints, I would bundle them up and give them to Tony; then, when he reached Pearl City, he would give them to the conductor of the train for Honolulu, and eventually they would find their way to Jack.

About this time, we got our new captain. He was an old fellow who had been all through the South Seas, and knew them like a book, and whom we will call Captain X——. He was an ideal sea-captain of the old school — the kind that is rough and headstrong. He and I had a little set-to at first, but later ignored each other as much as possible. About this time, too, Gene Fenelon, a young fellow of thirty, came from Oakland to take Bert's place as engineer. He and Jack had known each other for some years, and were good friends. We took a great liking to Gene, who was really a clever fellow, though, as will be seen, he did not last long at this particular job. He had been for eight years assistant manager of an European circus, and spoke several languages fluently. Bert and Gene and I would go of nights up to the Hawaiian Yacht Club, and coming back would frighten the very birds off their perches by our vigorous sea-songs. During the day we were busy around the boat, scraping the masts and painting the galley, and developing and printing Jack's negatives.

I myself spent a couple of days in Honolulu at this period, doing some special camera work, and trying my luck at surf-board riding. This is said to be one of the greatest sports in the world, but as it takes several months, at the least, really to learn it, I can hardly testify as to that. But I do know that I was nearly drowned, and managed to swallow a few quarts of salt water before the fun wore off. Jack stayed at it for some time, and got so sunburned that he was confined to his bed. Let me say here that it is my honest belief that only the native Hawaiians ever really learn the trick in all its intricacies, despite the fact that, at several contests held, white men have come out victorious.

For my part, I found swimming and fishing at Pearl Harbor much better sport. The fish bit readily. I have caught as many as twenty in five minutes. In the water, nearby, were turtles as big as a wash-tub. One day a shark twenty-two feet long was killed, and the day after one eighteen feet long.

Once, toward evening, Tochigi, Gene, and I were out rowing in a little canvas boat. It sank about a quarter of a mile from shore. Not that we cared much, for we had on nothing but swimming trunks, but we went lively when we discovered that a little hammer-headed shark was close to us, circling around in the water. He was too small to do us any harm, but his little protruding eyes looked so fierce that we all made haste for shore. This place was full of these little hammer-headed sharks, as well as of turtles and devil-fish.

It may sound rather strange when I say that we were in the habit of wearing only swimming suits, but we lessoned from the people we saw about us, and many of them were more simply garbed even than that. Mr. and Mrs. London, however, usually wore Japanese kimonos. And our captain dressed like a tramp.

Captain X—— was a horrible example of what ill temper will do. His half-breed son declared that he was born angry. At any rate, he seemed aboard the

Snark to have the idea that he was working Kanaka sailors, and would have sworn at us continually had we allowed it. It may be that he had cause to be irritable, for he had once been beaten out of a great fortune. X—— had been plying around the South Seas for twenty years, and once had discovered a small island covered with guano — about twenty million dollars worth of it. X—— beat back to Honolulu with all haste, that he might arrange to take the island in the name of the United States. He was given the proper authority, and with a small crew he hastened back to his wonderful find. Daylight was breaking dimly as he approached; there was sufficient light for him to see a small Japanese man-of-war slipping in the gloom toward the cherished island. When he and his men landed, they were met by soldiers, who told them that the island was now formally in the possession of the Japanese government. I really think that this would be enough to sour any man's temper. Another time, he drifted around for weeks in a small ship, nearly dead for water, and with half his crew lying corpses on the deck. He escaped when wrecked off the coast of the island of Maui. One of his occupations was "shanghai"-ing South Sea Islanders for work on the Hawaiian plantations; and a favourite trick was to cheat the natives when buying copra — he would put his knee under the sack while weighing it, thus making a two-hundred-pound sack lose half of its weight. He was a regular old skinflint; but whatever his merits

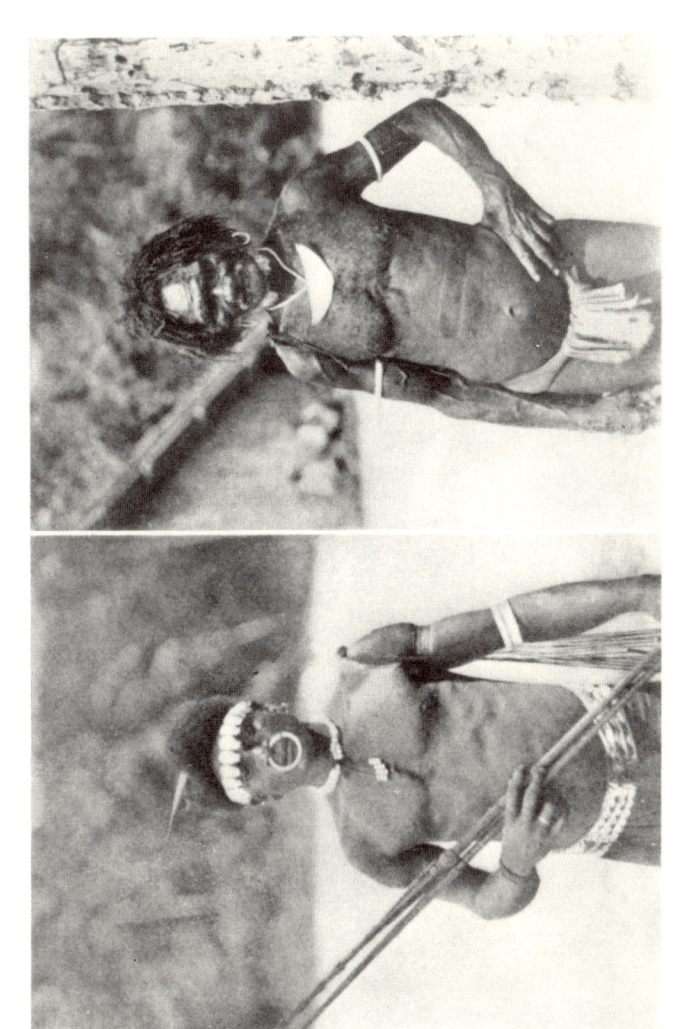

A Man of Roas. Solomon Group, Island of Malaita

Chief of Florida Island, Solomon Group

or demerits, one thing was certain: he had been everywhere in the South Seas, and had the records to prove it.

Much work was being done on the *Snark*. Men came from Honolulu and put everything shipshape. They got the seventy-horse-power engine to running, also the dynamo of the small engine, painted the *Snark* again, cleaned the rigging, scraped the masts and spars, and stopped the leaks. Best of all, they put the engine of the gasolene launch into condition. We used to make little trips in the launch by night. All this time, Jack and Mrs. London were making visits to the neighbouring islands, so that we saw little of them.

Oftentimes, in the evening, I would spend an hour or more watching the beauties of the Hawaiian scenery when bathed in the soft beams of the moon. In the harbour lay the *Snark,* looking as if lighted by electricity where the moonbeams were mirrored on her freshly painted sides and her polished metal, and further away was the shadowy shore-line, fringed by groves of cocoanut palms, and still further back, fading away into the night, were the majestic mountains.

"The *Snark* will never be able to heave-to," we were told. "She catches too much wind aft, no matter how the sails are trimmed." But with the seventy-horse-power engine in running order, the danger was vastly minimised, for with its aid we could cut through a storm like a knife.

The boat was taken to Honolulu for a thorough

overhauling. Of course, the crew went too. My stay in Honolulu was one of the most enjoyable periods of my life, despite the growing enmity between Captain X—— and myself. None of us liked him; even Jack was wishing for an opportunity to let him go. He was an eccentric person, to say the least, and had all the latest variations in his vocabulary. Being particularly sore on me, he used to take his spite out by calling inanimate objects about the vessel the names he really intended to apply to the erstwhile cook of the *Snark;* and when our repairs were complete and the *Snark* was taken out for a trial trip, all the crew, except Captain X——, knew that Jack was dissatisfied with Captain X—— and would appoint a new captain at the first opportunity — presumably Mr. Y——, who was then on the boat as a common sailor. Hence his control of us was rather broken; during the trip the entire crew absolutely refused to be ordered about any; but, carried out the work that was necessary to take the *Snark* out in the bay and back again, while Captain X—— remained at the wheel, seemingly much disgruntled. Entering the harbour, as a result of this misunderstanding between the captain and crew, the *Snark* was so manœuvred that she bumped into a trading-steamer, and then into a bark, at both of which times the *Snark* was slightly injured — several holes were made in the stern. As soon as we touched the wharf, I telephoned to Jack to come down, as the opportunity was at hand

A Pacific Paradise

for him to discharge the profane captain; and this Jack did, with neatness and despatch, as soon as a cab could bring him from the hotel.

During President Cleveland's administration, there was considerable agitation about the annexation of Hawaii to the United States. The natives had become somewhat dissatisfied with Queen Lilioukalani, because she refused to allow them to frame a constitution. They felt that she wished to be the entire government. The natives dethroned the queen, and elected Mr. Frederick Doyle as their president, and they framed a constitution as similar to that of the United States as they could possibly get it. At this time a Mr. Thurston, a prominent land-owner and one of the most influential men on the island, took a hand in the administration of public affairs. It was his advice that led to President Doyle's trip to the United States, which resulted in the annexation of the islands to our country; and the Queen's palace became the United States Government building. Mr. Thurston's plan of annexation was a good one; it prevented the islands from falling into the hands of the Japanese, who were rapidly gaining control of them. Hawaii was civilised before the western line of the United States; the grass huts had disappeared before California was developed. This progress in the Hawaiian Islands was due to the conscientious efforts of the early missionaries; but there is now to be found upon this island a class of people who are the descendants of a few of the earlier missionaries (who were of a distinctly mercenary turn of mind and secured for their private use some of the most valuable lands of the valley). The descendants, known as the " missionary class " now live in ease and comfort without putting forth the slightest effort to help develop the islands or assist in the betterment of anyone but themselves. Of course, they are not missionaries, nor have they ever been missionaries in the true sense, as they are not supported by any church organisation, but live off the natural richness of the land appropriated by their missionary forefathers.

During the development of the islands, it was necessary, in order to secure suitable grounds for the rapidly growing and beautiful city of Honolulu, to fill in and raise above its former marshy level the entire end of the Nuuanu Valley; and this large drainage canal still disposes of the water from the upper valley. The city of Honolulu now boasts of as fine hotels as will be found anywhere in the world in a town of that size, and the business section of the city is built upon as solid a basis as any town of possibly twice the size. In 1778, Captain Cook estimated the native population of Hawaii as four hundred thousand. The 1900 census showed only about twenty-nine thousand natives on the island. In their place have sprung up thousands and thousands of Japs, Chinese, and half-castes.

With all its development and advancement, there

are still interesting spots in the city of Honolulu. One will occasionally see a Japanese 'rickashaw, or see a Japanese mother carrying her naked baby in the streets. The Chinese section presents about the same weird style of Chinese architecture as will be found in many of the large cities in the States, where the Chinese population still holds to its original manners and customs. After the annexation of the Hawaiian Islands to the United States, which took place in 1900, the business advancement of the islands was very rapid, in spite of certain peculiar laws enacted by the members of the first legislative body. This body was composed of natives who had no other idea in mind than to get their names on a statute-book as the makers of law. One of them even proposed an act to regulate the rise and fall of the tides. Of course, he had an idea that this legislative body, backed by all the authority of the United States government, could accomplish any act it saw fit to. Another member proposed a bill creating the office of State Entomologist, as he had read somewhere that an entomologist was a bug-man; he had himself appointed to the office, and a few days later came with another bill asking that the position of State Entomologist be declared vacant, because there were still bugs in his coffee. But these minor defects in the first legislative body were rapidly overcome, and now the people of Hawaii hold dear to their hearts two flags, one the stars and stripes of the United

States, and the other the red, white and purple of Hawaii. In their decorating, the two flags are always in evidence, equal prominence given to each.

We paid a visit to the crater of an extinct volcano, called The Punch Bowl. Out at Waikiki Beach the surf-board riding could always be undertaken by such as liked it; and there were other amusements. Once, at Thomas Square, I heard the Royal Hawaiian Band play, while a Sunday School gathering of Japanese children sang. After they had finished, a Kanaka class sang. All those three hundred children were dressed in their native costumes. It was very enjoyable, even if we couldn't understand a word of the songs.

We were in Honolulu over the Fourth of July, that is, all but Jack and Mrs. London. Several American transports, with fourteen thousand troops, lay in the harbour. The celebration of the Fourth of July was a moral event in Hawaiian history; and the parade was one of the most splendid I have ever witnessed. As a fitting climax to the day's festivities, a picked baseball team from among the American soldiers challenged, and were defeated by, a picked-up aggregation of Japanese boys.

The development of the city of Honolulu under the American flag is just as perfect and complete as in any city in America. In fact, the street-car system of the city of Honolulu is the most perfect in the world — all fine, big sixty-foot observation cars, especially fitted for the passengers to enjoy to the utmost the tropical

A Pacific Paradise

scenery along the delightful suburban routes. The fire departments are fully equipped with the most efficient and modern machinery, and their runs are just as awe-inspiring as those of the city departments of our land.

The equable climate of Honolulu has tempted many of the wealthiest people of the United States to select it as a spot for permanent residence. As I think I have mentioned before, the temperature varies only about ten degrees, so that Hawaii is a veritable Paradise of the Pacific. Beautiful homes are springing up along the shady streets, some of the more elegant ones costing many thousands of dollars. The Japanese seem fully to understand the use of the picturesque and beautiful trees found on the islands. The parks are as pretty as any in the world, little pagodas and brilliant-coloured trees and grasses usually so disposed in landscape gardening as to carry out quaint Japanese patterns. Some of the mammoth trees burst into a mass of bright flowers, and they, too, will be found to be set in varied designs. Here will be found the famous banyan tree. One peculiarity of this tree is its method of throwing down from the horizontal branches supports, which take root as soon as they touch ground and enlarge into trunks and extend branches of their own, until one tree will cover an acre or more of ground. A single tree has been known to cover seven acres. The pleasant drives naturally stimulate the breeding of fine horses. One may see here equipages as superb as are to be found in Paris or London.

As a natural result of the religious basis upon which the original civilisation of Hawaii was founded, there are many fine churches, mostly constructed of lava. Volcanic lava forms a very solid and permanent building stone, being much heavier even than granite, and susceptible of a very high polish.

Upon the island are several volcanoes. Scientists have figured out that one of these is the progenitor of the island of Oahu, and certainly, whatever the validity of their claims, Oahu is entirely of volcanic origin. Japanese now farm inside the crater of one extinct volcano, which is more than a mile across. The volcanic mountain called Diamond Head, the first point of land observed by sailors approaching the Hawaiian Islands, is as beautiful a bit of mountain scenery as will be found on any sea-coast. On the island of Hawaii are the two largest volcanoes in the world, Mauna Kea, thirteen thousand eight hundred feet high, and Mauna Loa, thirteen thousand six hundred feet high.

Thunderstorms are rare and hurricanes are unknown in the Hawaiian Islands, hence the deep large bays form very favourable shipping ports. Their position puts them in direct line of vessels trading between western North America on the one side, and eastern Asia and Australia on the other. This is responsible to a great extent for its commercial development. Regular steamers come to Honolulu from San Francisco, Vancouver, Yokohama, Hong-Kong and Sydney, and the various ports of minor significance. Hono-

GROUP OF ROAS WOMEN, SOLOMON ISLANDS

lulu is also a station of the Pacific Commercial Cable, and has direct communication with the United States and the Orient. During our stay, the cable ship *Relief* came into the harbour. We saw ships of every sort, from the little fishing craft, Jap *sampans,* up to brigantines. One of the most interesting of all was the transport, *Thomas,* with several thousand American soldiers on board. Sailing-dates of one of the large steamers are always big days; thousands of people flock to the wharf.

Before leaving Honolulu, Captain X—— did everything in his power to make me uncomfortable, for he considered it my fault that he had lost his position. He called me a mutineer and told Jack that I was not of much account, anyway. As the time drew closer for us to think of leaving Honolulu, we set several dates for our departure, but always at the last minute something went wrong with the engines, and we were compelled to postpone sailing. Tochigi told me several times that he thought he would quit — he could not help but dread the seasickness he knew would afflict him — but each time I persuaded him to remain, reminding him that it would be a sorry trick to leave me all alone to fight the sickness.

Whenever we set a date there would be a crowd of people at the wharf to see us off, but each time we were obliged to set out a sign, *Sailing postponed,* until the people in Honolulu had ceased taking us seriously; and one man asked Jack why he did not buy him a house instead of living at a hotel — that it would be cheaper. The Honolulu press came out with several amusing articles on the *Snark,* and even reprinted the old refrain of " Not yet, but soon." This, with other articles, made us dislike to go upon the street, on account of the comments, as we were pretty well known by them. One day, while in King Street, one of the principal thoroughfares of the city, I heard even the newsboys crying: " When will the *Snark* sail? — Not yet, but soon."

But after spending several months in Honolulu and the suburb of Waikiki, we managed to leave the harbour on a day when few people expected us to be ready. The engines ran splendidly, until we were out of sight of Honolulu; then the suction pump on the big engine carried away.

Jack was angry, but said he would not go back to Honolulu if the boat were sinking, so we set sail and during the next three or four days sailed down past the islands of Molokai and Maui. At the island of Maui, the natives were catching mammoth turtles that are sold in the Honolulu fish-markets; as a matter of fact, these natives are regular fiends for turtle-flesh. They catch their prey in a peculiar manner, creeping upon them as they lie on the sandy beach warming themselves in the sun. Two or three Kanakas will steal down upon a turtle and flop him over on his back, in which position he is powerless.

After nearly a week of sailing, we came in sight of

one of the largest active volcanoes in the world, Mauna Loa, or, as the crater is called, Haleakala. This was Captain Y——'s first landfall, and I must say the way he brought the *Snark* head-up into the wind and lowered anchor was a marvel to us landlubbers, who up to now had been sailing the vessel as a boy would float a tub. Captain Y—— sailed and anchored the *Snark* as a ship should be sailed and anchored. He gave his orders in a tone that left nothing for us to do but obey; not that his orders were delivered in the manner of Captain X——, but instead in the strong, clear tones of a man who was used to giving orders and having them obeyed.

Kailua is the fifth largest town on the island of Hawaii, and contains possibly one hundred persons. The main business street of the town often appears utterly deserted, as the natives say no one but fools and Americans will venture out in the heat of the day. The main business house is an American saloon run by a Chinaman; the bar fixtures consisting of a counter and a large refrigerator, which I am quite sure never had any ice in it. Gene bought a glass of beer, but it was so flat and warm that he could not drink it.

The volcano of Kilauea is situated on the leeward side of the island of Hawaii, which makes it very dangerous for sailing vessels. Captain Cook, whose monument stands a few miles below this volcano, discovered the Sandwich Islands, or Hawaii, while searching for the Northwest Passage. He determined to build here his winter home, and study conditions among the islands while waiting for the snow and ice to melt, that he might get through to Bering Strait. As the natives had never seen the like of the saws and axes and hammers used by the ship's carpenter in building this house, they stole them. Not that the innocent people knew what stealing was — they had merely planted the tools in the ground in the hope that they might grow and produce more tools. Captain Cook, following his usual drastic methods, seized the old King, whom he intended to hold as a hostage for the return of his property. During the fight, several of the natives were killed, and Captain Cook was himself captured. When the sailors found that Captain Cook had fallen into the hands of the natives, they sent word that the King was to be held until Captain Cook was returned. Captain Cook *was* returned; at least, as much of him as could be found after the feast. The body was brought aboard the ship in pieces, was buried, and a monument erected. Beside the grave is the grave of a Kanaka who used to boast proudly that he had eaten the big toe of Captain Cook, for, as the natives afterward explained, the captain had really been eaten, and the body of a native substituted.

In the days gone by, the natives used to call the feast of human flesh the long-pig feast. They still have these feasts, only instead of human flesh they serve the flesh of the wild boar, which is plentiful on the island. Instead of roasting the pig from the outside, as we do, the natives dig a hole in the ground, and, after making a fire, pile stones on top of the fire until they are red hot, then put the stones on the inside of the pig and bake him from the inside out, and serve the meat with *poi*.

Like Oahu, the island of Hawaii is entirely of volcanic origin. The two large volcanoes on this island, Mauna Kea and Mauna Loa, formerly had craters at the tops, which have soiled over, and new craters have opened up far down the mountainsides. In many places the surface of the ground is nothing more than lava, still in the exact condition the latest eruption has allowed it to cool in, and seamed with fissures that opened up as it cooled.

Kailua is one of the most lonesome, desolate spots in the Hawaiian Islands. I had a great deal of time in which I had nothing to do, for, as I have said, the crew absolutely refused to eat my cooking any longer. I used to sit on the lava coast and try to see across the several thousand miles to America, where there were people to whom I could speak; I did not understand these people here. As Tochigi had finally settled that he could not fight down his seasickness, he had decided to remain in Kailua until the steamer could take him back to Honolulu. I was very sorry to see Tochigi go, but I appreciated his reason, and so offered no more resistance. Gene I did not get very well acquainted with; and Captain Y—— seemed too much like a boss for me to be friendly with him, but afterward he thawed out and we became the best of friends. During the week that we lay in Kailua anchorage, Tochigi and I made long trips into the interior and along the coast, where we saw some of the large rice and coffee plantations. The Chinese are the only ones in the islands who have any success with rice; we saw the young sprouts in the artificial marshes they have made. The natives never make any attempt at farming, except to farm fish. They have large artificial fish-ponds that they stock with mullet and crimps, and there is trouble if any person tries to catch fish out of another man's pond. Fruit here, as on all the islands, is very plentiful. There are no seasons for it; it grows the year round.

The famous Kona coffee is raised on this side of the island of Hawaii — in fact, this is the only place in the islands where coffee can be raised, as elsewhere the wind would disturb the coffee-tree and cause the bean to shatter. The coffee is hulled by the old and primitive method of allowing a large log to beat the coffee until it is hulled.

A pleasant way of killing time was to do a little amateur sailing with our life-boat. Gene and I knew practically nothing about sailing such a small boat, and when we got on the bay all the natives hunted shelter, terrified by our manœuvres; and when we clumsily ran on the beach, there was much amusement among the natives who were loafing on shore. Mr. and Mrs. London decided to go across the island to Hilo, on

A Pacific Paradise

the Puna coast, on horseback. So only Captain Y——, Gene, and myself, and a white man we had picked up in Honolulu, were left to take the *Snark* around the island through the main strait to Hilo.

Little Tochigi, who had been but a bundle of Japanese misery every minute at sea since leaving San Francisco, now said good-bye to us. As we heaved anchor and sailed out of the bay, the last thing we saw of poor Tochigi was his diminishing form sitting alone on the seashore, watching the *Snark* disappear from his view.

The day before we left Kailua, a small trading sloop came into the harbour and was still anchored when we left; in fact, we later found that we had a whole day's start on this boat; but during the time that the small crew of the *Snark* was fighting head-winds and tide-rips in the main channel, this vessel drew up and passed us and was in Hilo Bay a day before us. After we got to the Puna coast of Hawaii, we could see the prettiest shore-line, rich with tropical fruit trees and luxuriant vegetation. Scores of waterfalls, some of them hundreds of feet above us, were scattered all along this coast, clear into Hilo Harbor.

We dropped anchor in Hilo five days from Kailua. The harbour here is too shallow for the largest steamships to draw up close to the wharf, but the *Snark*, being so small, was able to anchor just at the mouth of the Waikaiea River. In the heart of Hilo's little fishing suburbs, the town of Waikaiea is about one mile along the seashore from Hilo proper, and is inhabited almost wholly by Japs, Chinese and Kanakas. Before going further, I had perhaps better explain this word " Kanaka." In the Hawaiian language, *Kanaka* means man, and *Wahine* means woman, but all Hawaiians, both men and women, are called Kanakas by the white people, so the word is generally understood to mean native Hawaiian.

The people of Waikaiea are nearly all fishing people, everyone taking a hand in the fishing. The men go out in their boats just before sundown, and fish all night long. At five o'clock in the morning the womenfolk are waiting along the little river-docks to unload the fish. The fish are carried into one of the fishmarkets, where the children sort out the different kinds into piles. There are large tanks for the turtles and octopuses; and big hooks are suspended from the ceilings by pulleys for the larger fish that are too heavy for handling. Then the auctioneer sells the fish to the highest bidder. The big sharks weighing two and three hundred pounds often bring less than a ten-pound fish, as the fins are all that is used of certain kinds of sharks. I have seen devil-fish, or octopuses, that were thirty feet from the end of one tentacle to the end of the opposite one. The fish are usually bought by Japanese or Chinese fish-runners. Immediately after they have secured all they can carry, they start off at a dog-trot, which never ceases until

A Pacific Paradise

each has reached his district for selling, sometimes ten or fifteen miles up the country.

To get to Hilo from the *Snark,* the best way was to walk along the sandy beach clear into Hilo, for the damp sand was always cool and refreshing, and the sea breeze blowing made one want to take off his shoes and roll up his trousers, and splash along in the water, a thing I did many a time. Truth is, people, after a few weeks in the Sandwich Islands, start doing things they would never think of doing in the staid old United States. The climate seems to make one younger, for it is always spring in Hawaii.

On a quiet morning some strangely wonderful sights may be seen. In the clear water one can easily make out many-hued fish, and coral, sponges, coral-crabs; and, under the sponges, small octupuses or devil-fish from the size of one's hand down to the size of a silver dollar.

Hilo has about five thousand, mixed population. Here, as among all the islands of the group, the Japanese predominate, with Chinese a close second. The white people on this side of the island live mostly outside of Hilo on plantations; and as the brown population sleeps through the heat of the day, the business streets are deserted until late in the afternoon. Then the streets spring suddenly into life, and for several hours are thronged with people of all nationalities. The clubs and saloons are crowded, the band plays nearly every evening, and everyone settles down to enjoy himself.

Off the business streets, the residence district seems like a park. The roads are well paved, electric lights are strung at every crossing, hedges and fences are of trees that usually bear flowers throughout the year. Homes are mostly of the bungalow style, with large porches running clear around the house. These porches are used as dining and sleeping rooms the year round. In fact, the people often give more thought to the *lanai,* as they call the porch, than to any other part of the house.

The lawns around the bungalows are studded with fruit trees that are usually laden with ripe fruit at all times. The small boys never care to steal fruit here, as there is so much of it that anyone may help himself to fruit wherever he finds it.

The fine public libraries, churches, and a good opera house at Hilo are as truly modern buildings as any I have seen in the United States. A large pineapple factory is located here, and one steamer makes regular trips from San Francisco to get the bananas that grow wild along this coast.

Hilo supplies the United States with more canesugar than any city in the world. Large sugar-mills are located along the water-front, in order that ships may load by gravity right from the mill. The sugarcane is raised back of Hilo, and as far back as twenty miles into the mountains. The sugar-cane is sent to the mill in long flumes that are filled with water, and the cane laid in the flumes goes down to the mill at the rate of twenty miles an hour.

The manager of the Waipalia sugar-mill invited Jack, Mrs. London, Captain Y——, and me to go for a flume-ride one Sunday, when there was no cane in the flume. Cabs were secured, and we were driven away back in the mountains to a good place to start from. Before leaving Hilo we had donned our bathing suits. Making a good seat of cane for ourselves, to guard against possible nails, we all got in the flume and started off. There is no more exciting sport in the world than flume-riding. Often, we could look down inclines, from one hundred and fifty to two hundred feet below. We rushed so fast that had a nail ever gotten in the way, it would certainly have ripped off a lot of skin, but we could not stop, for to have done so would have thrown us from the flume.

The rice fields looked like ordinary wheat fields. The rice is threshed by the primitive method of cutting the heads off the stalk, laying them on a large piece of volcanic rock, and letting in Chinese with bare feet to stamp upon it until the grain is hulled. Rice is an important factor in the Hawaiian farming, as the Japs and Chinese live upon it almost wholly. No rice is exported; the orientals consume the entire output.

As the rice must be planted in the water, the rice fields tend to breed mosquitoes, which become so annoying that it is often necessary to burn a powder called *buhack* all night long, in addition to having the regular mosquito netting over the bed.

About a half a mile outside of Waikaiea River is a small island a mile in circumference, called Cocoanut Island. On this island is a family of native fishermen who still cling to the old way of fishing with spears, instead of hook and line, and they never employ the large nets used by the oriental fishermen. Instead, they use a small hand net, so that they can catch the particular kind of fish they want. They will not eat an ordinary fish, but they have their favourite variety, which are hard to catch.

Fish are so plentiful here that a child can catch as many as it wants. Even a Kanaka child would eat only certain kinds, but to the *Snark's* crew they all tasted alike; and we ate whatever we could catch — even shark, and the tentacles of the octopus.

On one side of Cocoanut Island is a large sandy beach that is fine for surf bathing. On the other side, the large lava rocks go almost straight down, making a fine place for diving. Nearly every afternoon I would go over to the island for a swim, and usually had the whole beach to myself, except Sundays, when the island was crowded with bathers. One day, on going to my favourite lava rocks, off which the diving was fine, I found the place occupied by a person whom I had never seen before. I was so surprised that I could only stand and stare. She was a full-blooded Hawaiian girl, and from what I could see of her she

A Mission School. Boy in white shirt is the Teacher, the rest are Members of the Class

was good-looking, too. Of course, I could not let a chance like this go to waste, so I made several photographs of her, and when I asked her to stand I was more than sure she was good-looking. She did not like to stand with the sun shining in her eyes, so we hunted a shady spot, and I used up the rest of the film in my camera.

But it must not be supposed for a minute that the native girls are the only good-looking girls in Hilo. Some of the Japanese girls with whom I had a photographing acquaintance were as *chic* as are to be found any place. One in particular, who was head saleslady for the Hilo Drug Company, was not at all bad-looking. To see these little Japanese girls gliding through the streets — gliding, for their walk is such a funny little trot that that is the only word to describe it -— I say, to see them gliding along makes a man ashamed of his own uncouthness when he chances to meet one of them, and must, for manners' sake, walk up the street with her. One girl I knew was born in Hilo, but her parents would not let her wear clothes of American fashion, so she looked like any native Japanese, but spoke excellent English. American clothes usually spoil the looks of a Japanese, for the Jap form will not take to our garb at all.

These Jap girls do not at first sight seem to be extravagantly dressed, but for Sunday- and evening-wear, a Japanese girl's dress will oftentimes cost double the sum the clothes of a stylish American girl cost. At least, this is what the new cabin-boy we got in Hilo, a Jap named Nakata, told me, and I suppose he ought to know.

In the mountains are herds of wild cattle; and near Hilo are large ranches, where the best cattle country in the world is found. Here, too, will be seen the only genuine American cowboy. The cowboys we have in the States are for exhibition purposes only. But here the big open valleys and mountains, where the cattle breed, are so extensive that when the cattle are rounded up only an expert cowboy would be able to manage them, for by that time they are nearly as skittish as the wild cattle. With every round-up, the men say they catch many wild cattle which have attached themselves to the ranchman's herd.

Gene and I made long excursions with the launch up the little creeks and rivers, and always returned with a load of fruit. Mr. and Mrs. London were staying with friends in Hilo. The sailor had been discharged, so that Captain Y——, Gene and I were the only ones aboard the *Snark*. We ate at a Chinese restaurant, and as there was little work to do, we found ample time for exploring. Gene wore only sleeveless track-shirts and swimming trunks, and became so sunburned that wherever exposed, his skin was of almost Ethiopian blackness, in strange contrast with the protected skin. During this time I became as black as Gene, but I seemed to tan all over. Jack did not tan at all;

every time he became exposed to the sun he blistered so badly that often it would lay him up in bed.

Finally, through a mutual agreement between Gene and Jack, Gene decided that the trip was too much for his delicate constitution, and Jack decided that he must consent to Gene's going. So Gene got ready to go back to San Francisco.

One day I got a call from Jack over the telephone, telling me that I was promoted to the position of engineer, and instructing Captain Y—— and me to look out for a new cook, a new cabin-boy, and a new sailor. I don't believe I would have traded positions with the President, or King Edward, that day. I was in a greater state of excitement than at the time of securing the position of cook. A Dutchman named Hermann — which is all the name we ever got out of him — was secured for the crew of one sailor. Hermann was one of the real deep-water sailors, of the kind that is rapidly passing away. He was about the best-natured fellow I ever worked with; in storm or calm he was always the same, always singing in one or another of the half-dozen tongues he could speak. We secured the cook and cabin-boy at the same time. Wada, a Japanese, could speak fluent English, and was a very good cook. He had been in almost every large port in the world. Nakata, whom we hired for cabin-boy, was likewise Japanese, and could not speak a word of English. All we could understand of his vocabulary was *pau,* which means finished, and *pilikea,* which means trouble. But when Nakata reached Australia, one year and a half later, he could speak very passable English, and could write quite well.

The principal photographer in Hilo was a young Chinese boy, who did excellent work. He used to make pictures of the *Snark* to sell; and wherever Jack went, the Chink would be on hand to photograph him. In the end, Jack could only get rid of the boy by consenting to pose for a number of pictures, which were afterward published in a Chinese magazine, with certain descriptive text beneath each one. I have no doubt Jack is a very big man in their eyes.

The time was rapidly nearing for us to leave. The engines were in good repair, we had fuel and provisions aboard, and practically every one of us was anxious to be off. Our way led now to the Marquesas Islands; and the trip, sixty-one days across the trackless Pacific, in which we sailed four thousand miles in order to advance two thousand miles, was to prove the greatest adventurous event of my life. And it ended by our landing in the world's Garden of Eden.

But before going further with the voyage, I must devote some consideration to one island of the Hawaiian group to which as yet no attention has been directed, Molokai, the Leper Island.

CHAPTER V

MOLOKAI, THE LEPER ISLAND

IN telling of Molokai, the Leper Island, I might as well confess at the outset that I was never on it. But Jack London was, and everything here set forth was gotten direct from him or from others who had intimate knowledge whereof they spoke. Not many persons, outside the officials of the Board of Health, have ever been allowed to leave the island of Molokai, once they had entered the Settlement. Dr. Pinkham, president of the Board of Health, who has the entire managing of the island, was an ardent admirer of the literary works of Jack London; and he so managed it that both the Londons were allowed to visit Molokai, in order that Mr. London might properly describe the life on this island, and thus correct the Kanaka notion that Molokai is a place of torture. Dr. Pinkham's decision was a wise one. Much has been written in the past of the horrors of the Leper Settlement, but almost without exception these expositions have been wild and lurid — as London put it, the work of sensationalists, most of whom had never laid eyes on a single one of the things they described in such exaggerated and undependable detail. But there are a great many persons among English-speaking peoples who have learned that Jack London always tells the truth as he sees it.

Dr. Pinkham knew that if London were to go to the Settlement, his account of it would present conditions as they actually are, not as they are shown to be in the distorted articles of the yellow press. And so, permission was granted.

But when I tried to follow, the doctor, though my very good friend, stopped me. He could not take me to the island of Molokai, because he had no excuse for doing so. I was not a noted writer — I was merely a sightseer; and to take a sightseer to Molokai would have lost him his position. For that matter, the Hawaiian citizens and the Honolulu press did criticise him severely for taking Mr. and Mrs. London to the island.

But while I have never seen the lepers in their Settlement, I have seen hundreds of cases of leprosy all through the South Seas. Furthermore, I have discussed the disease and the managing of Molokai with Dr. Pinkham, than whom surely there could be no better source of information. Leprosy was a constant topic of conversation, morning, noon, and night, with the little crew of voyageurs on the *Snark*; we were all deeply interested; and of this, as of every other island subject, Jack London had almost encyclopædic knowledge. In fact, leprosy was his hobby; he was an untiring defender of segregation. What of my own experiences, and the memory of other men's experiences, and what of all that Jack London told me at this time, there has been bred in me a profound conviction that my own knowledge of leprosy is considerable — certainly greater than that of many who live all their lives within a stone's throw of Molokai. In the very nature of the thing, I was bound to learn, and learn more than could any ordinary tourist, even though my actual observation might not extend quite so far as did the observation of the specialists, the members of the Board of Health, the executives, and those visitors, few in number, who have had the privilege of setting foot within the Leper Settlement.

And so, at the beginning, let me add my testimony to that of Jack London, in saying that the horrors with which Molokai is associated in the average mind, *simply do not exist.* The sensationalists have done their work well. To the four corners of the earth they have disseminated their ghastly fictions, with a persistency truly wonderful; and the people of every nation, hungry for things that are gruesome, have pounced greedily on all that was offered. As a result, their minds are full-fed with every variety of deceit, from mere harmless fables to the most inexcusable lies, and to such an extent that the truth, even when shown to them, may find little room for lodgment. Nevertheless, I am optimistic enough to hope that a pinch of real fact may leaven a mountain of misrepresentation, and that, in time, the people of every civilised country will come to know just what sort of place Molokai is, and just what things take place there.

It is strange that the greatest misapprehension exists among the people of Hawaii. Living next door, as it were, to the segregated unfortunates, many of whom have been recruited from their own ranks, it might be supposed that they would be the very first to disburden their minds of delusion. Not so. In the city of Honolulu, there are many who still credit the idea that Molokai is the place of life-long confinement, inhuman torture, and melancholy death. The word "Molokai" spells for them nothing but the most unmerciful disaster. The very name is enough to send the hot blood rushing to the heart, and to strike laughter from the lips. Truly, to their unhappy conception, Molokai is but the valley of the shadows, wherein shines never a ray of light to brighten the path of him who must tread its sombre way.

Much of this sentiment is due to demagogues, who stir the people constantly with their recital of the lepers' wrongs. Indignation often runs high when some particularly outrageous abuse is instanced. The natives are almost inconceivably credulous, and, unfortunately, they will not take the trouble to test the truth of demagogic assertion. However, a campaign of education has been begun; persons long resident in the Leper Settlement have been shown by the bacteriological test to be free from the imputed disease; and, returned to friends and families, they shatter by direct evidence the absurd fancies theretofore current. More and more the value and necessity of segregation is being impressed upon the Hawaiian natives' minds.

Molokai, the Leper Island

Jack and Mrs. London were at Molokai a week; they spent the Fourth of July there. I went with them down to the wharf to catch the leper-steamer, which makes weekly trips. It is almost always sure of at least one passenger, from the receiving station at Kalihi, where suspects are put through the bacteriological examination; and of course Superintendent McVeigh is usually on board, to take charge of the lepers and see them safely to the island.

A number of new lepers were to go that day, and the wharf was crowded with friends and relatives, come down to say the good-byes and to see the poor patients off. It was not a happy sight. I shall never forget it. Such stormy scenes of grief are terrible. Men and women and children were there; and on the faces of those who were to stay was great sadness, on the faces of those who were to go sadness and something more: a sick look, a lurking dread in their eyes, a pallor not natural to human flesh. As the time drew near for departure, a sudden stir came over the crowd; grief grew more vociferous. The babel of voices, hitherto somewhat subdued, rose first to a hum and then into a sharp murmur. Somewhere a rich native voice, low-pitched and beautiful, began softly singing the song of farewell. *Aloha oe — aloha oe,* was the refrain. Wheresoever the departing lepers might roam, through all their days of enforced segregation from those who loved them and whom they loved, affection and best wishes would be with them.

Then came the bustle of going aboard; last handclasps; tears; voices that shook with emotion; and though the sad hearts could not be seen nor heard, their beat somehow found its way into the scene; misery bound the many hearts into one, and their pulse was united by some mighty bond of sympathy. A harsh cry from the steamer now stirred everyone into action; the lepers broke sorrowfully away from their friends and families, whose grief burst out anew, and hurried aboard. Such was the parting — not a happy thing to see, not a thing one can forget.

At this point I was compelled to go back to the *Snark,* leaving Mr. and Mrs. London to make the trip to Molokai on the leper-boat. Two hours must elapse ere their arrival. Jack carried with him his camera, and took a number of unique and interesting pictures of the island and its inhabitants. Some of these pictures are here reproduced.

As the leper-boat approached the island, he secured some good views of its rocky coast. Owing to the fact that there is no anchorage close up, the leper-steamer must stand on and off a half-mile from shore, and the landing is made by shooting the surf, through a very dangerous passage, to a little wharf that extends about two hundred feet out into the channel. As they came near, a sound of music floated to them over the water. The return of Superintendent McVeigh is always considered an occasion for rejoicing, among the lepers. A number of the leper men and

MOLOKAI, THE LEPER SETTLEMENT, HAWAIIAN ISLANDS

Molokai, the Leper Island

women, gathered on the beach, play stringed instruments and sing happy songs to make the arrival of the new lepers as pleasant as possible.

Jack told me afterward that it was much different from what he had expected. He, too, had fed his mind on the writings of the sensationalists. Once he had read an account which told of Superintendent McVeigh (his host on this occasion) crouching in a grass hut and surrounded by lepers wailing through the night for food, which the cruel superintendent withheld. The funny part of it, Jack explained, was that Superintendent McVeigh's house was not of grass, but of wood, and the lepers, well-fed and comfortable, did no wailing at all, but were remarkably happy and contented folk, following their various chosen pursuits by day, or loafing if they desired, and filling the night with the melodious music of their *ukeleles*, banjos, guitars, violins, and other stringed instruments, to say nothing of beautiful songs sung by the singing societies. And another thing: when we were sailing along the windward side of Molokai on the *Snark*, Jack had pointed to the island, and said it was the pit of hell, the most cursed place on earth. But he never spoke so after his visit. His eyes were opened.

The Leper Settlement is divided into two main villages. These are on a peninsula extending from the north side of the island. To left, right, and front is the water. At the back towers the giant wall of the *pali*, varying from two to four thousand feet in height.

Besides the villages, there are a good many seaside and country homes. Many of the lepers are well-to-do, owning horses, fishing-boats, buggies, carts, and other property. One woman is said to have several good houses, which she rents.

In all, I believe there are over eight hundred souls on the island. The population is a mixed one. Dr. Pinkham told me that most of the lepers are Hawaiians, or part-Hawaiians; next in number come the Japanese; and the Chinese are third. (It is thought that the Chinese imported the disease into Hawaii.) There were also three negroes, a few Portuguese, a Norwegian, and about seven Americans. Americans, however, seldom catch the disease, and then almost always by inoculation. Jack met several of the American lepers; he afterward mentioned a Major Lee, once a marine engineer for the Inter Island Steamship Company, and then working in the new steam laundry of Molokai; Mr. Bartlett, formerly in business in Honolulu, now keeper of the Board of Health store; and another, whose name I have forgotten, but who was a veteran of the Civil War — a crack shot — and at that time in his sixty-fifth year. Then there are the non-lepers. Of these are the *kokuas,* or native helpers, and the priests; Protestant ministers and their wives; the resident physicians, Dr. Goodhue and Dr. Hollman; the Franciscan Sisters at Bishop House, and their Jap servants; two principals and four Brothers at Baldwin House, and sev-

Molokai, the Leper Island

eral domestics. Superintendent McVeigh's assistant, Mr. Waiamau, is a pure Hawaiian, himself stricken with leprosy.

In the two villages there are churches and assembly halls. Yellow writers to the contrary, there is not a grass house in the Settlement. The buildings are of wood and stone, and are very comfortable. There are stores for such as care to engage in business. Some of the lepers fish, others farm; there are splendid grassy pastures for the horses, which roam by hundreds in the mountains. The lepers have their fishing-boats and a steam launch. Again, there are painters and carpenters. Almost every trade is followed — even stock-raising and dairying are carried on. There are artisans of every variety. In such a large gathering of men and women and children, there is of course great diversity of taste and ability. Usually, those who have been actively engaged before coming to Molokai prefer to follow the same pursuits after their arrival.

But let it be emphasised that not one of these people needs work unless he elects to do so. Being wards of the Territory of Hawaii, all things necessary to life and comfort are supplied to them free. If, by their own efforts, they are able to make a few dollars, they are just that much ahead of the game. Lepers who live outside the two villages draw from the government a fixed amount of money as a " clothes ration order," in addition to a weekly allowance in provisions.

Of course, many of the lepers have property elsewhere, from which they derive an income; and some of them are looked after by friends.

There are over seven hundred buildings in the Settlement. Among them are the six churches: two Protestant, two Mormon, and two Catholic. The Young Men's Christian Association building is particularly good. The lepers even have an electric plant, and a *poi* factory, to say nothing of a courthouse and jail.

Social life is brisk on Molokai. An athletic club has been founded; also glee clubs. Weekly band concerts are given in the pavilion. On the afternoon of the Fourth of July, Jack and Mrs. London had the pleasure of seeing a merry parade, and were appointed the judges at a horse-race. On the morning after their arrival, they attended a shoot of the Kaluapapa Rifle Club. On the day the Londons climbed the two-thousand-foot *pali* and looked their last upon the Settlement, an exciting baseball game, played by the doctors, the lepers and the non-lepers, was in progress, on a very good baseball diamond. There are even visitors' houses, kept clean of disease, where, at certain intervals, the lepers may meet such of their friends, relatives, or business agents, as come to see them. And when one adds to all this the consideration that Molokai enjoys a better climate than even Honolulu, it will be seen that the Leper Settlement cannot be such a very terrible place after all.

After the Londons returned to Honolulu, many persons expressed amazement at their temerity in venturing wilfully among the afflicted of Molokai. They had not even held aloof from the lepers, nor worn long gloves; instead they had shaken hands with scores of them. To such of the staid people of Honolulu as still clung to their chamber-of-horrors notion, the act was the very height of foolhardiness. It was inconceivable. But among the more intelligent Hawaiians, no such horror of leprosy obtains. They realise how feebly contagious it is. In the Settlement, lepers and non-lepers mingle freely; at a shoot of the Kalaupapa Rifle Club, the same guns are used by those afflicted and those free from the disease; in horse-racing, the same horses are ridden by all; and in baseball games, bats, gloves, and masks are freely exchanged. Not easily does the *bacillus leprae* pass from body to body. Only is there danger when one has open wounds which might come in contact with leprous flesh. The usual precaution, after being with lepers, is the washing with antiseptic soap, and the changing of clothing. And as to the Londons' trip, two very important things were accomplished by it. In the first place, Jack's longing to see the much-talked-of leper retreat was satisfied; and that meant much. And secondly — more important — probably the first detailed and absolutely truthful account of the Settlement was given to the world in the article Jack wrote soon after, entitled "The Lepers of Molokai." That article, now reprinted in his " Cruise of the *Snark*," covers so thoroughly this visit to Molokai that it is needless for me to say much more concerning it. But my own observations as to leprosy in the other islands of the Territory of Hawaii, and the many things told me by the better-informed class of natives, may not be without value.

Segregation is imperative. By its means, leprosy is on the wane in Hawaii. When a person is suspected of the disease, he is summoned to Kalihi, in the outskirts of Honolulu and put through a thorough bacteriological test. If the *bacillus leprae* is found, after a careful examination by the bacteriologist, the suspect is further examined by a Board of physicians appointed for the purpose; and if he is pronounced a leper, preparations are made for taking him to Molokai. Plenty of time is given him in which to administer his business affairs. Every courtesy is shown. And after being sent to Molokai, he has the privilege of being again examined, at any time, by competent authority, to determine the exact condition of his disease.

As I have said, leprosy is very feebly contagious. But throughout the world, there is widespread fear of it. Considering the horribleness of the disease — for horrible it is, beyond the power of the most unprincipled inkster to exaggerate — and its absolutely incurable character, one cannot wonder much at the sentiment existing among all peoples in countries where

Molokai, the Leper Island

any of its forms are known. To be pronounced a leper seems, to the average person, virtually to be pronounced dead. But not decently dead! Were it so, the added horrors would not be there. No, the leper's death seems many times more dreadful than mere ordinary dissolution, because of its slowness and the awful form it assumes. The average person shrinks from death, but absolutely recoils from the same dark thing when it dons the robe of this, of all diseases the most foul. Furthermore, some deaths are swift — mercifully swift, and not unlovely. Leprosy is usually slow, vile, hideous. One dies by inches. Terrible in contemplation, what must it be when fastened insidiously upon one's flesh!

But no more of this, lest I, too, be adjudged one of the purveyors of things needlessly dreadful. But remember this: when Jack London, or I, or any other man, says that the horrors of the Molokai leper life have been exaggerated, it is not meant that the disease itself has been exaggerated. No one denies that leprosy is an awful thing. But anyone who has ever seen the leper colony of Molokai, or knows anything about it, will most strenuously deny that the conditions under which these people live are bad. Jack said, on his return to the *Snark,* that, given his choice between living out his days in any one of those " cesspools of human misery and degradation," the East End of London, the East Side of New York, or the Stockyards of Chicago, or going to stay in Molokai, he would, without hesitation, with gratitude even, choose Molokai.

For he knows that the people of Molokai are happy. They live at ease, *while they live*. But not so the people of the other places. Theirs is one long, mad struggle for mere existence; life is a turmoil, a riot, a nightmare. On Molokai, food is plenty. No fight is there. The days are peaceful and the nights are happy. All is music and beautiful scenes; fresh breezes are always blowing from over the sea. The men and women of Molokai do not freeze through a bitter-cold winter, nor do they swelter in a raging summer's heat. While they live, they live in Paradise. No wonder Jack London knew, without debate, which place he would choose.

The lepers themselves are satisfied — and what better testimony could be asked? Since the bacteriological test was put into effect, a number of persons once declared lepers and sent to Molokai have been found to be wholly clean of the disease, and been returned to their homes. They have never ceased bewailing their expulsion from Molokai. "Back to Molokai," is the lament of all who have once tasted of the island's delights and then been shut out from them.

One of the most unfortunate things about leprosy in the Territory of Hawaii is the fact that the friends and relatives of lepers so often hide them away when

Molokai, the Leper Island

the disease first appears, and keep them hidden until they are in a terrible condition. One day, when I was walking along a little-frequented part of the beach, not far from Pearl City, on the island of Oahu, I saw a small child playing near the water. As I drew near, its mother came rushing toward it, gathered it up in her arms, and ran to her hut, about fifty yards away. At the time I was puzzled, but I was afterward told, in confidence, that the child was a leper, and that the mother was determined to keep it from the attention of the Board of Health.

It is best for the lepers themselves that they be taken to the Settlement, where they can receive proper medical treatment. Outside, they can do nothing but lie and await inevitable death. But in the Settlement, the surgeons can make occasional operations, and hold off the ravages indefinitely. Some lepers, stricken in their youth, have lived happy lives, and died of old age, when thus protected. Leprosy is very intermittent in its action; after once appearing and being treated, it may not show itself again for years. But if not treated, it gallops.

I well remember the case of a leper in the United States a few years ago. The newspapers exploited the case sensationally, but I think there was nevertheless an element of truth in what they printed. The leper was a tramp. How he had contracted the disease, no one knew. But it is said that he lived altogether in a box-car. This car he was never allowed to leave. The railway company was desperate. Time and again they tried to force him out at different stations, but each time the men of the town cried a veto to the scheme. Thousands of miles that leper tramp travelled. In the whole country, there was no spot of earth big enough for him to set his foot on. In the box-car he was, and in the box-car he must remain. Not that he starved. People flung food to him as they fling food to dogs; also, there were occasional donations of clothing, reached out to him on long poles. At last the railway company, grown doubly desperate, hit upon an expedient. They unhooked the car one night, and left it standing on a siding, about a mile from a little mining village. But the trick failed. The next freight that pulled up that way was met by several hundred black-looking men, armed with rifles; and when that train pulled out, it carried with it the leper's box-car and the leper. I never heard what became of the car, nor of its occupant. But the story was a gruesome thing, and well illustrates the difference between a leper's fare outside the Settlement, and inside the Settlement.

Now as to leprosy itself. No one knows what it is. It is classified according to its manifestations. Delve we never so far into the remoteness of antiquity, we will find records of leprosy. Fifteen hundred years before Christ, it was widely known in the delta and valley of the Nile. It flourished throughout the Middle Ages. To-day it is common in Asia, Africa, South

LEPER BAND AT MOLOKAI, THE LEPER ISLAND OF THE HAWAIIAN GROUP

Molokai, the Leper Island

America, the West Indies, and certain isolated localities of Europe. Little was known of it in the ancient days; but little is known of it now. It is parasitic — that much is certain. Dr. Armauer Hansen discovered the *bacillus leprae* in 1871, but no one has gotten much further than that. Its only alleviation is surgery, but this is sometimes without avail. Leprosy is of three well-defined kinds: There is Running Leprosy, the most horrible of the three. It shows itself mainly as shiny ulcers, which throw off a highly offensive perspiration. In this kind, the fingers, ears, nose, and eyes are often eaten away, leaving a hideous bundle of flesh that but faintly resembles a human being. Dry Leprosy, the second variety, does not take such an offensive form. It resembles a very bad case of eczema, affecting the feet and the hands more than any other part of the body. The skin becomes thick and reddened, while the fleshy part rapidly disappears, leaving the fingers crooked and hard, like claws. The third kind is known as Nervous or Anæsthetic Leprosy. The nerves of the body cease to do their work and become so deadened that a finger could be scraped to the bone with a nutmeg-grater without the least pain. This kind of leprosy makes its victim appear gnarled and twisted as with rheumatism.

The period of incubation is not definitely known. Probably it is some years. Now and then, however, there is a case in which the disease develops with great rapidity, and is steady in its ravages. Various internal remedies have been tried, among them chaulmoogra oil, arsenic, salicylate of soda, salol, and chlorate of potash. While these prove of efficacy in some cases, there has never been a well-authenticated case of cure. Years may pass before the proper remedial agent shall have been discovered.

One of the most interesting spots in the island is the grave of Father Damien, the name in religion of Joseph de Veuster. In the days when segregation on Molokai was first being tried out, many of the lepers sent to the island were in an advanced stage of the disease and were consequently helpless. Being unable to take care of themselves, they lived in misery for years. Some of the deported unfortunates were too feeble to build themselves grass houses, and lived like wild beasts, anywhere they could find shelter. At this time, the young Belgian missionary, Father Damien, undertook to assume spiritual charge over the lepers. He worked for several years in the Settlement, and with his own hands built huts for those unable to build their own. He nursed the advanced cases, and with the help of the stronger lepers dug drainage canals, and took off the malarial water which had been a curse up to this time. He asked small donations from the government, which were reluctantly given, and he persuaded several other priests and two nuns to help him, and gradually built up the present sanitary Settlement, which has more perfect conditions

Molokai, the Leper Island

for sick people than any sanitarium, hospital, or detention camp in the world.

After about ten years of the most noble work any missionary ever attempted, Father Damien contracted leprosy, and for the next twelve years was not allowed to leave the island. But he carried out the work he started, and during the last months of his life, when he was one mass of gnarled, decaying flesh, he lay in his bed directing that his work go on as it had when he was well to oversee it. And on the day that he died, he asked to be brought out in the open air, that he might see the fruit of his labours — the thing for which he had given up his life. To-day, none can deny this man honour. He was a hero. By his sacrifice, he has been and will be for years to come the means of saving the lives of others. The United States government gladly took up the work that he laid down unfinished, and Molokai is now better managed than Father Damien, in his most optimistic dreams, might have hoped. It is good to know that when, not long after, a calumniator took up his pen to make light of the work of the dead priest, and to vilify him personally, Robert Louis Stevenson, himself a great writer and a great man, was there with all his energy in the defense.

Leprosy is often accompanied by elephantiasis; in fact, some medical authorities use the terms synonymously for the same disease. All through the South

Seas, where lepers and elephantiasis victims mingle with the other natives in their villages, the ones afflicted with elephantiasis are looked upon with more horror than the ones with leprosy, as the natives say elephantiasis is more catching, and that it develops more rapidly. At one island I was on, in the Society Group, it is estimated that one-tenth of the population has elephantiasis, or *fey-fey,* as they call it. Leprosy is not painful until it reaches an acute stage, but elephantiasis is accompanied by considerable pain from the first forming of the tumor, which tumor sometimes weighs one hundred pounds.

It will be noticed that I have not attempted a full description of leprosy. The symptoms once set forth, I fear certain of my impressionable readers might begin to experience them, just as hypochondriacs, after reading a patent-medicine almanac, appropriate to themselves all the diseases therein described. The doctors have enough to do; far be it from me to add to their troubles a swarm of pseudo-leprosy cases. Besides, such an enumeration could do no good. These things are depressing. Let us forget them, or, at least, the worst of them.

CHAPTER VI

THE LONG TRAVERSE

"It will be a long traverse."

"Yes, but what of that? The *Snark* is equal to it, and so are we."

"It will be a difficult traverse."

"So much the better."

Jack and Mrs. London were sitting at the cabin table, poring over their maps and planning the further voyage of the *Snark*.

"The Marquesas Islands lie two thousand miles away, as the crow flies," Jack went on. "But there are a good many things to reckon with. It will not be all plain sailing. Let's see — we mustn't cross the Line west of 130° west longitude. To do so might get us entangled with the southeast trades, and throw us so far to leeward of the islands that we couldn't make them. Then there's the equatorial current to be considered, and a few other things. But we'll do it. We'll do it."

Mrs. London glanced across the table at him and nodded her assent.

"October 7, then, is the day," Jack announced; and we set to work.

Again we were kept busy almost up to the hour of sailing. The boat was provisioned and fuel put aboard. We stowed away vegetables, salt-horse, codfish, salt pork, canned goods, potatoes, and a hundred and one things. We expected that it would take us at least two months to make our next anchorage, and possibly longer. The element of uncertainty was large, what of the storms and calms we must look for. But we were confident of making fair speed, for had we not a powerful gasolene engine with which to cheat the wind?

During the wait, we ordered a full wardrobe of clothing made, as we could hardly expect to find any stores down in the South Seas. Our working clothes were made like a Japanese fisherman's knee-trousers and sleeveless shirts, but the most comfortable dress for lounging was Japanese kimonos. My kimonos were made by two Hilo friends, in the latest Japanese fashion; and by the time we were ready to sail, I had a large camphor-wood chest full of clothing.

Gene Fenelon left on the little island steamer *Keaneau* on the same day that we sailed from Hilo. We had made many friends in Hilo, and on the day of our departure, the wharf was crowded with the most cosmopolitan gathering that ever assembled to see a ship off. Here again the people prophesied that we would never reach port, for this voyage was considered the most foolhardly we could attempt. But we were not to be deterred. We were looking for Adventure and trying to see the out-of-the-way places

The Long Traverse

that other people did not see, and, naturally, we wanted to make a trip that others could not make.

Before quitting land, I packed up a box of curios I had purchased in the Islands, and shipped it by steamer back to the States. Good fortune had attended my buying. In the box were reed sofa-pillows, deerskin rugs, an Aloha Nui (a pillow signifying lots and lots of good luck), a grass water-carrier, poisoned arrows, hooks used by natives in catching devil-fish, one tapa *hula* blanket, *hula* dresses, calabash dishes, native combs, opium pipes, and other interesting things. Jack and I determined from then on to get all the curios we could. Captain X—— had once assured us that down in the South Sea isles the natives would trade their very souls for gaudy cloth or for trinkets, so we laid in a big supply of red handkerchiefs, bolts of cheap but brilliant-hued calico, and worthless pocket-knives. I even sent back word to the jewellery store in Independence to have a consignment of highly polished " junk " jewellery shipped ahead of me to the Society Islands.

At last came the hour for our start. I think we all had deep regrets at leaving Hawaii. The months spent there had been happy ones, and it was a sorrow to part with our friends. In Honolulu, the Elks had been particularly kind to me, even giving me a letter to put with the two I had previously received. It seemed to me as I stood on the *Snark's* deck taking my last look at Hawaiian territory that I could subscribe heartily to the words of Mark Twain: "No alien land in all this world has any deep, strong charm for me but that one; no other land could so longingly and beseechingly haunt me, sleeping and waking, through half a lifetime, as that one has done; other things leave me, but it abides; other things change, but it remains the same; for me its balmy airs are always blowing, its summer seas flashing in the sun; the pulsing of its surf-beat is in my ear; I can see its garlanded craigs, its leaping cascades, its plumy palms drooping the shore; its remote summits floating like islands above the cloud-rack; I can feel the spirit of its woodland solitudes; I can hear the plash of its brooks; in my nostrils still lives the breath of its flowers that perished twenty years ago."

It was just after dinner on the 7th of October that I started the engine; the shore lines were cast off, and amid the cheers of our friends we slowly turned our bow to the south, and one of the most remarkable cruises ever attempted had begun. We ran along the coast of Hawaii until nearly sunset; then the course was set to southeast, and by dark we were out of sight of land. I stopped the engines and went on deck to enjoy the pleasant evening. It was a strange sight that met my gaze. Jack and Mrs. London, Nakata and Wada were all leaning over the rail, as seasick a crew as ever I have seen, and Captain Y——, our full-fledged deep-water captain, gave up the wheel to

Hermann just as I came on deck, and joined them. Hermann and I sat back in the cockpit and made remarks about people with weak stomachs coming to sea. And I started to enjoy myself at their expense. But gradually the sea got rougher, and I began to feel queer; then I stopped enjoying myself and went below to bed, while Hermann called down sarcastic things from above.

During the next week, not much work was done aboard this ship. The wind was gradually becoming lighter, and we knew we were nearing the doldrums, or horse latitudes. The air was growing warmer, so that we all slept on deck; and when the weather was not too rough, we would place large canvas windsails below and catch all the fresh air there was.

Jack was writing a new book. While in Honolulu, he had told me of it, and he was then preparing his notes for it.

"Look here, Martin," he called to me one day, at the Seaside Hotel.

I came to where he was sitting.

"Look at this," he directed, holding out a sheet of paper. "There's the title of something new I'm going to write. And I'm going to make you half-hero of it, what's more."

I looked at the paper. On it was the title, "Martin Eden."

Jack then went on to explain. The name was a combination. Jack had used my Christian name and the surname of an old friend of his called Eden. The story, he said, would be drawn largely from his own experience; it would treat of the struggles of a young fellow who was determined to " make good " at writing; of his eventual success; and of his unhappy death. But it was to be more than a story. Through it was to run a certain cosmic undertone that would make of it a record of universal truths. Beyond the mere recital of details incident to the plot would be a biological and sociological significance. The thing would be true, not only of Martin Eden, but of all life, of all time. In a way, a value would be put upon life and the things of life that would ring true, even though the view-point would not be that of the smug bourgeoisie.

When he was not too sick, Jack worked on this book. I think he found much pleasure in it. Of evenings, if the weather was fair, we would assemble on deck, and Jack would read aloud to us that day's instalment. Besides this, we had the five hundred books of the *Snark's* library to draw upon, so that we never lacked for reading.

But fair weather or foul, one thing was continual. The roll of the boat was always present. The lunge, the dip, the surge — over and over, never changing, never ceasing. Body and brain, we rocked. Strange antics the horizon line played, shifting in all manner of angles. Sometimes there was no horizon line — great towering waves would blot it out, interposing their foam-capped crests in leaps and tumbles, swelling and subsiding.

Finally, after about three weeks of slow sailing, the wind played out altogether, leaving us rolling on a glassy sea for another three weeks. We kept our head turned to the east as much as possible when there was breeze enough to steer, and sometimes I would run the engines for a few hours, but we were saving with the gasolene, as we feared we would be unable to get any more for a long time to come. Every time I had the engines running I noticed that they seemed to decrease in power, until finally they were not developing half the speed they should. On going over them, I found that the exhaust-pipe had been connected up wrongly. The engines' being below the water-line allowed the water to run back into the cylinders, causing them to rust, and naturally they lost power. After showing Jack the trouble, I suggested that it would be better to shut down the engines entirely until we got to a place where we could get the exhaust-pipe changed; he agreed with me, and for the rest of this trip we were compelled to depend solely on the sails.

The Sailing Directions for the South Pacific says:

Sandwich Islands to Tahiti.— There is great difficulty in making this passage across the trades. The whalers and all others speak with great doubt of fetching Tahiti from the Sandwich Islands. Capt. Bruce says that a vessel should keep to the northward until she gets a start of the wind before bearing for her destination. In his passage between them in November, 1837, he had no variables near the line in coming south, and never could make easting on either tack, though he endeavoured by every means to do so.

The variables we encountered in 11° north latitude. This was a stroke of real luck. The variables were our hope; without them the traverse would be maddeningly impossible. We stayed in the immediate neighbourhood of 11° north latitude.

The variables were extremely uncertain. Now we would have a fair gust of wind, just sufficient to raise our spirits and set us betting on the speed such a wind made possible; and now all wind would die away, leaving us almost motionless on the smooth sea. It was in such moments of despair that we realised the immensity of the task we had set for ourselves. In years and years, no vessel had attempted to cross the Pacific in this particular waste; several vessels had tried it, but they had either been blown far out of their course and landed in the Samoan or Fiji Islands, or else had never been heard from again. A grim possibility stared us in the face. What if all winds failed us; what if progress were impossible; what if we were doomed to sail and drift in this deserted ocean space for months and months, until death put an end to our sufferings? It might happen. Who could tell?

But all things come to those who dare. We had dared mightily. And mightily we reaped of our sowing. We did the impossible. We cheated the chances,

The Long Traverse

we defeated the odds that lay against us. The *Snark* and crew put in safely to Taiohae Bay, in the Marquesas Islands, sixty-one days out of Hilo, Hawaii.

By the time we were calmed in the doldrums we were all seasoned seamen; and I never again saw one of the crew seasick.

From the time we left Hilo up to now, we had made no effort to catch the fish that were so thick on every side of us, but now that we were feeling fine and enjoying life, we each got our fishing tackle and started to fish. When there was no wind, we lowered the sails and spread the awning — there was no use letting the sails tear themselves to threads by flapping around while the ship rolled. It did not take us long to become expert in fishing, for we soon learned the kinds of baits and hooks to use for the different kinds of fish. We vied with one another to see which could catch the greatest number. One of us need only say that he would bet fifty cents or a dollar that he could catch a certain kind and amount of fish in less time than any other person aboard could perform the feat, and everyone would start in with hook and line. I've seen Jack London throw aside "Martin Eden" and join us. Often Jack would come up on deck, and say: "See that big fish over there, the one with the spot on his back"— or any other way to distinguish a particular fish —"Well, I'll wager I can catch him inside of five minutes." I would take him up, and then his sport would begin, trying to keep from catching other fish when only a particular one was wanted. Some idea of the trouble he had will be conveyed when I say that I have seen thousands and thousands of fish, anywhere from one to fifteen feet long, on every side of the *Snark*. It was no longer sport merely to catch fish — we must catch some particular fish. One variety, the dolphin, the prettiest fish in the world, we would try for with rod and reel and sometimes a quarter of a mile of line. This fish we could easily harpoon, but that would not have been sport. We caught many sharks, from which we used to cut out steaks and throw the bodies overboard. Hermann, like all deep-water fishermen, wanted to pull the sharks aboard and cut off their tails and then throw them, alive, overboard; for a sailor hates a shark worse than anything in the world, and will never miss a chance to torture one. At last Jack gave orders that no more sharks were to be caught, for they dirtied up the deck, and besides, some of the larger ones had broken up things on the deck with their tails. A large shark could easily kill a person with a well-directed blow of the tail. But it was interesting to see the different species of shark. Further along we found a number of different kinds.

An interesting thing about a shark is the way it turns on its back to bite. The mouth is set back under the nose, so that the shark must turn clear over with the white stomach upward in order to feed itself. Another remarkable think about a shark is its

Santa Cruz Natives in Catamaran Canoes

The Long Traverse

almost unbelievable vitality. I have cut out a shark's heart and let it lie in a dish, where I have timed it to beat for two hours. Up on deck, the shark itself would be flopping and twisting — through some muscular reaction, I suppose.

On board we had a full set of harpoons and granes with which to catch bonita. The bonita are the swiftest fish in the sea; no matter how fast the *Snark* sailed, they kept up with us without difficulty. Often, if we would slightly wound a bonita so that the blood would start, the whole pack would jump on this fish and have him eaten before we were out of sight. Again, we have hauled them from the sea with fresh-bitten holes in their flesh, as big as a teacup. Bonita are called the cannibals of the sea.

Thousands and thousands of flying fish could be seen. It was these that lured the bonita. For be it known that the flying fish are food for many deep-sea creatures, and for the swooping sea-birds. Incidentally, I might mention that on occasion they proved also a delicious diet for the crew of the *Snark*. Our boat was continually stirring up the flying fish, causing them to essay flight, but ever the birds swooped and drove them into the voracious maws of the bonita.

The sharks we caught by bending chain-swivels on small rope and attaching big hooks. The shark steaks were very good to eat, when properly prepared. We ate also pilot fish, and remoras; in fact, the sea yielded up its creatures abundantly to our larder. Once we spied a big green sea-turtle, sleeping on the surface and surrounded by a multitudinous school of bonita. Hermann got him with granes. That turtle later appeared on our table, and toothsome he was! I think he must have weighed a full hundred pounds.

The dolphin proved good sport. We used an entire flying fish as bait, strung on a tarpon hook. The dolphin leap and fight and buck in mid-air when caught, turning the colour of rich gold. Many of them are heavy, being usually right around four feet in length.

A passenger on a steamer never sees any kind of fish other than bonita, unless it be an occasional whale or a school of porpoise, for the swish of the propeller frightens the fish so no one can ever experience the real excitement of good fishing at sea, unless he is on a sailing vessel. And when a fellow tells you of the fish he has seen from the deck of a steamer, enlarging upon their extraordinary length, their abundance, their gorgeous colours, just set that fellow down as a prevaricator.

In addition to " Martin Eden " Jack wrote on other work. There were his magazine articles, short stories, and other things to be attended to. He had now made up his mind to make a study of the South Sea Islanders, a fancy which, as the event showed, was never fathered into action. I have often wished he had had the opportunity to spend more time among the primitive people with whom we later came in contact. Jack

London, what of his animal stories, or tales of creatures closely approximating men, yet with all the simplicity of animals, has often been termed a "primitive psychologist." Had conditions favoured, I really believe he would have given to the world some studies of the strangest creatures in existence, making plain their mental processes and throwing light upon their manners and customs in a way never before attempted. But it was not to be. We were not wanted in the South Seas, as we were later to be shown.

We drifted at the will of the currents and tides for a couple of weeks, until we had just about reached the Equator; then storms were frequent, driving us to the westward further than we wanted to go. For eight or ten days we had miserable weather. A squall would show up on the horizon and a large black cloud sweep over the sky. Had we been in Kansas and seen such elemental disturbances, we should have hunted the storm-cellar. These storms would last from ten minutes to an hour. The little *Snark* would lay over in the sea while salt-water would pour over the decks and sweep below, leaving everything drenched. Many times the boat buried her rail and deck, but she did not turn turtle. The *Snark* was stanch.

Now entered the first real discomfort. And it was a serious one. It was November 20, and we were in the doldrums. It was night, and a storm was raging. One of the Japanese left a water-tap open that connected the deck tanks, and in the morning not a drop of water was left in any of the tanks, and only about ten gallons below.

We did not know what to do. We had been forty-five days out of the Sandwich Islands, had not sighted any land or a sail, and were in the uncertain doldrums and not half-way to the Marquesas Islands. Jack immediately ordered the remaining ten gallons of water put under lock and key, and one quart of water per day was our allowance.

One has no idea how small an amount a quart is until he is put on such an allowance. Before the middle of the afternoon, we would have our water drunk. Our thirst raged. It grew worse because we knew there was nothing to assuage it. At meals, when tins of provisions were opened, we tried to buy each other's share of the liquid from the can.

The days crept by. Our thirst grew almost unbearable. We spoke of nothing but water. We dreamed of water. In my sleep, a thousand times I saw brooks and rivers and springs. I saw sparkling water run over stones, purling and rippling, and a thousand times I bent over to take a deep draught, when — alas! I awoke to find myself lying on the deck of the *Snark,* crying out with thirst. And as it was with me, so was it with the rest of the crew. It seemed a monstrous thing that there should be no water. The situation grew more serious with every passing hour. It seemed such a needless misfortune that had befallen us. We had started out with over a thousand gallons of the precious fluid — had even installed extra tanks on deck, that we might be assured of a sufficiency — and here we were, with a quart a day apiece! and our thirst raging and crying out in our throats!

How we longed for rain! None came. At last, after nearly a week, we saw a storm blowing up, and black clouds gathering. Here was promise! We rigged lines on either side, between the main and mizzen riggings, and from this spread out the large deck awning, so disposed that it would catch and pour into a barrel as much water as possible. The storm swept on toward us. We gazed at it with parted lips. Gallons of water were descending a few hundred yards away from us, and the heart of the squall was making directly for us, while we stood there and exulted. And then, to our infinite disappointment and dismay, the squall split, and the two parts drew off away from us.

Twelve hundred miles from land, and no water!

Death leered at us from the dark sea. There seemed no possible chance for us. And what did Jack London do?

Almost dead with thirst himself, he went into his cabin and wrote a sea story about a castaway sailor that died of thirst while drifting in an open boat. And when he had finished it he came out, gaunt and haggard, but with eyes burning with enthusiasm, and told us of the story and said:

"Boys, that yarn's one of the best I ever did!"

That night a heavy, soaking tropical rain came on; we spread the awning again and filled our water tanks; and as the big barrel ran over with the gurgling water, Jack said:

"I'll not kill that sailor; I'll have him saved by a rain like this; that'll make the yarn better than ever!"

That water was the best we ever tasted. We couldn't deny it. After seeing that we had a good supply, we set all the sail we could crowd on the boat and crossed the Equator. When the sun rose next morning, and we awoke for the day's duties, we knew we were out of the doldrums.

During this time Nakata was rapidly picking up English; in fact, I never saw a person pick up the language so fast. When asked if he was happy, he would answer: "I'm happy, happy, happy!"—which seemed to be the truth, for he was always in a good humour, and was never too tired to do more work. Nights, when we would be called out of our bunks to help on deck during a storm, Nakata would come up smiling, while the rest of us would come up grumbling. It has often been noticed how soon a small party will get grumpy if they are together for a long time, but we were an exception to the rule; our days were spent amicably up on deck, and in the evenings Mr. and Mrs. London and Captain Y—— and I went below to play cards.

In the diary I kept on this part of the trip, I find these interesting entries:

Sunday, December 1, 1907.—Have started studying Henderson's Navigation. The rest of the crew are up on deck, watching the fish that keep up with the *Snark*. They look like thousands of comets, swimming so fast that their shapes are not distinguishable. The way we are gliding along is fine.

Monday, December 2, 1907.— Sliding along at seven knots. A large frigate bird followed us all day. They never go far from land, so we were glad to see him, for he presages a landfall. The funniest little mascot has been after us for a week: a little, pale-green fish, about a foot and a half long, who is having the hardest time to keep up, wriggling his tail as if it was awfully hard work to swim so fast. Bonita and dolphin slide through the water with hardly any exertion, but this little fish is so hard put that we wonder what he gets to eat.

Tuesday, December 3, 1907.— Captain says we are three hundred and sixty miles from land — and still going! It is funny to see us crowd around the chart at noon, as the captain puts our position on it. We are drawing closer to the islands all the time, until it seems that we should see them now, they look so close on the map. Captain, Jack and I got away out on the flying jib-boom and had a contest to see which would catch the most bonita. They caught more than I, but I caught the largest, thirty pound. I must make a picture of the little craft from there; she looks good, and the spinnaker-boom improves it. Jack discovered to-day that last Thursday was Thanksgiving. Just one year ago to-day that I left home to join the crew of the *Snark*. Heaven only knows where we will be next year at this time.

Wednesday, December 4, 1907.— Still sliding along. Took off the mizzen sail this afternoon, for with the wind aft it only cut off the wind from the main and caused hard steering. Fish were so thick around us this afternoon that the water looked as if it were boiling and sounded like a waterfall. The bonita must have struck a school of small flying fish near the surface. Captain got out large charts of Nuka-hiva and the bay we are going into, so we are all excitement; expecting to sight land to-morrow night. Clothes are brought out and brushed and aired, and brass is being scoured up, and still we slide along. Am getting along well with my navigation.

Thursday, December 5, 1907.— I just got through giving Nakata a lesson in English. He knew no English at all at the start of the voyage, now can understand most anything told him; talks pretty well, too. Fish is getting to be a tiresome subject by this time, but must tell of the thousands of big five to thirty pound fish leaping in the air and swarming through the water so that their noise can be heard above the splashing of the boat here below. Jack shot several, which were eaten before they could sink — wounded ones

Canoe House in Solomon Islands

eaten alive by their own kind. As we were all leaning over the stern watching them, two monster sharks appeared, one at least fifteen feet in length. Then all the bonita vanished. I have a bet with everyone on board that I sight land first. It's only about seventy miles away. How good it will seem after two months on the *Snark!* I am going to print pictures up till midnight; then two hours at the wheel, and if the air keeps as clear as now, I think I'll win my bets. Got launch to running just as I was about to give it up. Now I'm busy painting and oiling it, while Hermann is painting and varnishing the boat.

Friday, December 6, 1907.— Midnight. We are anchored in the prettiest bay I ever imagined. But let me begin at the first. My brain is so full of things to write that I know I will never do them justice, for I have not the time or paper. Early this morning captain awoke us with "Land ahoy!" and in the quickest time anyone ever got on deck we were trying to make out in the hazy atmosphere *land.* At last we succeeded. Ua-huka was straight ahead, and away in the distance could be seen the ragged crags of Nuka-hiva, the island we were heading for. How good those big green mountains looked! Only men who had been sixty days on the sea could appreciate the scene. In a few hours we were within three miles of Ua-huka, seven miles long and thirty-three hundred feet high. It looked like a big rock. Soon Nuka-hiva loomed up straight ahead. It seemed as if we were in another world as we sailed past several low cocoanut islands, sometimes going so close that with the glasses we could see villages of grass houses, and we knew that at last we were in the real South Sea islands.

By five o'clock we could make out the two sentinel rocks, between which we must go to get into the bay. It was nearly midnight as we sailed up the coast of Nuka-hiva. A fine bright moon had been shining earlier in the evening; but just as we had sighted the opening of the bay (called Taiohae Bay on the chart), a squall struck us and we were in the most dangerous position we had ever been caught in: rocks and reefs on every side, so we could not turn back. We did the only thing possible — drove right for the place of which we had sighted the opening, and left to luck that we would find it. Luck was with us. We sailed in the opening, just missing a large, rocky island at its mouth. We passed so close that thousands of sea-birds were sent crying and frightened off their rocky perch. After getting inside the bay, the mountains on every side shut off the storm, and the wind dropped so low that we were an hour getting from the mouth of the bay to the upper end, where the water was shallow enough for anchoring.

At last we are at anchor. It seems that we must be in paradise. The air is perfume. We can hear the wild goats blatting in the mountains, and an occasional long-drawn howl from a dog ashore. It is so near morning now that the cocks are crowing; and we are so proud of ourselves for doing what the Sailing Directions said was impossible, and so happy at seeing land again! Well, now we shall get a much-needed rest.

CHAPTER VII

IN THE MARQUESAS

AT last we were in the real Marquesas Islands, the islands we had heard so much about, the islands that very few white people ever see — for here there is only one way of communicating with the outside world, and that is by two trading schooners that make four trips a year from Papeete, Tahiti, one thousand miles away, and an occasional bark or brig that drops in here for copra.

When the sun peeped over the mountains, we awoke to the prettiest sight imaginable. All about, sloping steeply upward, were green mountains; at the end of the bay ahead, palm trees of all kinds were clustered. We saw a number of white houses, with low white roofs; and, further back on the mountains, one considerably larger house, where the French Resident lived. Our deck was covered with a sweet-smelling pollen, which had settled aboard during the small hours of the morning. Near us was a small, old-fashioned bark — Norwegian, we found out afterward — with painted imitation square port holes, such as are seen on old galleons. Her hull was down in the water, showing her to be loaded, or nearly so. We were surprised to see this vessel, for we had expected to have the bay to ourselves. From a distance, several big, brown, grinning men inspected the *Snark;* and when we invited them aboard, they climbed over the rail, bringing bunches of bananas, oranges, papaias, and various other fruits, all of which they gave us. I lowered the launch and soon had it running, but it was nearly noon before we had a chance to go ashore. The natives were constantly swarming around us, all talking at once and trying to talk to us. The big, good-natured fellows were doing their best to make us feel at home. With each presentation of fruit, a speech was delivered, which always ended in a grin and a handshake. We had learned enough of the Hawaiian tongue to understand a little of what they said, for the languages are very similar; and we could gather that each one was wanting the pleasure of being our guide.

These people were the most hospitable and kindly of any in the South Seas; they entertained us lavishly; expense was no object to them; and our money was of no value to us, as here no such medium of exchange was in use. These people gladly prepared the most gorgeous entertainments when they found that we were bent on a mission of friendly inquiry and honest research into their customs and manners.

At last Jack made them understand that we were not needing assistance, but would gladly avail ourselves of their hospitality when we got ashore. Finally, we did go ashore, but only to stagger and roll so that walking was almost impossible. In those sixty-one days at sea, we had practically forgotten what walking was. The whole village of nearly naked islanders was awaiting us on the beach. How those kind people did bustle good-naturedly around us! With the whole crowd following, we made our way to the only trading station on the island, "The Societé Commercial de la Oceanie," a branch of the biggest trading concern in the South Sea islands.

We were quickly relieved of our escort when the two white men of the place came out and said a few words in the native tongue. All the people stopped out in front while we went inside. Mr. Kriech and Mr. Rawling, two Germans, were the agents for the company here, and during our stay they did all in their power to show us the interesting spots on the island. Everywhere we were stared at by the natives. Mrs. London attracted more attention than did we men. Few white women had ever been seen here before. A Mrs. Fisher had lived here thirty years, and had boarded Robert Louis Stevenson while he was at Nukahiva.

The storekeeper accompanied us to the French Resident's, where he acted as interpreter. The French Resident spoke no English. He was a queer, fat little man, with a good-natured face. When we first saw him, he was wearing overalls, and had no coat; on his feet were wooden shoes, and on his head a military hat. Upon observing us, he quickly donned a faded old uniform coat, and was all dignity at once. He did not even look at our papers, for he declared that

In the Marquesas

the word of so important a man as Monsieur London was better than any credentials we could display. He made us highly welcome, and did not even charge us the usual twenty-franc hunting license.

Shortly after, Captain Luvins of the bark *Lucine* came in, and to him Jack broached the subject that had brought us to the island. We wanted to see Typee Valley. Arrangements were immediately made for us to go over to this famous valley, which for years and years, in fact, since he was a little boy and had read Herman Melville's "Typee," Jack had longed to visit. Mr. Kriech secured horses and guides for us, and we started next morning before sun-up.

When I think of those early mornings in the Marquesas, I seem to smell anew the sweet flowers and the copra. The soft still morning air leaves something in one's nostrils that makes one want to go back again. I believe that all four of the white people on the *Snark* will drop anchor in this bay again. I know I will . . . sometime.

We started early next morning, Captain Y——, Mr. and Mrs. London, myself, a native guide, Captain Luvins, and two girls we did not know were going, and to whom Jack did not take very kindly at first, until it was explained that they were the daughters of the chief of the Typee tribe, and that their going assured us a welcome in their valley. We were each mounted on a small Marquesan pony, with provisions for four days in our saddle-bags. We started off a narrow path and headed straight for the mountains. We climbed for hours, often going around the corner of a mountain on a little path, where we could look hundreds and hundreds of feet down a sheer precipice. The little ponies were as sure-footed as goats, and finally, at nearly noon, we reached the summit of the mountain, the mountain that divided off the different tribes. Looking down one side, we could see Hapaa Valley. Back of us lay Taiohae Bay, with the Norwegian bark and the *Snark* lying at anchor. Straight ahead spread Typee, the wonderful valley Herman Melville so vividly described as a paradise. We had fought the elements and suffered for sixty-one days in order to win to this place, and see whether it was really the perfect spot that Melville described it, or whether, like certain who write about our Pacific coast states, he was but a delightful romancer. But we found that Melville had told the truth — that if he had not told the whole truth, it was because he had not described all the beauties of this bewitching valley of leisure and abundance, so far from the United States, where white men toil and grind incessantly.

We rode until late in the afternoon through the groves of bananas, thousands of big yellow bunches that would never be picked. Our horses stumbled over cocoanuts in the path. At one place, one of the native girls pointed out to us what she called a short-cut. We followed her directions, and rode right through a cluster of hornets' nests. The girl, who remained at a safe distance, stood and watched us fighting the hornets and being royally stung, and laughed heartily at what she considered the cleverness of her practical joke. Just how much intrinsic humour there may have been in the situation I am unable to say — being so closely involved in it — but I am sure that the girl was the only one who did much laughing. The rest of us were busy swatting hornets, as were also our horses busy in dodging.

Finally, we came to a clearing where the old village of Typee had once stood. But now only the foundations of the buildings of this once strong tribe remained to show where they had been. The cocoanut trees we found growing in the fantastic arrangement that Melville had spoken of, but the natives were gone. Everything was quiet except the chirping of the birds, and the rustling of palm-leaves. We rode on until we came to a frame house that had been built by a trader, but he had left, and now a family of natives lived in this old house on the edge of Faiaways Lake. How delightful this little lake looked, with the background of mountains, but how sad this one family! When we came to them and asked for a drink of water, the woman brought a large gourd full to the brim, and as she extended it, we saw upon her flesh the curse of the islands, leprosy. The man came out, dragging a big heavy foot behind him. He had elephantiasis, and the children that played in the yard showed signs of leprosy.

Perhaps we should have gone back without seeing any more of the Typee tribe, had not the girls urged us on. We shortly came to another clearing — the new village of the valley. Here we found about twenty grass houses and perhaps fifty or seventy-five people, all that remained of the once strongest tribe in the Marquesas Islands.

About thirty years ago, there were six thousand natives in this valley, with nearly as many in the opposite valley of Hapaa. But the two tribes were continually at war, until the Hapaa tribe was totally exterminated. Then came ships in search of sandalwood and copra, and came also missionaries. With them they managed to bring leprosy and elephantiasis, and a venereal disease that, in the tropics, is worse than either of the others. As a result, the native hosts are gone, and only the few remain. Still, these people we saw looked healthy enough, though here and there we could see a leper lurking in the background.

Better had it been had the natives never seen the missionaries. What happened in the Marquesas has happened in many other South Sea islands, and no doubt is happening to-day. My conscience smote me. To think, the very pennies I had given in Sunday School for foreign missions had contributed to the calamitous end of the inhabitants of this beautiful garden-spot!

After the girls had told who we were and what we wanted, a large house was put at our disposal, and the women brought mats for us to sit on, while the men started a big fire and roasted several pigs. Others brought fish and *poi* and eggs and chicken. The feast was spread out on the ruins of an old stone house, and we sat down to eat. Only we white people and the two chief's daughters and the chiefs were together. The other natives would come up respectfully and gather their portion, then withdraw to a little distance and eat. Of all the various kinds of edibles I have tried in different places of this world, I think none could compare with this. The fish was served raw, but it was good. The *poi* had been buried in the ground until it was slightly fermented. The natives climbed the big cocoanut trees and picked the young nuts for us to drink; and when we had finished eating, they got out their queer musical instruments made of logs, part of the natives danced and others sang, and I lay on my mat when I had finished eating and watched these happy people until it got too dark to see. I could not help thinking of my friends at home, who were bundled in heavy clothes, trying to keep warm, and going to moving-picture shows and dances, and persuading themselves that they were really having a pleasant time. What a contrast between their lot and mine!

That night Jack and Mrs. London slept inside on sleeping-mats thrown on the floor, while the rest of us slept outside on mats thrown on the ground. No mosquitoes or insects bothered us. There were no reptiles for us to be afraid of. The soft-treading natives came and went all night long. Bright and early next morning, we were awakened by the natives' getting breakfast. When the meal was over, we went swimming in Faiaways Lake, and that day we explored the valley, and tried to buy curios. But they would not sell to us. They forced us to take presents of tapa cloth and ornaments of sharks' and porpoises' teeth, and corals, while we made presents to them out of our stores of tinned provisions.

One thing that I tried hard to bring out in photographs was the gorgeous tattooing of the natives, but their skins and the tattooing colour being so near the same shade and hue, the camera cannot catch so subtle a distinction. I tried many exposures, without success.

After the boys are old enough to stand the pain of tattooing, they are started on, and it sometimes takes years to complete them. When they are completed, their eyelids, nose, every part of the body, are covered with fantastic designs. Tattooing seems to be the only really serious thought of these people, except worshipping their big stone idols, several of which we saw in the valley.

One of the girls who had come with us was named Antoinette. She was the last left of royal blood on Nuka-hiva, and she owned nearly all of Typee Valley and most of Hapaa Valley, but she received little revenue. There is much copra, but no one to gather it. Copra, I may explain, is the dried kernel of the cocoanut, valued at about twenty-five cents a hundred.

MARQUESAS ISLANDERS

While we were here, one woman brought in a large piece of tapa cloth, which she sold for five dollars Chile. Chile money is the common currency here. It is about half the value of American money, and comes in very handy. Of course, this tapa cloth could never have been bought elsewhere for such a sum, but in the Marquesas quality is not considered in setting prices — only quantity. Natives gave us calabashes, *hula* dresses of human hair, then more tapa, until Jack was loaded down. I bought a fine big piece of this cloth, which is made from the bark of cocoanut trees, pounded into a pulp, then flattened out and dried. Once it was used for making *pareus,* but now they wrap their dead in it.

At one place, the girls told us that near the mouth of a river nearby was a large cave, in which were petrified bodies. It had once been an old burying ground, they said, but now a big stone had blocked the way. I had heard of this cave, and knew that Stevenson had once tried to force his way in after petrified eyes, of which the natives had told him. But my own opinion is that cave, bodies, and petrified eyes are all myths, although they are myths in which the natives place belief.

In telling of Typee, the Garden of Eden, I want to lay special stress on this one thing: if ever there was a Garden of Eden, it was right here in this valley. Nowhere else in the world is the climate so perfect, nowhere else in the world can be found the myriads of delicious fruits, nowhere else is there such a profusion of wild cattle, goat, turkey, and chicken, to say nothing of the different species of ducks, cranes, storks and pigeons. One thing that struck me as strange was that the thousands and thousands of pure white doves which soared and floated over our heads showed absolutely no fear of us. It was evident they had never been molested.

Big ragged mountains rose on every side, over which were scattered waterfalls that started high up in the mountains and fell so far that before the water had reached the bottom it had scattered away in mists that floated down the valley in rainbows. Turning one's eyes at any time up the mountains, one could see the wild goats feeding or watching one in wonder, and see the occasional wild cattle that swung up precarious paths and out of sight, and the wild chickens that stalked about in search of food. One could reach up on either hand and pick the delicious fruit, ripe from the trees. A climate so perfect that no words can describe it, other than to call like unto the Garden of Eden, is here. The natives are like big happy children. They do not steal, gossip about one another, nor carry grudges. Instead, they sing, dance, hunt, fish, and live together as brothers in a life of perfect peace.

On my return to my own country, one provincial (and so narrow-minded) man went so far as to tell me that he thought the United States had the most perfect climate in the world; that it was the most perfect country in the world; that he couldn't see why people should poke about looking for something better — for his part, he would see what he could of the States, and settle down and be satisfied. Then he started telling me of the Road of a Thousand Wonders, the place where there are oranges and flowers the year round.

Now you who read, of you let me ask: Have you ever seen this Road of a Thousand Wonders, this place where the oranges and flowers blossom the year round? What was your impression of it, if so? Did it come up to your expectations? Were you disappointed? And are you satisfied that in seeing it you have seen all that is worth seeing on this whirling sphere of ours?

Now, I have seen the Road of a Thousand Wonders. And I have been in Typee, the Garden of Eden. The very thought of comparing the two places makes me sad for the frailty of human judgment.

Our stay in Typee Valley was one of the most delightful experiences of a voyage that contained much of the delightful. It was with a profound regret that we left it, and with the determination that some day our eyes should again feast upon its many beauties, and that again we should partake of the hospitality of those who had made us so royally welcome. Back we came to the *Snark,* filled with pleasing memories.

The Marquesas Islands lie in Latitude 10°, so close to the Equator that ordinarily the sun's rays would have been almost unbearable, but among all the South Sea islands the trade winds that blow every month in the year, coming from over the sea, keep the temperature about the same as a fine spring day in America.

The *Snark* lay at anchor close in to the shore. Jack and Mrs. London secured a small frame house, the one that Robert Louis Stevenson had lived in while he was in the Marquesas. And they secured board with Mrs. Fisher, the same old woman who had cooked for Stevenson. Many of the older natives would tell stories of the time *Tusitala* (which was Stevenson's native name, signifying " story-teller ") had lived here. He was a great hand to entertain, and as anyone can see from his writings, he loved and was loved by all the natives with whom he came in contact. The Polynesians never had a better friend than Robert Louis Stevenson. He has done more to give the Americans and English a good name in the islands than has any other man.

After the first day in Taiohae Bay, the *Snark* was deserted most of the time. There was never any danger of quitting the vessel with no one on board, for we had left the only persons who needed watching, back in America. Hermann was a great hunter. He usually started off early in the morning, and returned in the evening with birds of every variety, and he would sometimes return with wild goat. Once he shot a wild cow. It seemed a shame to kill the cattle, for such a little of the meat could be used, and the rest would

In the Marquesas

spoil in a day. Jack and Mrs. London went hunting one morning, and returned about noon with the native boys who had accompanied them bearing fourteen goats.

But the great attraction for the natives was our graphophone. When evening fell, they came about us in swarms to hear the playing, and they could never get over the belief that we had a little dwarf caged in the " talk-box." At times, there would be as many as two hundred brown people squatting on the grass, and they would never leave until we stopped the graphaphone. In the Hawaiian Islands, we had secured records of *hula-hula* music, which so delighted the Marquesans that sometimes we would have half a hundred dancing in front of the machine.

The natives who lived nearby in a small grass hut came to the house one day with the request that we play the graphaphone for them to dance by. Jack left his writing, and all that afternoon while he played these men practised different steps, and I believe a new *hula-hula* was originated that day.

The men, understanding nearly half of the Hawaiian language, sang with the graphaphone, keeping time by clapping their hands and swaying their bodies. They would anoint themselves from head to foot with cocoanut oil, until their skin was shiny. The cocoanut oil emitted a faint, pleasant odour, which, once smelled, is never forgotten. They would dance as fast as their limbs could carry them, the womenfolk keeping time with their hands. Even the children imitated them. A native Polynesian can no more keep from dancing when he hears music than a duck can keep away from water.

The house where Jack lived was tended by an old man and a woman, who were covered with tattooing. The man's face looked like a convict's uniform — brown and blue instead of white and blue, with long stripes clear across the face. The woman had a trick of pulling up her dress and showing the tattooing on her legs whenever she saw anyone admiring it on her feet. Very immodest she was, but then, there is no such thing as modesty among such people as these. I think some staid persons I have seen in America would be vastly shocked by the things that take place in the Marquesas.

These natives are considerably larger than the average white person. Their skin is a light brown colour; their hair is thick, straight and black. Dark eyes and eyelashes make them appear a fine, handsome race. The only unfortunate thing is their tendency to age so soon. At fifteen the girls are fully developed women, and at twenty-eight or -nine they are old women. They seem to have no vitality; though they look strong and healthy, if one were told that he was going to die, and had the idea impressed on his mind, he would be sure to lie down and die.

They have no morals at all. Their marriage contracts are so flimsy that if one wants a divorce, he needs only to apply to the chief; and a couple can be married and divorced in the same day. There were few white men here, but all had native women, and were continually changing. The girls, from fourteen years up, make their homes with first one native and then with another. If they want to marry a man they say so, and if he refuses them they call him "missionary." I was sitting on a barrel in front of the trading store one day, when several young *vahines* (women) came up, and tried to talk to me. One grabbed me by the arm, and pointing to the others: "She wife — she wife — she wife — me no wife!" One girl had a white baby of which she was very proud. To my mind, the girls here were better looking than the Hawaiian girls, but they were much more lax in their notions of becoming conduct.

All of Jack's photographic supplies were spoiled, so I was kept busy printing pictures from mine. Once, while I was engaged in this work, a girl came in the house, without knocking, and was tickled nearly to death watching me develop velox. After that, she came and went whenever she wished, but always dispensed with the formality of knocking.

We had aboard the *Snark* a full set of dentist's tools, which Jack had had no chance to use up to this time. His entire experience of dentistry had been gained by practise on a skull he had purchased in Honolulu. He was always wanting someone of the crew to act as patient. Wada had once pulled a tooth with a string before Jack could get to him, and Jack never forgave Wada for that.

One day I found an old Chinaman — the only Chinaman on the island — groaning on the beach with the toothache. Here was Jack's chance; I rushed off and told him. He urged me to hold the Chinaman until Nakata went aboard for his tools. Then the Chinaman was led to the back of the house. The poor old fellow was shaking with fright. After Jack found, by reading in his little dental book, the proper forceps to use, and was ready to start on the operation, I cried for him to wait until I got my kodak. Mrs. London ran for hers, too. When I yelled "pull," Jack pulled mightily, and he nearly fell over on his back, the tooth came out so easily. But we got the photographs!

The most amusing thing I saw while here was the jail. It was a little old wooden shack, so small that it would hold only two or three persons — and not then, if they wanted to get out. The French government used Nuka-hiva as a penal settlement. Some twenty or thirty prisoners were kept here, and they were the happiest prisoners I ever saw. Why, they didn't need to stay in jail unless they wanted to, so they had built grass houses. One of the long-term men had married, and not only did the government feed him, but it fed his wife as well — better food than the natives ever got, and it was cooked, too. They were supposed to work, but the old jailor was as lazy as they, so I don't think any of them ever did a stroke. Tom the Jailor had once lived in Papeete, Tahiti, and was the proud possessor of an old suit of clothes. These clothes were only worn on state occasions; the rest of the time he dressed like any other native. Tom could speak a little of the English language, and he used to bring all his family around to the house so he could show off his knowledge of the white man's talk. One day I was enquiring about a string of porpoise teeth made in the form of a necklace that his daughter was wearing, and Tom took it from her and gave it to me. These porpoise teeth are very valuable and are used by the Marquesans in lieu of money.

The Norwegian bark of which I spoke had been anchored in this bay for six months. The captain owned the vessel, so he could stay as long as he wanted to without anyone's complaining; and I don't think his ten sailors wanted to leave any more than he did. They all had native girls to whom they seemed to give more time than to the loading of copra. And I think it probable they would have been there yet had it not been for a queer little comedy that I saw enacted.

A large stone idol stood back in the mountains, that the natives were very superstitious about. They believed that anyone touching this image or even going into its shrine cast a spell on them. Now the captain of the bark did not know this, and as it was a very fine piece of work, he decided to take it back to his country with him. His ten sailors cut a large cocoanut tree, and the image, which weighed two tons, was made fast to the middle. It took two days to get it down to the ship. During this time not a native was to be seen, and it was not till the work was done and the sailors tried to go back to their girls that they knew of the superstition attached to the idol. The girls would have nothing further to do with them; so a few days later they set sail and started on their long journey, first to stop at St. Helena, and then on to Norway.

As our launch drew too much water, we used to borrow small native canoes with which to go out in the bay, and were able to come and go without difficulty. One night Hermann arrived astraddle an overturned canoe. He had been to some kind of feast ashore, and had mounted the wrong side of the canoe. Hermann often did these little things.

Our favourite loafing-place was the German traders' headquarters. Here the natives would bring curios for us to buy. It was our custom to buy knives and sticks of tobacco of the Company at white man's prices and trade them to the natives at brown man's prices. For instance, a knife we would buy of the trader for twenty-five cents, we would trade to the Marquesans at $1.00 value. Four hundred per cent. is the regular scale of South Sea profit.

The copra that I have mentioned is the principal article of South Sea commerce. The natives collect the cocoanuts after they have fallen from the tree, and after hulling them, cut the nut in two in the centre, and

THE OLD HOME OF ROBERT LOUIS STEVENSON,
MARQUESAS ISLANDS

the pieces are laid in the sun until the meat is dried and broken away from the shell. It is then ready for shipping. Soap-oils and perfumes are made from copra. One company that has stations in the Marquesas, the Society, and the Taumotu Islands, collects fifty thousand tons of copra every year.

The cocoanut trees grow anywhere they can find sand to hold their roots; even places where no other vegetation will grow the cocoanuts thrive. They must have plenty of water — the soil makes no difference.

Near Mr. London's frame bungalow were numerous mountain streams where the natives bathed. Some of these people seemed to spend most of their time in the water. Captain Y——, who liked bathing but was a little bashful, used to have a hard time finding a place where he could swim unobserved. One day, he and I were bathing close to the house in a spot where we thought we were safe. When we started out, we heard a snicker ashore, and there stood two native girls, watching us. We sank down in the water, which just struck us to the chin. Captain Y—— told the girls to go away, but they didn't understand, and when he threw a shell at them, they thought it a new game, and threw it back. Finally, we made a wild dash for our clothes, and finished dressing back in the jungle.

The girls here make ornaments of land-snail shells, several of which ornaments I now treasure among the curios I brought back with me from the South Seas.

The healthy appearance of these people is due to their method of living: sleeping in their grass houses is nearly the same as sleeping in the open air. They eat fruits and fish and very little meat — in fact, very little of what they eat is cooked. They grind the different kinds of fruit together and make *poi*. The leaves of certain trees and grasses are made into salads. One salad that they prepare only on state occasions is made by taking the heart from a young cocoanut tree; but a handful can be secured from each tree; and as it kills the tree, there is an unwritten law that this salad can be made only with the chief's consent.

Tom the Jailor was a polite old fellow, especially polite to Mrs. London. He would bring fruit to us nearly every morning, and would help at any work we were doing, although, like Rip Van Winkle, he was too lazy to do any work for himself. Once, when Mrs. London asked him his age, he said he did not know, although he knew he was still young, to prove which he climbed one of the tallest cocoanut trees nearby, and brought us the nut. The young nut, rich with milk, could also be eaten with a spoon, and was much better than when dried.

I wish it were possible for me to describe Taiohae Bay. Photographs give no idea of its beauty. And I know no description can do it justice. Viewed from our ship as she lay at anchor in the harbour, it presented the appearance of a vast natural amphitheatre overgrown with vines. The deep glens that furrowed its sides seemed like enormous fissures graven by the disruptive influences of time. Very often, when lost in admiration of its beauty, I have experienced a pang of regret that a scene so enchanting should be hidden from the world in these remote seas, and seldom meet the eyes of devoted lovers of nature.

Besides this bay, the shores of the island are indented by several other extensive inlets, into which descend broad and fertile valleys. These are inhabited by several distinct tribes of islanders, who, although speaking kindred dialects of the same tongue, have from time immemorial waged hereditary warfare against each other. The intervening mountains, generally two or three thousand feet above the sea-level, define the territories of each of the three tribes.

The bay of Nuka-hiva, in which we were lying, is an expanse of water not unlike in figure the space included within the limits of a horse-shoe, being perhaps nine miles in circumference. From the verge of the water, the land rises uniformly on all sides, with green and sloping elevations and swells that rise into lofty heights. Down each of these valleys flows a clear stream, here and there assuming the form of slender cascades, then stealing along invisibly until it bursts upon the sight again in large and more noisy waterfalls, and at last demurely wanders along to the sea.

CHAPTER VIII

THE SOCIETY ISLANDS

ONE thousand miles to the west of the Marquesas Islands lie the Society Islands. Both groups are of volcanic origin. Stretching between them are the low coral reefs of the Paumota Archipelago. In order to get to the Society group, it was necessary for us to go through the thick of these low reefs.

Robert Louis Stevenson was lost for nearly two weeks among these lagoons; whaling and trading ships avoid them; and navigators have given them the name Dangerous Archipelago.

We had been in the Marquesas Islands a little over two weeks when Jack decided that we had better be getting on. So word was sent out to the natives that on a certain day we would want fruit and fowl; and on that day, canoes were coming and going from daybreak to twilight, and by evening our decks were littered with good things of every shape and colour; the life-boat had been filled with oranges; sacks containing pineapples, yams, and taro were piled on the deck; the cockpit was so full of green cocoanuts that there was barely room left for us to steer; and there were bananas of every stage of ripeness, from very green to very ripe, hung upside down to the davits.

We had expected to start away on December 17,

but we did not do so, for late in the afternoon a white spot showed on the horizon at the mouth of the bay and gradually got brighter until the schooner *Tameraihoe Tahiti* dropped anchor close to us. Here was news, and we could not leave until we knew what was going on in the world. The schooner had met the steamer in Papeete, Tahiti, two months before, and had some three-months-old San Francisco papers aboard.

There were three white men on this ship. One was such an interesting subject that I must tell of him. He had come years before, when only a young man. He was in the employ of some trading concern that he still worked for, and on his rounds among the islands he had met and fallen in love with a native girl, but she only laughed at him, saying that he was not nearly so good-looking as the natives, because not tattooed. Now, the girl's brother was just learning this art, and as he thought the white man's skin would be fine for practise, he persuaded the trader to be tattooed. The man quit the company, and for six months lived in a native house in the mountains while the boy practised tattooing on him every day, until the work was done and the skin healed up. Then he made his way to the girl's home. At first the girl was frightened; then she nearly went into hysterics, and ridiculed him; and finally, she insulted him in the worst possible manner — she spat upon him, and ran away into the jungle. And the tattooed white man never saw her again. Now he is one of the wealthiest men in Polynesia; pearl shell, copra, and sandalwood have reaped him a fortune that is of no use to him, for he can never return to civilised people again.

On December 18 we left Taiohae Bay, at seven-thirty in the evening. We started thus late because we had to wait for a land-breeze to spring up before we could set sail. The trading vessel gave us three salutes with their cannon as we started. Owing to the lightness of the breeze, we were an hour getting out. All the time the vessel was giving us three salutes, while Hermann kept the shotgun hot answering. As long as I live, I shall never forget that clearing. The full moon was just rising over the mountains, making it almost as light as day. We caught the trades just out of the mouth, and soon were flying southeast at six knots. No one was seasick; it seemed almost as if we had not been ashore at all, but were still on the long traverse from Hilo.

The days were very hot. We accordingly changed our working hours, getting up early and laying off during the extreme heat. I say "working hours," but the truth is that extremely little work was done at all. Jack wrote as usual, Mrs. London did her typing, and all took their tricks at the wheel, but most of the time we just lay around on deck and read or chatted.

For the first two days or so we skirted the shores of numerous small islands of the Marquesan group, but we soon left them behind. On the fourth day out, squalls began to blow up every few minutes, looking like storms as they came up over the horizon, but always fizzling away in a little rain. That evening the wind suddenly shifted from east to west, sending the sails across deck with a boom, almost enough to tear the masts out. As it was, it carried away a stanchion on the rail, and the boom tackle.

Everybody's nerves were on end, what of the nasty and uncertain weather. According to the chart, we had a coral reef about fifteen miles on either side of us, making this a bad place in which to encounter a storm. Early on the morning of the 24th, we sighted cocoanut palms on our port side, but no land at all, only the tall palms above the horizon. We left them behind, and soon picked up another island, but could see only the palms as before, though more of them. The barometer had been falling for thirty-six hours, and numerous quick squalls swept over us. All hands were kept on deck all of Christmas Eve and all of Christmas Day. No one seemed to realise that it was Christmas, for the heat and squalls and barometer together had greatly worried us. This was the middle of the typhoon season, and we were in the most dangerous part of the world for storms.

The day after Christmas we sighted the tall cocoanut palms growing on the first of the Taumotu Islands; then for two days longer we could see the tops of the palm trees on every side, but during this time we could catch no glimpse of land, as the islands rise only between two and six feet above the water, and cannot be seen over five or six miles away.

Jack had decided that our first stop in the Taumotus would be on one of the largest of the atolls, known as Rangiroa. Early on the fifth morning we sighted what we supposed to be this atoll. We had not been able to make observations since leaving the Marquesas, for the sky had been overcast with low, black, threatening clouds, so we were navigating by dead reckoning only; and as the currents and tides are known to be very treacherous, it was merely blind guess-work instead of real navigating.

All morning and most of the afternoon we coasted along about a mile from a low coral reef, on which the surf thundered and pounded. The strip of land was only about a quarter of a mile wide, but one hundred miles in circumference, forming an atoll with a large lagoon in the centre. We sailed within a mile of the low sandy beach before we could make out an opening, and Captain Y—— finally decided that this was not the lagoon we were looking for, but that the one ahead was, so we sailed up the coast of this island, so close that we could plainly make out the remains of a schooner that had been wrecked upon the reef. Perhaps this old hull was the monument of human lives, the last relict of those who had sailed her. This did not prove to be the atoll we were looking for, nor did the next, or the next; we were getting among

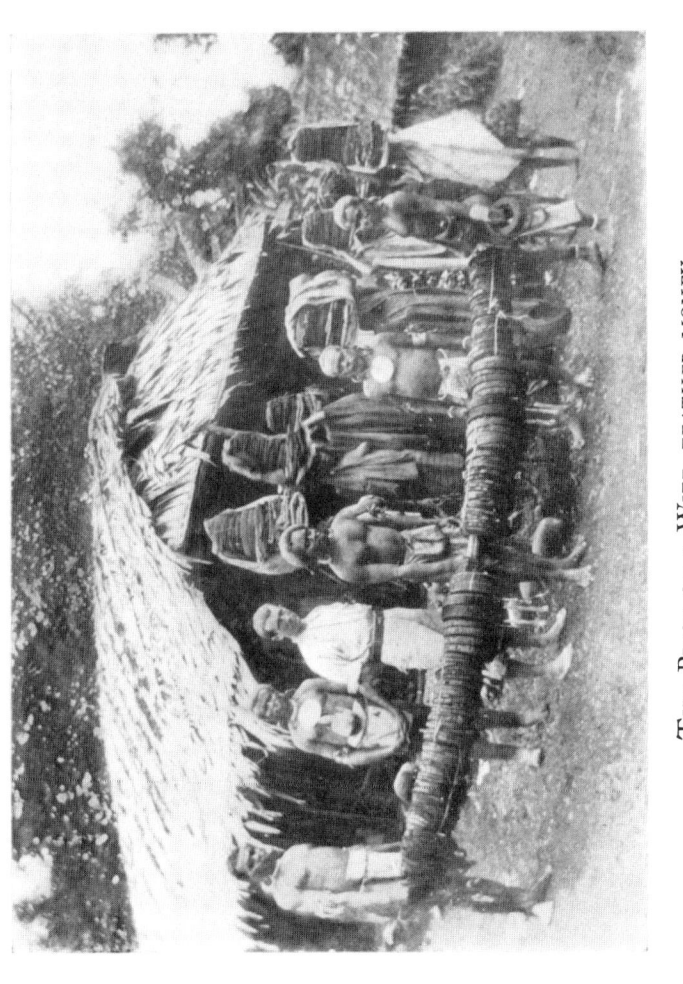

THE PRICE OF A WIFE, FEATHER MONEY

islands so thick that it was necessary to carry double watches at night on deck. Captain Y—— acted like a man driven crazy, for the ship was in his care, and the currents and squalls were so deceptive during this time that he was almost entirely deprived of sleep. One day we had sighted several small sails to the leeward of us; on trying to get to them we found our way blocked by a reef just on a level with the water, so low that had it been night nothing could have saved us from being wrecked. While we were trying to get round the reef, the sails disappeared beneath the sky-line, and we were still in a dangerous position. Little islands scarcely large enough to bear one cocoanut tree would spring up ahead, and then we must spend valuable time beating around them. It was not the island itself that we were most afraid of, it was the reef that we knew always surrounded the island, sometimes over a mile from the land.

Large merchant ships have spent weeks and weeks trying to get out of this group. Little pearling luggers pile up on the white coral by the hundreds, every year. Something like two thousand of these small pearling vessels are scattered through these islands. Pearl shell is the only article of value to be found. Every season, scores of lives are lost in the hurricanes that sweep over the islands; the sand, being so close to the water, will often be levelled off to the waterline. The only safe place during such storms is on some sort of boat in the centre of the lagoon.

The atolls are all about the same shape — that is, circular. The land, about a quarter of a mile in width, will sometimes form in such a large circle that it will be impossible to see across the lagoon. However, we could see the whole of the atoll of the ones we sailed past.

We had been tangled up among these islands for seven days. There was no sun, no stars, from which to work our observations. We had now given up all thought of anchoring anywhere in the Archipelago — if we could only get away, far away, we would be more than satisfied. Even had we wanted to anchor, it seemed impossible, for the openings made by the run of the tide as it ebbed and flowed were too small for us to enter, and the reefs around the outside of the atolls were too rough for us to give a thought to. We knew that if we worked to the south, we would eventually get out. Had the islands been properly charted we could easily have located our position, but as it was, all was confusion and guess-work. In this duty, as in most others, the French had been very remiss. It was too late in the season for many pearling boats, and very few traders ever attempted these passages, although I afterward saw in Papeete several old Kanaka captains who had worked through these lagoons as the Indians used to locate themselves in America — more by instinct than through any practical knowledge.

It was on the seventh day out that we saw clear

water ahead. That night we sailed out of the reach of any cross-currents, and we now had clear water ahead to Papeete. All sail was crowded on, for the barometer was still acting queerly, and we did not relish the idea of being caught in a hurricane in so small a vessel. During this trip, we had not tasted one bit of meat. The fruit of every variety, and the yams and taro, made food that, for health, in the tropics has no equal.

Nakata was the biggest banana-eater I ever saw. He would keep his Japanese stomach filled with bananas all the time. Once he made a bet with Jack that he could eat twenty bananas in half an hour. He managed to eat a dozen with no difficulty, but after that he had to force them down, and he got stalled on his eighteenth banana. He just could not force down another one. One night, while it was his watch on deck, he got hold of a tin of salmon which gave him ptomaine poisoning. He was doubled up on deck for several hours while I poured mustard down him, but next day he was all right again.

On the morning of the ninth day we sighted the island of Tahiti, and raised a signal for a pilot. A Frenchman came out in a large whale-boat, manned by twelve big Tahitians. The wind was light, so that we did not get inside Papeete Bay until nearly noon. Papeete Bay is more like a lagoon with a narrow passage, than it is like a bay. About one mile across, the water is so deep close to the shore that a ship can make fast to a cocoanut tree on the beach.

We had been expected in Papeete for a couple of months. Sailing authorities had given us up as lost.

I shall never forget that scene as we tacked back and forth against a light headwind; hundreds of little pearling luggers tied to the shore all around the bay, a French man-of-war tied up to a small wharf; an American warship anchored in the centre of the bay; and back on the gradual slopes of the mountains the city of Papeete, the capital of the South Seas, a city so gay that I can only compare it by calling it the Paris of the South Sea islands.

The American warship saluted us as we passed under her stern, and a couple of hundred American sailors set up a cheer that was worth all the hardships we had been through to hear. And to see the old Stars and Stripes again! Surrounded by flags of other nationalities, our old flag looked better than ever before; and no words can describe our feelings as those white-clad jackies cheered the crew of the *Snark*. We wanted to show our appreciation of their welcome, but the best we could do was to bare our heads as the big flag on the stern of the warship was raised and lowered three times.

Then as we passed the warship, a little canoe with two passengers bore down on us. One of the passengers was a big, sunburned white man, with long hair and beard, dressed only in a native loin-cloth. He

The Society Islands

urged along the native who was paddling the canoe, while he stood upright waving a big red flag. When he got close enough to be understood, he yelled: "Hello, Jack," and Jack, recognising him, answered: "Hello, Darling." Then the Nature Man, as Darling is called, came alongside. We could not let him aboard, for the doctor had not passed us yet, but that did not hinder his piling baskets of fruit on our deck, and jars of honey, and jams, and jells, of his own make. He was so glad to see us that he cried; and as I leaned over to shake hands with him, it seemed that I had clasped the hand of a friend, and so it proved. Ernest Darling, the Nature Man, was one of the best friends I ever made in the South Sea islands. I came to know him well during our stay at Papeete, Tahiti.

The Society group comprises about twenty-five small islands, the greatest of which is called Tahiti. On the windward side of Tahiti is located the city of Papeete, the largest settlement in Polynesia.

Papeete has a population of five thousand. About one thousand of the population are French; five hundred are Chinamen, and the remainder are natives, with a sprinkling of New Zealanders, Australians, Germans and Americans. The city lies at the foot of a large mountain, and is fed by the finest supply of fresh, cool water of any city in the tropics. This water, coming from the high mountains, rushes down past Papeete as cool and clear and pure as spring water. At the outside of Papeete are large cocoanut groves and sugar-cane plantations. In the city are several first-class business buildings, and the French have built splendid bungalows; but inside the town the natives live in their grass houses, and always will, I suppose, for a frame building is too close and confining for them — they will invariably select a grass house in preference to a frame. These islands belong to the French, than whom there are no people in the world with better ideas on making clean, pretty cities. As a consequence, they have in Papeete well-kept, parked streets, and cultivated lawns.

The tropical ferns and trees are excellent for decorating, as the trees are easily trained to any shape, and they use the rare figures to advantage. The traveller's palm is one of the rarest of the palm species, and is used quite extensively in decorating the government grounds.

The French government in the South Seas is as funny as a comic opera. In their love of pomp and display, the officials parade the streets in blue and gold uniforms, with medals pinned to their coats. The man-o'-war *Zelle* is stationed here to keep down rebellions, but even to think of these quiet people's rebelling is amusing.

The *Zelle* makes regular trips among the other islands, and the first class battleship *Catinet* makes one trip a year to Papeete from France. Each ship carries something like two hundred men, who just about turn Papeete upside down when they get ashore. It seemed to me that the officers had very little control over the men, for they came and went from the ship whenever they felt like it, and the ships, as compared with the American warship *Annapolis,* were about the dirtiest, most ill-kept fighting vessels I ever saw. I have heard the French sailors talk back to the officers when they had been ordered aboard the ship; and one sailor told an officer to go to h——, that he intended to stay ashore all night. Should an American sailor ever return so much as one word to an officer, he would most likely be court-martialled.

About one hundred sailors were busy one day beaching a large coal-barge near the *Snark,* with six or eight officers overseeing the work. I stood on the rail of the *Annapolis* with several American jackies, watching the operation. The sailors were all talking at once, so loud that the officers could not be heard, and finally the officers gave up in disgust and let the men do the work to suit themselves.

But to me most interesting were the tiny trading schooners that ply between here and the hundreds of small islands within a radius of a thousand miles — dozens of them, some of such meagre proportions that a man can hardly stand between the rail and the tiny poop deck over the little hold. Yet, I have seen fifteen almost naked islanders squatted on the deck and poop, with no room to lie down, in which position they would probably remain until they got to their destination, some minor coral island in the low Archipelago. It was always amusing to watch one of these vessels unload, for the cargo was sure to be queer.

One schooner I noticed had several bags of copra, several of pearl shell, four live turtles weighing about three hundred and fifty pounds — the largest I ever saw — and the rigging was hanging full of bananas. In addition, there were ten native men and women aboard. I wondered how they could make expenses, for the whole thing would not bring over twenty-five dollars. The turtles they sold for two dollars each, and the bananas at ten cents a bunch.

I think Papeete might easily be called the city of girls, for they outnumber the male population two to one. From the Taumotu and Marquesas Islands and the rest of the Society Islands, the girls come to Papeete when about fifteen years old to complete their education, which consists of playing the accordion and dancing the *hula-hula*. Playing an accordion is as much of an accomplishment with these girls as playing the piano is with an American girl. Every evening, from every direction, will be heard music and singing, and one will see crowds of girls, hand in hand, singing and dancing through all the streets. From eight o'clock in the evening until nearly midnight this merry-making goes on, like a continual carnival, every night. On account of the extreme minority of the men, the streets seem to be flooded with nothing but girls. They wear a loose white wrapper in the evenings, called an *au-au*. In the daytime they wear gaudy coloured *au-aus*. The French government compels the girls to wear these dresses inside the city limits, but outside they wear only the comfortable *pareus*.

After the first day we had anchored the *Snark* in Papeete Harbor, we secured Darling, the Nature Man, to stay aboard; and while Mr. and Mrs. London rented a small house, Captain Y—— and I rented a small two-roomed bungalow, while Wada and Nakata found accommodation elsewhere in the town. Hermann went on a protracted drunk, which lasted so long that Jack gave him his walking papers. He afterward secured the job of second mate on a small trading vessel.

We had been in Papeete but a few days when the steamer *Mariposa* made port from San Francisco, and we learned the first of the panic in the United States. Jack's business affairs were badly tangled, so it became necessary for him to go back to attend to them, leaving the rest of the crew in Papeete. No one was sorry that we were delayed, for we had just about decided that we should like to live here.

An interesting place was the market. Life in Papeete starts at five o'clock, when the market opens. Fish, fruit and vegetables are brought before sunrise, and at five o'clock sharp the people may begin buying. Two known lepers have their booths in this market, where they sell fruit that the Kanakas buy just as readily as from any other fruit vendors. For several hours the market square is crowded with buyers and with girls anxious to show their finery. It seems queer, but this is the time to show their clothes, for half the town is there to see them. The market is the most important place in Papeete. Even during the hottest part of the day, sleepy Kanakas will be on guard over the fruit until later in the afternoon, when the people come out again; and for the rest of the day until midnight the crowds loaf around here making small purchases of fruit, which is eaten on the spot.

Just imagine buying one of these big yellow bunches of bananas for what would equal ten cents of our money, and as many oranges as one could carry for five cents! But the best fruit, alone worth a trip to Tahiti, is the big red juicy mangoes, and another banana, the *fei*, which, when cooked, makes a substitute for the best pudding ever tasted.

I had secured the services of three French blacksmiths, who called themselves machinists, to help me on the engines. We took all the machinery from the engine-room, and completely overhauled it. Also, we installed new rigging on deck, swung our boats on their davits, and repainted the *Snark*, inside and out.

Our bungalow was just a block up the beach from the *Snark*, on a quiet, shady street where the élite of the city lived. As no one worked during the middle of the day, Captain Y—— and I stayed at home in our cool bungalow, eating fruit and reading, until late in the afternoon. We had always a bottle of cognac or absinthe, and plenty of tobacco, of which the natives who visited us partook freely. At our house, we saw the real *hula-hulas,* and heard native music and singing that tourists who happen to come to Papeete never encounter. Everyone smokes in the South Seas — girls, children, men and women — and all drink. The Kanakas would have drunk our cognac and absinthe like beer, had we allowed it. In the daytime, the girls came and squatted on our floor, making shell wreaths or weaving hats. Their toilet is very simple. On arising, they take a bath, slip on a *pareu,* over that an *au-au,* put on a wreath of flowers, wash their hair in cocoanut oil, tuck a flower under the right ear, and — the toilet is complete. They have a saying that only white people and fools wear shoes, so of course they go barefoot.

The girls gave a big *hula-hula* one day just back of our bungalow, in a big grass house built for the occasion. In the morning they got a large demijohn of orange beer from the mountains, and by evening were pretty drunk, but that did not prevent eighteen girls from giving the prettiest dance I ever saw, while four others played their weird music on tom-tom drums. One old woman kept shouting and jumping throughout the dance. At times they would shout in chorus, and all squat on the floor together, holding their hands over their heads and keeping time by rhythmical waving. Again, they would give short hops and yells, holding on to each other and keeping time by a peculiar scraping of their bare feet.

In the cool of the afternoon, I would start again on the engines, and work until dark, while Captain Y——, in his new white clothes, would promenade around Papeete, telling everyone that he was captain of the *Snark*. Captain Y—— was really a pretty good fellow, but he took himself too seriously. He was well liked by everyone who knew him. He was known throughout the Society Islands in a short time. In fact, it was impossible to see him without getting acquainted, for he *would* have everybody know that Captain Y—— of the *Snark* was in town; and as he was a pretty good spender and a sociable club fellow, the people were always glad to have him about. The two clubs extended to him and Jack and me honorary membership cards to their club houses. One, the " Circle Bouganville," gave dances and held social sessions, which we usually attended. We were always sure of a good time, though it got very tiresome saluting the many captains we found there. These " captains " strutted about the streets like peacocks, and gathered in the evening at the " Circle Bouganville " to drink until morning. There was always plenty of them! It was safe to call any man captain, for even if he did not hold the title, he would be so flattered that he would take special pains to speak to you at every meeting.

A Study in Ornaments

On the government grounds is a large bandstand. Here the band, pride of Papeete, plays several times a week. The band is small, very small, only a little larger than a tiny orchestra, and the music is horrible, but it supplies an excuse for the population to gather for a good time. Usually, a few *hula-hula* dancers have more attention than the band.

These people are great hands to bedeck themselves with flowers. The older people carry on a very profitable business during the evenings, selling wreaths. The Tahitians would no more think of going out in the evening without wearing flowers than the average man in the States would think of going without his shirt.

The Kanakas (the name holds even outside Hawaii) are very religious during church hours; the rest of the time they forget about it. The big Catholic church is the finest building in the town, being made entirely of coral cement. The other buildings are of wood.

Along the water-front the principal street, known as Broom Road, runs clear around the bay in the shape of a horse-shoe. One side of the street is lined with buildings. On the other side is the beach. At one end of the beach is a shipbuilding yard, where small pearling luggers are built and repaired. The rise and fall of the tide in this bay is so great that no dry dock is necessary. Some of the vessels have names almost as large as the ship. For instance, there is the *Teheipouroura Tapuai,* a mission schooner belonging to the Catholics.

The streets running into the market square are lined with Chinese stores, and the headquarters of the several trading concerns that send schooners among the other islands. The Chinese are the only ones that can carry on a retail business. The Kanakas are too lazy, and the white people could not live on so small a scale. About all the natives need is coloured calico, fruits, cheap overalls, and singlets. They make their own hats when they wear any, and a white coat is the only thing the French ever buy in the way of luxuries.

Now that I am back in America, I can appreciate their quiet lazy life better than I could then. To be able to sit or sleep under those big shady trees or to take a book out there to read, all the time with plenty of fruit handy, and with nothing to worry over, is a genuine luxury.

Now and then a sailing vessel will drop in from America or Europe or Australia, loaded with lumber, and ships of wine come from France. Every six weeks arrive the *Mariposa* from San Francisco and the *Manapaoura* from New Zealand, while warships of every nation coal here on their long journeys across the Pacific. It is only when the South American warships put into port that any real trouble begins, for the South American jackies always have fights with the French jackies. The Americans licked a few of the

Frenchmen while I was at Papeete, and after that there was peace for a while.

Papeete is the centre of the pearling industry of the South Seas. Hundreds of little sloops lie here during the hurricane season, while the captains strut about the streets. None of the captains can navigate. They sail entirely from dead reckoning, often taking weeks to go a few hundred miles, when a captain who could navigate would take only as many days. But they put no value on time. They simply look for an island until they find it. Every year, when it is time for the pearling vessels to come in from the Taumotus, there are always many missing which are never heard from again.

The pearl shell is loaded in large sailing vessels. Most of it is sent to Europe. The pearl divers are only after the shell, and not after the real pearl, as most persons think. If they are lucky enough to find a pearl, they are that much ahead, but fishing for the pearl alone would be a very unprofitable business.

CHAPTER IX

SOME SOUTH SEA ROYALTY

THE islands that we are familiar with as the South Sea Islands are properly called Oceania. Oceania is divided off in four distinct parts, known as Polynesia, or the eastern islands; Australasia, or the southern islands, including Australia; Melanesia, the islands lying to the north and west of Australia; and Micronesia, which lies to the north and west of Melanesia. The characteristics, the languages, and the customs of the people of each distinct division have no similarity.

The Polynesian people are supposed to be descended in mixed line from the Spanish and original Tahitians. It is certain that they have a strain of white blood in their makeup, for they have none of the negroid characteristics found farther west. They are a quiet, easy-going people, whom it would be hard to disturb. Their colour is a light reddish-brown, and they have black eyes and hair and well-rounded, intelligent faces. Very seldom is one of these people angry. It must be something out of the ordinary to arouse their anger, but when once aroused, they lose their heads entirely, they make no discrimination between friends and foes, and they are best given a wide berth until their fit of temper has passed.

Among the inhabitants of any community, will always be found some characters of sufficient strength and uniqueness to distinguish them from the herd. In the South Seas, they are usually chiefs, or old retired sea-captains and beach-combers, who hold this position in the Australasian, Melanesian and Micronesian sections, but in the Polynesian section the place of honour unquestionably belongs to Helene of Raiatea. Hers was the greatest power, though it was not a vested one. She seemed a true South Sea queen.

Raiatea is another island of the Society group, and Helene's home. She was the most prominent personage in these islands, and a typical Polynesian. I had ample opportunity to study her — her every mood and whim. Helene of Raiatea was known to all successful traders, and we were advised to be pleasant to her, as the success or failure of many a trader has depended on the smiles or frowns of Helene of Raiatea. It is needless to say that we took the advice, and invited Helene to be guest on board the *Snark*. Helene had no royal blood, nor was she of chieftain stock, but many a chief or king had less power than she.

She had been born with more energy than the average Kanaka, and a constant mingling with the white people had given her ideas above her class. A little over the average height, her figure was admirable. Her skin was a light olive colour; she had two perfect rows of teeth and a brain that seemed never to be still.

We had heard of her in the Marquesas Islands, and I was anxious to make her acquaintance. During the hard fight getting through the Paumota Archipelago, we had forgotten about her. On the first night ashore, as I was walking about the town in company with the captain of one of the German schooners, my mind was on other things. Life was gay in Papeete. There were singing and dancing in the streets, accordions everywhere, girls and boys strolling hand in hand or eating fruit on the sidewalks. We had paused in the centre of the market square, where life was the merriest. Young people would stop their games to see who that strange person was and what he was doing in Papeete. I felt self-conscious as I moved along, the cynosure of hundreds of pairs of eyes. Of a sudden, a white-clad girl from the throng laughingly grabbed my hand, and as if to ask a question, she said: "*Iaorana*, Missionary," which means: "Hello, Missionary." With these people, everyone is a missionary until they find out otherwise, and they always greet a stranger as a missionary when he first lands. The captain with me explained in their native tongue who I was, and then I seemed to be taken in as one of them. Helene drew us to the side of the street and made known that I could buy her some flowers and fruit, and the captain and I squatted on the sidewalk and ate watermelon, while she chattered away, asking questions of the captain as fast as he could answer them. Several other girls halted enquiringly, and Helene with a gesture

Some South Sea Royalty

told them to be seated with us. Then I bought more flowers and fruit, and I commenced to wonder if I was not "getting my leg pulled," until I paid the whole bill and it amounted to something like ten cents. As I had never had such a good time on so small an amount of money, I got generous, and nodded to another group of girls to join us, but I saw Helene frown at them, and they turned away. This was the first I saw of Helene's power, but later on I observed that the white people as well as the natives treated her with vastly more respect than the ordinary Kanaka ever got.

On the day after I first met Helene, I had occasion to go to Lavina's Hotel, where the Londons were staying. I found Helene seated on the *lanai*, trying to make Jack understand what she was saying. When I came up the walk, she jumped to her feet, and said, "*Iaorana oae*," and I noticed that she no longer called me missionary, nor was I ever called missionary again. I'm sure I never gave any of them cause to mistake me for a missionary; in fact, after the crew of the *Snark* had become acquainted in Papeete, I'm afraid the real missionaries did not approve of our keeping open house to the natives. But the good-natured, hospitable people did us so many favours and were constantly making us such generous presents of fish that we made them welcome whenever they wished to visit us. They would bring Jack bunches of their cooking bananas from the mountains; and then Jack would lay down his writing, pass around cigarettes, and talk to them. We easily picked up their language, for it is so simple that little effort is required in its use. Through the kindly services of Ernest Darling, the Nature Man, and Helene, we soon were talking without any difficulty. The Tahitian language has only about fourteen letters in its alphabet. There are no singulars nor plurals, no modes, no tenses. Every letter is pronounced. We were able to speak intelligibly after a little practice.

Helene was an every-day visitor at the bungalow belonging to Captain Y—— and myself, where she would wear only the native *pareu*. This was allowable, as we lived outside the centre of town. Had we been resident closer in, the French government would have forced all the native girls who came to see us to wear *au-aus*. At times, Helene would bring certain of her friends to the house, for they were always sure of finding tobacco there. As I have said, all through the South Seas the girls smoke as much as the men, and think nothing of it, for the habit has been with them since the very introduction of the weed. And now it has such a hold on them that no worse punishment could be inflicted on these people than to deprive them of their tobacco.

One day while Jack was in California, Helene came to the house wanting to borrow a dollar to buy medicine to take to her mother. The French physician stationed here charges one dollar to take a case, and for that will supply the medicine and attend to the case until the patient has no further use for him. A small lugger had just come in from Raiatea, Helene's home. The captain had been instructed to return at once with Helene and the medicine, and I was at the beach that afternoon when the boat sailed. I must say that I was glad that I had sailed on a nice big boat like the *Snark,* instead of on one of those little luggers. Raiatea lies over a hundred miles away from Papeete. And the boat was so small that none of the fifteen passengers could go below. But Helene did not seem to be afraid, and in ten days when she returned, she brought a couple of dozen big watermelons, for she knew that watermelons were the best present she could give us.

One Sunday, Helene and I decided to go out buggy-riding, thinking that we could make some good pictures. Early in the morning, I went to the stable, and was assured by a big, lazy Kanaka that in one hour he would send me the best he had, and I wondered what it would be, for all I could see was an old cart, a broken-down hearse with the glass sides smashed in, and a buggy made of parts of a wagon and another buggy. At present it had one wheel off. But in two hours I found out. When I went to the gate, I saw the Kanaka beating a poor, starved horse which would not move out of a walk, and which stopped by our bungalow. Well, we drove, I think, about five miles that day, when the horse refused to go further. The top fell off the buggy, and the harness broke several times. But anyway, we got some fine pictures.

On one of the regular trips of the steamer *Mariposa,* while getting my hair cut by the ship's barber, as I sat in the chair I noticed several pairs of ladies' shoes in boxes on the shelf. I don't know what use the barber had for them, but it gave me an idea, and as soon as I could find Captain Y—— I told him of it, and then we hunted Helene and took her aboard and fitted her out with shoes and stockings. It was laughable to see her strut around Papeete that day. The shoes hurt her feet, for she had never worn shoes before. None of the native girls in Papeete had ever worn shoes. That night she walked around the market square so long that soon she was limping. Next day she was again barefooted, and I never saw the shoes again. In that she was like all the natives, childish; they are anxious for something new, but soon tire of it when they get it.

I would sit for hours telling her of the rest of the world; of circuses, of trains, of tall skyscrapers. She would listen as quiet as could be until I had finished, and then ask questions. But it was not until a man with a moving-picture machine came to Papeete that I had the delight of seeing the height of her enjoyment. At one end of the square, an enterprising Frenchman built a frame building which he called "Folies Bergere." Here every Saturday night he

Some South Sea Royalty

gave moving pictures. I took Helene, and Captain Y—— took Taaroa, another native girl. I never enjoyed a show so much in my life. I secured seats near the front, in such a position that Helene would miss none of it. From the first picture to the last, her face changed from expressions of astonishment and delight to horror and fear. The whole audience was in the same state of excitement. There were reels of film showing large cities and railway trains, and magic pictures that none of these people had ever seen the like of. It was many a day before the natives could understand that it was not supernatural. And with my meagre knowledge of their language, I was hard put to explain to them how it was done.

They were like frightened rabbits when the fire department came charging down the street. When the swift-rushing teams got close, looking as if they would plunge out of the screen and into the audience, screams went up and there was nearly a panic in the house. How they laughed at the comic films! But the last thing was supposed to be the devil in hell, pitching people into the fire. Since seeing that, they were afraid of the least sound. Afraid of the *deipelo,* they said; and we could not convince them that the picture was not real, for, they argued, if it was not real, how could anyone take a picture of it?

When Jack came back from California, we learned that we had been lost at sea, and that the *Snark* was a very unseaworthy craft, anyway. Throughout the

States, newspapers and magazines had persisted in reporting us dead, every last one of us. I was told that an Oakland bank had even begun an agitation to wind up the affairs of Jack London, deceased. And of course the prophets of disaster had welcomed this evidence of their own amazing foresight, this news of prophecy fulfilled.

The engines of the *Snark* were still giving us trouble. The big one was just like a watch that seems all right, but won't run. It looked in fine condition, but often refused to start, and developed a hot-box on some one of the four cylinders when run for any length of time.

One night, along in the early part of March, Captain Y—— came to me and asked me to stay on the *Snark* for him for a little while. Away outside the reef was a ship, just barely to be seen, that was shooting skyrockets and cannon, as an evidence of distress. It was thought to be one of the Maxwell trading schooners, one month overdue from the southern Taumotu islands. A little gasolene schooner was chartered, and Captain Y—— and some others went out to it. It was not the trading vessel after all, but (to my great surprise) the Chinese war-junk *Whang-Ho* which I had been aboard of in California. They were sixty-eight days out of Frisco for New York; but the *Whang-Ho* was never intended to be handled by modern sailors; she had been blown to Papeete, leaking badly — the men, we afterward found out, had been obliged to pump her night and day. There were eight

Some South Sea Royalty

in the crew, all Americans. Captain Y—— went aboard, and made them pay one hundred and twenty-five dollars to be towed in. Once safe on land, the men swore they would go no farther in the ancient junk.

The natives watched the *Whang-Ho* with considerable awe. Never had they seen anything like it. Certainly, the ship was the strangest thing afloat — great eyes were painted on her square bow, the Chinese thinking that a boat needs something to see with. The big galley aft was painted yellow, and the tall, tree-like masts were brilliant red. I believe the *Whang-Ho* had once been in royal service in China.

Speaking of royalty, I think Ernest Darling might well be called the King of the Open Air. He never lives indoors — if he can help it. While at Papeete, we learned his story, and an interesting story it is.

Twelve years before, he had been lying on a deathbed in Portland, Oregon. It seemed that nothing could be done to save him. He was a wreck. The doctor told him what had caused his breakdown. Overstudy, was the medico's verdict; overstudy had put the final destructive touch on a constitution already broken and enervated by two attacks of pneumonia. His body was irreparably wasted, and his mind was fast going.

Ernest Darling lay on that bed of sickness, awaiting inevitable death. He could not bear the slightest noise. Medicine drove him desperate. The day came when he could stand it no longer. He tottered from his bed, escaped from the house, and crawled for miles through the brush. Here, in the silent spaces, close to nature's heart, he found rest and quiet. He bathed in the soothing rays of the sun, stripping off all clothing, clinging close to the moist earth as he bathed. Life, full and free, seemed to flow into his veins as he lay there. The sun was the real life-giver, he thought, noting his relief; that, with the balmy air, was all that he needed.

For three months he lived thus. He built him a primitive house of leaves and grasses, roofed over with bark. No meat passed his lips — only fruits and nuts, with occasional bits of bread. Every day he put on more weight, and the intolerable agony of his nerves subsided.

But at the end of the three months, the heavy rains forced him to return to Portland and take up once more his abode in his father's house. Then came the relapse. He lost all he had gained. A third time he grappled with pneumonia, and came out of the struggle nearer death than ever. His mind collapsed utterly. Ernest Darling was tried by alienists, found insane, and told that he had less than a month to live.

They took him to an asylum, where he was allowed to live once more on fruits and nuts. Again strength came to him. Leaving the sanatorium, he got a bicycle and went south to California, where he attended Stanford University for a year, going to his classes as simply garbed as possible. When winter came, he

MISSION SCHOONER TRADING AMONG THE ISLANDS AND "PREACHING" FROM THE VESSEL

was obliged to head further south. Several times he was arrested and tested for his sanity.

Finding that no one would let him alone, and not desiring to end his days in either an asylum or a jail, he made his way to Hawaii. But there was no relief for him. Here he was given his choice between leaving Hawaii or going to prison for a year.

Darling went to Tahiti. And there, at last, after all his wanderings and harassments, he found a haven. The Tahitians and French neither jailed him nor questioned his sanity. He spent his days in the open, on a tract of land he bought, near Papeete; and his food he picked from his own trees. When in town, he was busy in such simple shopping as he found necessary, or in expounding the principles of Socialism, in which he was a devoted believer.

We had lived in Papeete three months and a half before everything was ready for us to start again through the islands. We had decided to visit the island of Moorea first, then, on a special invitation from Helene, we were going to Raiatea.

Before leaving Papeete, we got a new sailor, a French boy named Ernest. Ernest was signed on the French bark *Elizabeth* as ordinary seaman. When our captain offered him a job on the *Snark,* he ran away from the French ship, and lived on fruit in the mountains until she had sailed, when he came down and joined us. He was eighteen years old, spoke little English, and was an all-around sailor. He had been round the world twice. He was very tall — one inch taller than I was — so that he was likewise obliged to stoop when he went below.

We were three hours and forty minutes getting out of Papeete Harbor and dropping anchor in Moorea Bay. On this trip, the engine ran perfectly; and it is hard to say which was the most pleased — Jack, Mrs. London, or I. I took Mr. and Mrs. London ashore in the launch, then came back and went to bed with a terrible headache, and did not have time to get a good idea of the bay until next morning. It is about three quarters of a mile wide, by one and a half long, and reminded me very much of Taiohae Bay in the Marquesas. All around range the mountains, ragged peaks with the sides one mass of green, with cocoanut palms half way to the top. The beach was a jungle of palms and bananas. With the glass, we could count as many as seventy cocoanuts on one tree. All day I painted the engine room, and that night walked with Ernest two miles along the beach to the village, which consisted of three Chinese stores and a bunch of grass houses.

Along the way we met Kanakas, looking very cool, dressed only in their *pareu* cloth.

"*Iaorana!*" they all greeted us, and with some joke passed laughingly on. When we got aboard, I started the searchlight, and turned it on the huts along the beach. The Kanakas would come out and watch us, and some of the *vahines hula-hula'd* for us. In the

Some South Sea Royalty

glare of the light, I could see Jack and Mrs. London eating in the open-air dining place of MacTavish, a white man, who boards any person who ever drifts to Moorea.

Next morning, I took the Londons out in the launch to make photographs; but in an hour the launch-engine stopped, and I had to land them, while I repaired it. I had it in good running order again in an hour.

During our stay, Kanaka men and women and girls paddled out, and we let them aboard. Great was their curiosity at the electric lights. One Kanaka wanted to turn them on and off so much that I had to switch the current off at the engine room, so that the lights went dead; but they could hardly keep away from the five-horse-power engine, which I ran most of the time in order to fill the storage batteries. I took some of the girls out in the launch, to their almost frantic pleasure. I towed an outrigger canoe with two girls across the bay, and as quick as they could paddle back they wanted me to do it again.

Darling, the Nature Man, and Young, a Socialist, had accompanied us. It was amusing to see Darling splash along shore in the shallow water, catching fish. At times he lay in the shade of a tree, resting. When a crowd of natives gathered around him, he would jump up and yell like an Indian war dancer, which performance always doubled the natives with laughter. They all like Darling, and he likes them. He told us that he knew he would be making a fool of himself among white people, but that he liked to amuse the Kanakas. Darling was full of energy — much different from the wraith of a man who had lain on his bed in Portland, Oregon, looking forward to nothing but death. He chopped wood for Wada and made trips up the mountains after fruit. He had the deck lined with half a dozen different varieties of bananas.

The next day I spent in reading and sleeping, except when I took the launch to go watch the Kanaka boys fish. They first catch a small fish among the coral banks, then bite out a chunk for bait; then another chunk, which they eat. I have seen them eat fish raw, just as they were pulled wriggling from the water. But usually they soak them in vinegar before eating. Raw fish is the favourite dish among the Kanakas. I tried to develop an appetite, but I fear I made no startling success.

We were a week at Moorea; then a casting on the engine broke, making it necessary for us to return to Papeete. It was just before we started back that a long canoe, filled with men and women, paddled past as and bombarded us with oranges until the decks were covered, then paddled away, its occupants laughing and shouting. Darling said the oranges were to pay us for being so good to them. The Moorea orange is nearly green in colour, and tastes the same as the California variety.

We had difficulty in getting away. I had a short circuit on the wires that I was puzzled to find; but when we were finally able to start, I beat my record coming over by forty-five minutes.

Arrived at Papeete, it took two days to put the machinery in order again. We then set sail for Raiatea. It was on April 4 that we cleared Papeete Harbor. The usual large crowd had assembled to see us off. After getting about five miles off the reef, I stopped the engine, which was running splendidly. We sailed all night with a fair breeze, and in the morning sighted Huahina, which we steered for, but kept one mile off the lee shore until we had left it far behind. Soon Raiatea was sighted. Its ragged peaks looked at a distance the same as Tahiti or Moorea. When about twenty miles off, I started the engine. We got through the reefs and anchored in the bay by seven o'clock.

On account of engine repairs having delayed us, Helene had given up our coming, and had gone to the mountains to visit relatives. But she heard that we were in the bay, and next day we were honoured by a visit from her. She came out to the *Snark* in a small canoe, and invited us ashore to her home. Jack had promised us every night off while at this island, so Ernest and I took the launch for shore. We took a five-mile walk along the beach and up the mountain to her mother's house. Along the shore, grass huts were built on stilts over the water. Kanakas sat, or rather squatted, all along the road, and each greeted us in the native tongue. We found the house away back among the mountains, a long, low grass house, with a huge waterfall made by a mountain stream in the rear. Oranges, limes, cocoanuts, papaias, guavas, bananas, and several kinds of fruit I cannot spell the name of, were thick for miles up and down the valley. We found Helene, her mother and her father, and several other members of the family, and were given a hearty welcome. Ernest talked French, Helene and her mother, Kanaka, while I used English, French and Kanaka — and we all used gestures. Her father could speak only the native tongue, and was an ordinary Kanaka. Her mother was a typical Tahitian. So I have never been able to understand why Helene should be so far above her class. Her environment had been no better; it must have been some strength of character, some intrinsic worth, that elevated her in station and in mind. Anyway, she proved that she was a person of authority on her own island when she ordered a big feast prepared in our honour, and the natives gathered with roasted wild boar and gave an imitation of their old-time " long-pig " feast.

We stayed at Helene's home until one o'clock in the morning. We remained four days on the island. Helene came to the village, to stay while we were in port. Later, we took a daylight trip to her mountain home, in order to enjoy the natural beauties. The scene from the waterfall was great. We had viewed some wonderful scenery in the Hawaiian and Mar-

Some South Sea Royalty

quesas Islands, but nothing to compare with this. There was not a sign of cultivation anywhere — everything in its wild natural state; and as for fruit, it was everywhere in abundance, buds, blossoms, half-ripe and ripe fruit on the trees at the same time.

Before going further with the voyage of the *Snark*, and while the *Snark* is still anchored at Raiatea Island, I want to tell of the comic opera war that once occurred here.

The natives of Raiatea, tired of the French system of government, pulled down the French flag, and raised the flag of England. They put the French officials then living in Raiatea adrift in open boats. These people made their way to Papeete and informed the governor, who had never seen any more active service than strutting around the streets of Papeete, and did not know what to do in such an emergency. The governor went to the British consul stationed here, and demanded that he cause the natives of Raiatea to lower the British flag. Now the British consul was only a figure-head, and had never attended to any duties other than signing pratique papers for the British ships that came here. Sometimes as many as two or three a year dropped anchor in Papeete. The rest of the time there was nothing to do. So now he was nonplussed. Long debates took place. At last it was agreed that both governor and consul should go to Raiatea and put down the rebellion.

The French man-of-war *Zelle* transported them to

Raiatea, and the two officials landed under the white flag of truce. The chiefs received them, and the two emissaries demanded that they raise the French flag. The chiefs refused, and gave the officers half an hour to get back to the ship. Then the warship shelled the village; but by that time all the natives had made for the brush; and finally, after five or six days' shelling, the sailors landed again and lowered the flag without opposition, for the Kanakas had realised that their fight was useless. But the funny thing about the whole business was that for at least four days the warship had been shelling an empty village.

The islands of Raiatea and Tahaa are in reality one island that has been cut through the middle by some volcanic disturbance. The distance from Raiatea Island to Tahaa is less than seven miles. The tides often sweep through here with such force that small canoes have spent days getting across the channel. Just as we were preparing to sail from Raiatea Island, a tiny outrigger canoe with a big sail hove in sight. In it was a big, almost naked Kanaka named Tehei. He invited Jack and Mrs. London to take a ride in his queer craft, an invitation they cheerfully accepted. They went over to Tahaa, the island seven miles away, and stayed two days, fishing and hunting. On their return, we set out with the *Snark* through coral reefs where a hundred feet either way would wreck us. At Tahaa we picked up the Kanaka Tehei and his wife, with two canoe-loads of fruit, a pig, chickens and *poi*. Jack informed us that Tehei had begged very hard to be allowed to go with us to the island of Bora Bora, our last stop in the Society Islands, and that he had yielded to his solicitations. Indeed, Tehei had wanted to go clear to Samoa, but to this Jack shook his head. Tehei had brought his wife, Bihaura, along. To her, also, was given permission to go with us to Bora Bora. Tehei and his wife returned to their house, and early next morning, with a light wind, we crossed the lagoon under power to the point where Tehei and Bihaura were to meet us. As we made into the land between banks of coral, we could see Tehei among the trees, running down toward the beach. He was afraid we would not see him, so he pulled off his shirt and waved it as he ran. Once aboard, Tehei informed us that we must proceed along the land until we got opposite his house. He took the wheel and guided the *Snark* through the coral, and we reached the beach. Here was another offering of fruit and fowl, two more canoe-loads awaiting us.

All the time that the fruit was being loaded in the cockpit and aft the cockpit, piled up to the railing, I had been letting the engine run free without the propellers in gear; the old engine had never worked better, and Jack was just commenting on how smoothly it was running, when it gave a mighty backfire and stopped, and in a very dangerous place, for the currents were running very swift through here and there was no wind that we might sail by. The crew on deck, with the help of several Kanakas, braced the long oars that we kept for the life-boat, and eight oars worked an hour while I toiled at the engine and finally got it running just as they were nearly exhausted. I threw the clutch into gear again, and with Tehei at the bow to look out for coral reefs, we slowly threaded our way out of countless reefs projecting only a few inches above the surface of the water. Canoes skimmed over the water ahead, showing us the way through the reefs.

Tehei was invaluable. Had it not been for him, I do not believe we would ever have gotten out of that maze of reefs. Now that I have a chance to think over that day's work, I don't believe that I ever had so much experience crowded into a single day before.

With the engines running smoothly, I would go on deck and look over the rail, down on remote bottoms where fish of every hue and colour played among the dense forests of coral. Islands were on every side of us, high rugged peaks, some of them a hundred miles away, and near us small low atolls covered with a riotous growth of cocoanuts. The day was perfect — very little wind, and with the awning stretched over the decks and all sails furled, we slid over the smooth surface of the water straight for Bora Bora. After we left the coral reefs behind, Tehei and Bihaura lay down on deck and went to sleep. Jack and Mrs. London were at work grinding out reading matter for the American public, the rest of the crew were asleep in their bunks, and I sat on the edge of the open skylight and divided the time between watching the engine and gazing over the dozens of small islands.

This was the real South Seas that I had read about, dreamed about, and had never expected to see. Numerous small canoes would put out from the islands and try to board us, but we moved too fast for them, and after paddling till they were out of breath, they would drift back.

At noon dinner was served on deck, entirely of fruit and raw fish. Then everyone went to sleep again, except Captain Y—— at the wheel and myself at the engine. About three in the afternoon the engine started backfiring and knocking so that I was kept in the engine room the rest of the day. With every backfire, the cylinders would lose gas until the engine room was almost unbearable to work in. But if we were to get to Bora Bora that night, I must keep busy with them. Our engine was a seventy-horse-power Twentieth Century, with four cylinders. I would run on two cylinders until they got hot, then turn them off and turn on the other two, and so kept up the hardest afternoon's work I ever did.

It was close to nine o'clock when we reached Bora Bora, and by that time I was nearly dead; but I kept working on the engines. I was doing the only thing possible, though the last few hours seemed a blank to me. The people on deck knew nothing about engines, so they could not help me. They were unaware that

I was nearly dead below. I think that during the last hour some power diabolical must have got hold of the engine. I lost consciousness and fell on the floor, and knew nothing till the big gong working in the cockpit gave me the signal to stop the engine. I aroused myself long enough to throw the switch and crawl through the hatchway; then I knew nothing more until several hours later, when I found Mrs. London bathing my face in cold water and the Japanese chafing my limbs with coarse towels. I was certainly near death's door, nearer than I can ever get without actually dying. They told me afterward that my heart was barely beating.

And I think I realise what it must be to be dead, for the only memory I have of that awful period is that I thought I was dead. The gas gave me a queer roaring sensation that seemed like some unearthly music; and had not the gong sounded when it did, I fear it would have been all the music I should ever have heard. How I roused myself enough to shut off the power and get on deck, is a mystery to me now. Many times, even after the lapse of several years, I awaken with that queer feeling of dying, and always I seem to be aboard the *Snark*. It was barely midnight when I gained consciousness, to hear the sound of music and of singing floating across the quiet lagoon.

Next morning I was still weak, so I did not clean my engines as I usually did after a long run, but went ashore to see the life of Bora Bora.

Some South Sea Royalty

The whole island rose up to entertain us, and the good people gave us ten days of the best time I ever had. Tehei's wife was of royal blood, and her influence caused the natives to make special effort for our entertainment. The night after our arrival, Tehei invited Jack, Mrs. London, Captain Y—— and me ashore, where we had a dinner such as surpasses description. Fruits prepared in every way a true Kanaka likes, sucking pig, chicken fried in cocoanut oil, watermelon, and raw fish! This last is one of the choicest of South Sea dishes. The fish, freshly caught, are cleaned and soaked an hour in lime-juice. It is delicious. Although we could speak very little with the Kanakas, we enjoyed watching them, and they enjoyed watching us.

After the meal, we went to a large oval, bamboo missionary-house, and watched an old Kanaka missionary drill what he called his *himines*. A score of girls, decorated with flowers, formed a semi-circle in front. Back of these stood the Kanaka men, and behind them the boys. Their music was more like grunts, but the wild, weird noise made my blood tingle. The boys kept swaying their bodies with the song and clapping their hands, at times beating themselves on the chest and chanting. This finished, a surprise was in store for us. Natives came in with chicken, watermelons, vegetables, fruit and fish, and made a pile that two boats the size of the *Snark* would find difficulty in floating under. Then a big Kanaka got up and presented it to us. Jack thanked them, but had to decline the greater part, for want of carrying capacity. Even as it was, our deck looked like a market.

Bora Bora is a marvellous island. Twenty miles in circumference, it is surrounded by dozens of smaller islands, each in turn surrounded by its own coral reefs. From our deck, I could count eight of these small islands, some only a few acres, others about three or four miles around, all covered, save for the sandy beach, with a thick green jungle of tropical trees. We were twenty-five miles from Raiatea and one thousand miles from Samoa.

Only three persons on the island could speak English. There were half a dozen frame huts; all the rest were of grass, or bamboo. The natives wore nothing but the red *pareus,* or breech-clouts.

We were anchored a half-mile out, but the launch made the trip to the beach in a few minutes. The whole deck was covered with awnings, and we ate and slept on deck. The three engines were running all right, though it kept me pretty busy attending to them; it took a good deal of electricity just at that time, for the fans were running almost without intermission, and I had connected drop-lights on deck, whereby we might see to read or write at night. The natives were unremitting in their attentions. They came out by canoe-loads, bringing us food of various sorts — that is, all but the women, who found the ship " taboo."

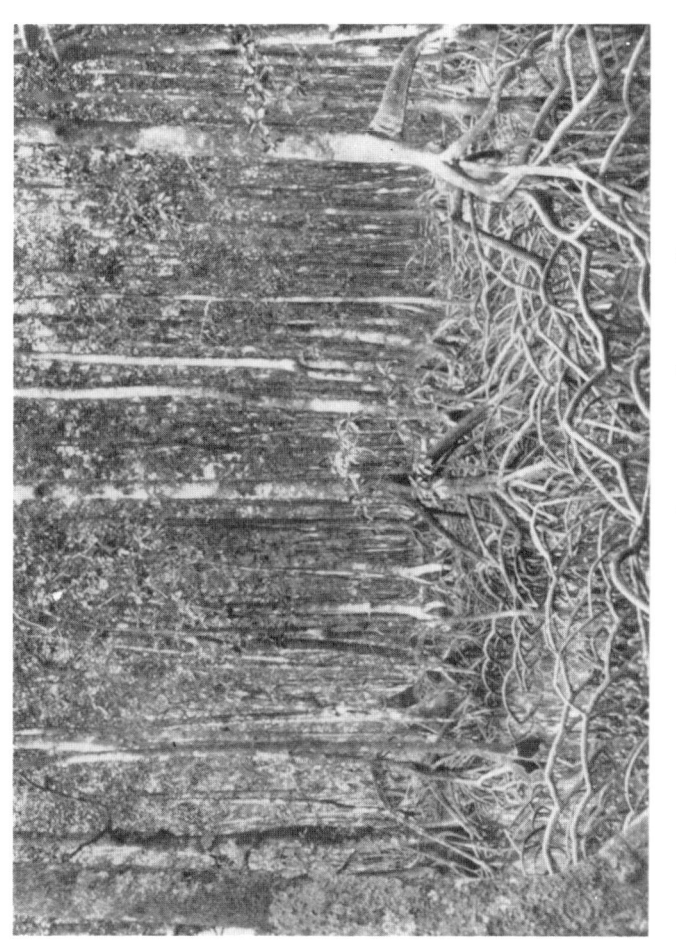

THE HAUNT OF THE CROCODILE, SOLOMON ISLANDS

Bora Bora was the most primitive place we had yet visited. All along the beach, the long outrigger canoes were propped up on logs cut out for the purpose. The beach itself was sown thick with forgotten graves. On the morning of the third day, Tehei came aboard, and informed us that he had planned a mammoth stone-fishing for us. It was to be the biggest in the history of the island. Runners had been sent to the interior of the island and around the coast. These men were telling every inhabitant of Bora Bora about the stone-fishing; and in the afternoon the people began to gather in the village, and that night we were invited ashore to a big entertainment, gotten up on the spur of the moment. We were given seats on the grass in the centre of the village green, and around us squatted brown-skinned and black-haired men and women and girls and boys. They would sing their weird, barbarous tunes and keep time by swaying their bodies and gesturing with the arms. Then a few of them would dance, while the crowd cheered — not such dances as we see in civilised places, but something so strange and indescribable as to arouse the disbelief of some who have never travelled in the South Seas. They would dance so slowly that they would scarcely be moving; then away they would go, like a mad whirlwind. The crowd urged them on. Finally, the dance would cease as abruptly as it had begun, while the dancers would sink down exhausted. On going aboard the *Snark* late that night, Jack remarked on the contrast between their easy, care-free lives, and the artificial, wearing lives of the so-called civilised people.

Early next morning we were awakened by the conch shells, signalling for the people to gather at the beach. This conch shell is used by heralds all through the South Seas. Once heard, the sound is never forgotten. I brought back a number of these shells, when I returned to America.

Going on deck, I saw canoe-load after canoe-load of natives putting off from the beach, and among them a big double canoe paddled by fourteen girls. Two men sat in the stern to steer, and on a little platform at the bow, dancing and singing, were Tehei and Bihaura. They had borrowed our large American flag, and had it waving at the bow. This canoe-load of the belles of Bora Bora came alongside the *Snark* and received Jack and Mrs. London, while Captain Y—— and I followed in the gasolene launch. I had nine kodaks and cameras arranged in the launch, so that I could use any one I wanted and use it quickly. From the *Snark* to the place of the fishing was about three miles. Riding in the launch, I often caught up with the other canoes, then stopped the engine and drifted back again, and sometimes I circled round the big double canoe. Jack once asked me if I did not wish I were among that bunch of girls, and he thought he was getting the better of me, until I ran alongside and three of the girls jumped in the launch, after which I sped on, with the

Some South Sea Royalty

laugh on Jack. The girls had never been in a motor-boat before, and they held on for dear life. The launch outdistanced all the other boats, arriving at the place of fishing half an hour before the rest.

After all the canoes had beached, the ceremony began. Tehei assigned to each of the fishers his or her duty; then nearly one hundred canoes, each with a couple of men, paddled out from the shore about three miles. And then, at a signal, the boats, which were spread out in a long line, moved slowly toward the shore, one man paddling and another rattling strings of shells in the water, and all yelling at the top of their voices. The men who paddled the canoes splashed as much water as possible, while their companions rattled the shells, the object being to frighten the fish toward the shore, where the water was shallow. They gradually closed in as they moved shoreward, while girls with nets of leaves waded out in readiness to close in on the canoes. The boats were an hour getting near the beach. As they approached closer and closer, the girls formed a palisade of their legs, and made a net of leaves. And Tehei, armed with a spear, stood in the corral formed by the girls. He was to kill the first fish, and it was to be presented to Jack London, along with the spear and an invitation to kill as many as he might want. Such is Polynesian hospitality. Tehei proudly made ready for the initial slaughter. But the canoes drew closer and closer, and Tehei rubbed his eyes in wonder. Then he dropped the spear. There were no fish to kill. Tehei hunted for fifteen minutes, and then, satisfied that there were no fish within that human palisade, he turned to Jack, the most forlorn looking person in Bora Bora. He was ashamed of himself, he was ashamed of the rest of the natives, and he was ashamed of the fish, and of Bora Bora. The poor fellow felt so humiliated that Jack hastened to invite as many as could crowd aboard the *Snark* to join us in a feast that night. This they were not slow in doing. That evening we fed them hardtack and tinned salmon, which they washed down with good old Holland gin. When they left, they declared that they had never had such a good time before.

And so the days passed in this land of abundance. Every day we were surrounded by canoes, anxious to see the *Snark* and her white crew. The natives were too polite to come aboard the *Snark* without being invited. One day, when I was drowsing lazily on deck, close to the engine room hatchway, so that I could keep one eye on the dynamo engine, which was chugging away filling the storage batteries for that night's run of lights and fans, and the other eye on the water, a big Kanaka paddled up close in his canoe, and asked politely if he could come aboard and peep — just peep — below into the engine room. Mrs. London, sitting on the rail, pointed to a big watermelon in the canoe, and made known to the Kanaka that I was inordinately fond of watermelon. Immediately, the native passed over the melon to me, and I took him be-

Some South Sea Royalty

low. His astonishment was supreme at the maze of machinery, lights that turned on and off at will, and the most wonderful thing of all, fans! Then I started the big engine for him, and he left the engine room with his head in a whirl.

That afternoon, canoe-load after canoe-load of watermelons came off to the *Snark,* and each time I would exhibit the engine room; and once, while a crowd of natives were on deck, I gave one two live ends of electric wire. With a yell he jumped overboard, and after that they were careful not to touch anything that I had aught to do with.

Bihaura, being of royal blood, had houses in several of the adjoining islands. The one in Bora Bora was her headquarters. One day while at her home, I noticed a large eight-day clock hanging on the wall. It looked as if it had not run for years. Examining it, I found that all it needed was cleaning, so I took it aboard and put it in good shape. Then I hung it again on her wall, and started it running. It was the only timepiece on the island. The natives would peek in at the door and watch and wonder. Next day, a Kanaka stopped me, with about half a dozen old clock wheels that he wanted me to make into a clock. I fell several points in Bora Bora estimation when I was forced to acknowledge that I could not tinker the old wheels into an effective clock: but next night I regained what I had lost when I made the graphophone talk.

Jack had taken the machine ashore, and was playing to several hundred people in the *himine* house, when the rachet spring slipped out of position, making it impossible to wind the machine. Jack send aboard for me, and I came ashore and straightened the spring in position, a thing Jack could have done had he thought of it. But he didn't think of it — and immediately I was restored to high favour among the Bora Bora natives.

After ten days of this delightful life, it was time for us to go. On the day of sailing, the natives tried to outdo all their previous generosity, piling the *Snark* knee-deep with abundance of fruit, chickens, vegetables, fish, and other good things. There were yams, taro, cocoanuts, limes, bananas, papaias, pineapples and pomegranates. The life-boat, the launch, and the deck were piled full. And when, at one o'clock on the afternoon of April 15, 1908, we set sail from Bora Bora, hundreds of natives came to the beach to shake our hands, and to wish us a safe voyage and a quick return.

We were genuinely sorry to leave. Our hearts' roots seemed to have found grateful soil in Bora Bora. The place is a happy paradise; and the life is one to envy. Everything seems to work for good to the natives. If a man's house gets old, and he wants to move, he need only spend a few days gathering palm-leaves and bamboo; then his new habitation can be built in a day. The man of Bora Bora need not cultivate his land — Nature does it for him. The earth bears prosperously, a hundred times more than can be eaten. What has civilisation to offer that can sway the balance of one's judgment in its favour?

When we sailed from this happy island, we carried with us a new member of the crew. Jack had yielded at last to Tehei's pleas, and had consented to allow him to go with us. Bihaura was taken back to Tahaa by six lusty Kanakas in a cutter.

We made our way straight out of the reef. It was a great relief to me to be able to be on deck, viewing the scenery, instead of down in the engine room. Tehei proved a valuable helper. He was a full-blooded Kanaka, thirty years of age, and could speak no English, but none the less, he was able to understand Captain Y——'s orders. For the first day and night, however, he spent most of his time weeping and praying, for he was unused to leaving home, and moreover was seasick.

I stayed on deck all afternoon, taking my last look at the Society Islands. We were now bound for the Samoan group, a ten-day run as we figured it. The *Snark* was so thickly packed with presents of all sorts that there was hardly room to walk, even though every toss of the boat sent bushels of oranges, bananas, and other fruits sliding into the sea. When I went to bed, the island we had so lately quitted was still visible.

On April 19, we were calmed. The sails flapped, the *Snark* rose and fell with the swell of the ocean, but we made little progress. That night Jack read to us an article he had written, entitled: "The Other Animals"—a reply to President Roosevelt and John Burroughs, who had charged Jack with being a "nature faker." Jack had intended to make no reply to the charge, but a big American magazine kept after him so persistently that he could not refuse. On the 20th, I spent some hours painting the engine room and the engines. These latter I coloured dark brown, with the pipes red; the walls I made a yellowish-brown, and the dynamo black. I then polished all the working parts like a mirror. And when I had finished, I called in the crew, for I knew that seeing the ship trim and shipshape always encouraged them. The next day I put in in developing and printing pictures for Jack. Nakata, Jack, Tehei and myself wore nothing during this time but *pareu* loin-cloths, and the rest garbed themselves as simply as possible, for the heat was overpowering. It did not prevent our boxing, however— Jack and I had five rounds in the evening, and I got a cut lip and he a scraped nose. Jack is an expert boxer, but I had the advantage on reach. While I was busy below, the men on deck painted everything above white, and looked to the condition of every shroud, halyard and timber. As Captain Y—— said, the little ketch had "put on her glad rags."

Everyone slept on deck, Jack and Mrs. London on the starboard side, Ernest, Nakata, Wada and Tehei on port, mid deck, captain aft the cockpit, and

Some South Sea Royalty

I slept away up in the bow. The southeast trades made life bearable on these hot nights; while we could not feel them on the sails, we could feel them on our faces, blowing gently and fitfully. Before going to bed on the night of the 25th, Jack read to us his latest story, "The Chinago," the scene of which was laid at Papeete. The night before we had heard "The Seed of McCoy."

The small crew of the *Snark* was now getting to feel more at home on water than on land. We were getting into the thickest of the South Sea islands; every mile we moved toward the west was bringing us among more primitive people.

The wind was so light that we moved along very slowly. The sea was almost as smooth as a mill-pond, and we progressed with all sail set wing-and-wing. There was very little work to do on board except to keep watch. We would lounge around on deck and eat fruit or play cards. Mrs. London had brought with her a small instrument from the Hawaiian Islands, a *ukelele*. This instrument is seldom seen outside the Hawaiian Islands, for despite its sweet tones, no other nation has taken up its use.

Mrs. London would play and sing in the evenings, while Tehei and Wada and Nakata would do their native dances. Sometimes Jack would read aloud his day's work. And all the time we were sliding west thicker into the heart of the South Pacific. We enjoyed this part of the cruise very much indeed. Jack had tops and skipping ropes aboard the *Snark*. The ropes gave us much needed exercise; and we all took boyish pleasure in spinning the tops. I have seen Jack London squat down and spin his tops by the hour, thoroughly absorbed in the fun. He said that this, like his cigarettes, soothed his nerves.

We were thirteen days from Bora Bora when we sighted the Manua Islands, with the largest island in the group straight ahead. The Manua Islands really belong to the Samoan Group, and are usually charted as such; but the three small islands, about one mile apart, are nearly one hundred miles from the Samoan group proper. The natives are the same class of people, and they speak the same language.

When Germany and England and America decided to stop quarrelling over their property in the South Seas, representatives of the three countries met at Apia, Samoa, and England agreed to take over some western islands, and quit the Samoan group entirely. So the group was divided between Germany and the United States. Germany kept the two large islands of Upolu and Savaii, while America took the large island of Tutuila and the small Manua Islands.

The natives objected to these powers coming here and taking possession of them; and for many years there was continual warfare in the German section. The United States had no trouble in the island of Tutuila, but in the Manua group, the old king at first refused to acknowledge their sovereignty. Old King

Tui-Manua made a trip to the United States, and after that he gave up the fight, for he saw the hopelessness of his position; his one thousand subjects in the Manua Islands could be wiped off the face of the earth in a single day. Old Tui-Manua was wise enough to submit; and he now governs the islands with nearly as much authority as he had before. The United States did not want the islands for the sake of ruling them, but they wanted a coaling-station at Tutuila.

We sighted the largest island, known as "Au," early on the morning of the thirteenth day from Bora Bora. As the wind was still very light, I set the engines to work, and by noon we were under the lee of the island, gliding along about one mile from the shore. A person who has never been in the South Seas cannot appreciate the pleasure of gliding along a tropical bay, just close enough to see the small grass villages and the dense jungles behind; the seas breaking over the coral reefs ahead, and the pure blue waters underneath; the tropical birds flying overhead, and canoes paddling along the shores. And with the exception of the rumbling of the sea over the reefs and the chattering of the birds, everything is still and peaceful.

Such were the conditions as the *Snark* moved along looking for an anchorage, but the coast seemed straight, and unindented by a bay suitable for anchoring; and the reef running outside and all along the coast kept us from getting very close to land. Finally, we slowed down until we were scarcely moving. We were undecided what to do; but suddenly a shout went up from the shore, and a big whale-boat was pushed down the beach, and as it touched the water, a score of natives jumped in. After fifteen minutes spent in getting across the reef, they headed for the *Snark*.

I have often thought what a fine cinematograph-picture that boat would have made, as it was tossed right and left; first its bow would seem to be pointing toward the sky, then down it would come while the stern went up. When the boat came alongside the *Snark* the natives were nearly exhausted from their hard work. They would not come aboard for a long time, but sat holding on to a stern-rope, trying to make out who we were. Tehei could not speak their language, and they could speak no English. We tried to tell them that we were looking for an anchorage, but it was not until Jack took several of them forward and pointed to the anchor that they understood. Then with a whoop they made fast a line from our bow to the stern of their boat, and with every one of the natives yelling at the top of his voice, we were towed into anchor close to the reef. The men, not knowing of the engine, felt that the only way for us to get in to shore was for them to tow us. We stowed everything, and after we had come to anchor we were surrounded by canoes of the oddest shapes. Jack and Mrs. London climbed into the big boat with the natives, and soon were ashore, but the rest of the crew remained on board to get things shipshape after the two weeks

Some South Sea Royalty

at sea. I got my engines in trim; then I bribed a native with a sack of Bull Durham tobacco to take me ashore in his one-man canoe. I say " one-man canoe," for their canoes are made to carry from one to a dozen men, and they are not safe with a single man more than they are built to carry. We got safely across the reef, when a wave broke over the boat, and we sank — and it was up to me to swim ashore while a hundred natives, standing on the beach, cheered; and it was their willing hands that drew me from the water. It was a rather embarrassing introduction to the natives of the Manua Islands; but I was such a funny figure when I surveyed myself that I had to laugh, too.

The natives crowded around me and laughed heartily at my condition, and one took me by the arm and led me to a large house in the centre of the grass village. The natives followed until they were a dozen feet from the house, when they stopped. Jack and Mrs. London, hearing the noise, came out of the house, followed by a tall, stately looking man, dressed in a white coat and *sulu*. There could be no mistaking this man: he was the king. The natives all bowed and salaamed, while I stood between the natives and the king, uncertain what to do. My clothes were a sight, drenched with salt-water. After a glance at me, the king and the Londons broke out laughing; then I had to laugh again; and then all the natives started laughing, and one, separating himself from the throng, stepped up and told the king about my adventure. I could not understand him, but I knew by his gestures that he was talking about me. Then the king motioned for me to step up on the porch, and we shook hands. Turning, he called for the queen to come out. She was an intelligent, fine looking woman, with excellent manners. After shaking hands, she called for the servant, and ordered that their native drink be brought. A pretty little girl came with *kava* in cocoanut shells; and after a toast by the king, we drank it down. It had a queer, bitter taste, but I managed to swallow it. I afterward found that I could not have offended the king worse than by not drinking the *kava* at one gulp. I was lucky in doing it just right. Jack and Mrs. London sat down on the porch, and left me with the king and queen. Now, I was not used to being entertained by royalty, so I did not know how to act. But I was relieved of a painful situation by all the natives rushing off to the beach, whither the king and queen followed them. The Londons and I went likewise; and we saw a small schooner drop anchor close to the *Snark*. She carried an English flag, which dipped in response to a salute from the *Snark*. Then they lowered a boat, and a white man was rowed ashore by a dozen native sailors. When the man landed, he shook hands with the king and queen, and spoke to them in their native language; after which he turned to us and spoke in English. He was the captain of the schooner and also the owner. Though he did not tell us his story, we afterward found it out.

HOUSES ON OUTRIGGER CANOES—SOLOMON ISLANDS

Some South Sea Royalty

Captain Young had come to the Manua Islands when a young man, had opened a trading station, and married a sister of the king. They had one daughter, who grew up to be the belle of the islands. Young had all the people in her favour; not that they were dissatisfied with Tui-Manua, but they were one and all fascinated by the beautiful girl. Tui-Manua got hold of a rumour that he was to be dethroned, and Captain Young's daughter was to be instated in his place; so he forced Young and his wife to leave the island. They lived on one of the other islands for nearly a year, when the girl took sick; and when she found she was going to die, she asked leave to die on her native soil. Tui-Manua, hearing of the case, allowed Captain Young and his family to return. The girl died, and Young erected a big monument over her grave. Now, while the king and the captain seem to be friends, they are constantly in secret fear of each other.

Tui-Manua invited us three from the *Snark* and Captain Young to stay for supper. We had new dishes that I was unfamiliar with, and we drank *kava*, while we were waited on by the king's servants; and afterward, when it got dark, the king ordered a big fire built in the centre of the village, and native men and women danced and sang for our entertainment, the while we sat with the king on mats thrown on the ground.

Next day, I went around the village making photographs, and going in and out of the natives' grass huts. In one place I found a tattooer working on a boy; and he asked to tattoo me, but to his great disappointment, I refused.

With the trader as interpreter, Jack made the king understand that we wanted to buy curios. The king sent runners to collect the entire village, whom he told to be on hand next day with things they wanted to sell. And next day Jack and Mrs. London and I stood in the centre of several hundred natives, buying mats and war clubs and tapa cloth; and I was lucky enough to secure a big, bushy grass fan, with which a native had been busy keeping the flies off the king. It has the king's name on it, and it is now reposing in the midst of the other things I brought home with me from the South Seas.

We lay anchored off the island of Au several days, while, in company with the king and queen, we were shown over the island by Captain Young. The day we prepared to leave, the king and queen gave us presents — one of the most valuable of these an extra fine piece of tapa cloth, which I still retain.

The day we left Au, the king and queen came off to the *Snark* and had dinner with us. Wada did gloriously, cooking for royalty, and Nakata was more polite than ever; and as we heaved anchor that afternoon, the boat bearing the king and queen circled the *Snark* three times, its occupants singing "Tofa-Mai-Feleni," the native song of farewell.

Some South Sea Royalty

Tui-Manua is the descendant of a long line of the most powerful South Sea Island kings. His father's authority stretched for thousands of miles around, and whatever he said took precedence over anything said by any of the lesser kings within this boundary. So it is rather humiliating to the present king to have to bow down to another power stronger than he. He is afflicted by a peculiar disease that is wasting his life away; and ere long we will hear of his death. The last of the true royalty of the South Seas will have passed from earth. I have met members of many of the South Sea royal families since then, but none deserved the name of king so well as did Tui-Manua.

CHAPTER X

THE SAMOAN GROUP

THE Manua Islands are only ninety miles from the island of Tutuila. This latter island is sometimes called Pago-Pago, after the village of Pago-Pago, which is on the southeast coast, and where the United States coaling station is situated. Either name is correct.

We were all of one night in sailing from the Manuas to Tutuila, and were calmed off the opening of Pago-Pago Bay for several hours in the morning. Then I set the engines in motion, and for a couple of hours we threaded up the narrow bay until it opened out into the prettiest land-locked harbour I have ever seen. Mountains were on every side. The village of Pago-Pago is set on the shores and up the mountainsides, with Governor Moore's residence on the highest point in the bay.

We sailed past the battleship *Annapolis,* the same ship that had given us such a pleasant reception in Papeete, Tahiti, one month before. We were expected, and the jackies and officers and the men stationed ashore were on the decks and lined up on the beach. The band, composed of Samoan (native) musicians, stood around the big flag-pole on the beach and played national airs while the flag was dipped in salute. It was a great day for us, and a great day for the *Annapolis,* when the *Snark* came in the bay. Just imagine three hundred Americans away down here on a little island in the centre of the South Seas, seeing no one from home for months and months! Sometimes even a year goes by with no American visitors. The *Snark* had been expected for weeks, and the minute we were sighted a boat-load of officers came aboard with invitations for everyone on the yacht.

We had not dropped anchor when the officers came aboard, and so busy were we, shaking hands with fellow-countrymen, that Captain Y—— forgot to give orders to drop the anchor until we were so close to shore that it would have been dangerous to do so on account of the coral reef. I had stopped the engines, and we were drifting in, when the officers saw our danger, and then some half-dozen of the highest officers on the battleship *Annapolis* got out in their boat with a line to our bow, and worked like coolies to keep us off the shore. When I had gotten the engines to running, they guided us to a place of safety.

These officers, who never got their hands dirty on their own ship, finally, after the anchor had been dropped, went ashore to doctor hands that were blistered; but they never lost one grain of respect from their men, who were watching from ashore, unable to help because of not having a boat handy.

The battleship *Annapolis* is stationed here the year round. The two hundred men who compose her crew live ashore in their own homes, while about one hundred men in command of the shore station have wives and families and nice little bungalows. Many of the sailors have Samoan wives, and many of them live what is known as *Fas-Samoan,* which means residing in grass houses and sleeping on grass mats thrown on the ground, and eating native foods. So far as I could see, they are the happiest lot of men in the world. Of course, life must have been very monotonous at first, but after they once got settled they formed a more contented colony than any persons of the same number in America. They have their clubs and baseball diamond; all the literature they care for they get every six weeks; they give balls and parties, and, as they are sure of their jobs, have nothing to worry over.

And it is certainly a pretty sight they make in their pure white uniforms. The Samoans that form the national guard are all dressed alike, in blue *lava-lavas* and white singlets. About one dozen of the chief officers have fine mansions. Governor Moore's is the finest of them all, and sits high above the rest. One officer owns an automobile, and many have motor-boats.

We lay in Pago-Pago Harbor one week. During this time we were living ashore with friends, that is, all but Tehei, who, not speaking English nor Samoan, preferred to remain aboard. We had been in the bay a couple of days when a big six-foot-one native came on board, and in excellent English said he was a Tahitian and that he had heard we had a Tahitian with us. We called Tehei. The big man went up and spoke to Tehei in his own tongue; and Tehei was overjoyed to find someone he could talk to. The big Tahitian's name was Henry — a native of Rapa Island. He was then captain of a small trading schooner that plied in the Samoan group. He and Tehei became close friends, and on the day that we prepared to leave, Henry struck Jack for a job. As Henry was acquainted with the islands that we intended to visit next, Jack decided to hire him. Ernest, the French sailor, was discharged. Ernest had proved a disappointment, so we did not regret the change. Jack bought him a ticket for Auckland, New Zealand (for no one can remain in Samoa without one hundred and fifty dollars in his pocket), and he left on the steamer *Nuvina*. Henry, however, was a very good sailor, having spent twelve years in the South Seas and in Europe in the French navy. He spoke French, English, German, and all the principal South Sea languages. Weighing nearly two hundred pounds, and six feet one inch in height, he was a mountain of muscle; and he knew more about every part of the ship than any person I have ever seen.

Henry's ship was turned over to a Samoan captain, and amid the cheers of three hundred Americans and a salute from the big guns on the *Annapolis,* we shoved out of the harbour under Henry's steerage. He kept the wheel all night, and early next morning we dropped anchor in the harbour of the largest city in Polynesia: Apia, Samoa. Several small schooners and a steamer were anchored close to us; and ahead, the white coral city that has been wrecked by revolutions and hurricanes a dozen times, until it now resembles an old European city with decayed castles. Between us, on the beach, lay the old hull of a German warship that had been wrecked here during a hurricane in 1889. The Germans had tried to dynamite it to pieces, but when they had broken nearly all the windows in the town and the old hull refused to budge, they decided to let it lie until it rusted away. But for twenty years it had defied rust and shown no sign of leaving its resting-place, and I don't believe the residents would allow it to be removed now, for it would not seem like Apia Harbor without that old hulk.

Apia has a population of about five thousand. About four hundred are Germans and Australians, and the rest are alien South Sea Islanders and native Samoans. Here the Germans have pursued the same policy as in all their larger possessions. They maintain a warship and a company of German soldiers on duty all the time. Their police system is entirely of natives, and they have a large standing army of native soldiers.

The city is built for about three miles around the bay. Most of the buildings are of white coral cement, showing up like white marble from the sea. Back from the sea are the native grass houses; in fact, a

Types of Solomon Islanders:
Only one degree removed from an animal

native of any of the South Sea islands will never live in any other than a grass house, from choice. He may live in a white man's house if he is a chief of royal blood, but he will usually have a grass house in connection, to go to when he can no longer stand the coral one.

Apia is a half-way station for steamers bound to and from Australia and America. Several steamers from New Zealand pay monthly visits to obtain copra. These steamers usually stay in the harbour for several days; and as the ships cannot draw up to the wharves, they must lie out nearly a mile while the copra is loaded from barges. The natives with boats do a profitable business carrying people to and from ships; and they hire out as guides and take the tourists to Robert Louis Stevenson's old home, and through the largest cocoanut plantation in the world. And when a steamer is seen to drop anchor, the professional entertainers give a big dance. The hat is passed around, and the natives always make a good sum of money.

Apia, Papeete, and Suva, Fiji, are practically the only places in Polynesia where money has a value among the natives. At Apia, the natives know its value so well that they devise every scheme to obtain it, and have developed their money-getting qualities as perfectly as Americans. The best scheme is their semi-annual boat races. Twice a year natives come from all over the islands and enter their boats; betting stands spring up on the beach, and every native who can dig up money will stake all he has on his favourite boat. At such regattas, there are usually excursion steamers from Australia and New Zealand.

Apia is a port of the most famous missionary steamer in the world, the *Southern Cross*. The steamer fits out every three months at Auckland and goes among the dark and little-known New Hebrides and Solomon Islands. Then she returns and puts such converts as she has found in a missionary school — later to be turned out as full-fledged missionaries and taken back to their homes, there either to backslide into a worse state of cannibalism than that of their fellows, or else to preach the word of God. When a savage from the Solomons does backslide, he is usually the most cannibalistic of his tribe.

Apia, Samoa, was the only real home that Robert Louis Stevenson ever knew. While a young man in Scotland, he was very seldom at home. He made walking trips over England and France, and came to America in the hold of an emigrant ship. After trying to settle down in California, he finally gave it up, and with his wife and her son, Lloyd Osbourne, he chartered the sailing-yacht *Casco* and spent several years cruising in the South Seas, at last settling down in Apia. About four miles back of the city he built his home on the side of a mountain, where he could command a view of the city and the surrounding bay. This home he named Vailima. Here, with his wife, and Lloyd Osbourne, his secretary, he lived the last years of his life. It was here that he wrote several volumes of South Sea stories.

Stevenson lost no time in making friends with the natives: it was the delight of his life to entertain them at his home. He would take part in their sports; and one chief, who had taken a fancy to him, lived at Vailima, and at certain hours every day he taught Stevenson the Samoan language, while Stevenson taught the chief English. At the top of the mountain, Stevenson built a little pagoda, where he went nearly every day to write. A narrow path had been cut up to the summit through jungles of bananas and guavas, and he would toil for hours in reaching the top. The natives had so much confidence in him that all their troubles and differences were brought to him for settlement. Except in the mornings, which he spent in writing, his time was entirely taken up with the Samoans.

Those who have read many of his works will notice that his characters are almost all big, strong, healthy people — just the opposite of Stevenson, who was always a thin, sickly man. In fact, people who knew him say that he had no use at all for a puny person.

The last year of his life was practically spent in bed, where he wrote his best stories. Along toward the end, the natives would gather in a body and stand around the house in silence, awaiting news of his illness. The last few days there were hundreds and hundreds of natives outside the house, awaiting the end, and when it came, early one morning in 1894, the natives set up the death chant, which spread along their lines until the whole island was wailing at once. Work suspended throughout the island until after the funeral.

Stevenson had requested that he be buried at the summit of the mountain. His coffin was carried by chiefs, while other natives with big knives blazed a road ahead for the procession, through the jungles and to the top.

Of course, the *Snark's* crew made a visit to Vailima, and then on up to the top, to the grave — nearly ten miles of toil.

At Apia, the German government boasts of the best outfitted observatory in Oceania. Here are all the latest astronomical instruments in charge of ten expert astronomers. It is a splendid set of instruments they have, but — as a native remarked — what is the use of them in Samoa, where there are no cable connections, and should the astronomers see a comet coming toward the earth, they would be so long in letting the greater portion of the people know that there would be no time to dodge!

Apia was the scene of slavery for many years. The schooners would leave here and go among the Solomons and Fiji Islands and steal the natives — *blackbird* them, as they call it. The natives were then brought to Apia and sold to planters and slave traders, until the German government put a stop to this illegal traffic; but even now, about five hundred blacks a year are brought into these islands, and while the dealers can always give a satisfactory recruiting paper for each native, it is doubtful if the natives ever knew what kind of papers they were signing.

It was in Apia that we learned an interesting piece of Tehei's history. One day while I was walking down the beach road in company with him, a white woman stepped up, and throwing her arms around him, nearly smothered him with her embraces. I thought she was insane, until she started talking with him in his native tongue; and then, turning to me, she told me that Tehei was once sailing in a pearl-lugger among the Taumotu Islands, in a boat captained and owned by her brother. A hurricane had surprised the small crew, and the boat was blown to pieces. The crew was drowned — all but Tehei, who, clinging to a hatch-cover, was washed ashore on one of the reefs where pearlers were at work, and a few months later returned to his home in an open boat that he had worked for while on the reef. He made his way nearly four hundred miles in this open boat, with only a lugger-sail for power. Tehei had never told of this adventure, but we afterward heard several remarkable exploits of his among the pearling islands.

Apia is full of interesting characters — old beachcombers and retired black-birders, captains and runaway sailors, and ticket-of-leave men from Australia. I know of one man, one of the greatest business men in the town, who is an escaped convict from the French penal settlement in New Caledonia.

The climate here is perfect. With a big wide sandy beach running for miles round the bay, Apia would be an ideal pleasure resort if the steamship connections were better, and if it were nearer to civilisation.

The entire crew of the *Snark* lived ashore while in Apia, although each one took turn-about staying on board at night. Everything possible was done to make our stay pleasant. Charley Roberts, a racehorse owner, who was ruled off the turf, first in England, then in America, then in Australia, and finally in New Zealand, had come to Apia that he might race horses undisturbed. He had two thoroughbreds shipped from New Zealand; and two aged horses were matched against Charley's thoroughbreds every few weeks; bills were gotten out telling of the big meet, and then the four horses would pull off race after race, always with the same result. Roberts' mind was wholly centred on this sport while we were there. Horses were his one passion. And as he had means, his relatives in Australia were content to have him race horses in Samoa. He got up a special race for us; in fact, he is always glad to have a meet. Anyone going to Apia should have Charley call a meeting of the Apia Turf Association — it would be heartily enjoyed all around.

After two weeks in Apia, we slowly sailed out of the

The Samoan Group

harbour late in the afternoon. Charley Roberts and some friends went out with us as far as they dared, and loaded us down with wines, and, most important of all, eggs.

It was just sundown on one of the most perfect of South Sea evenings that we cleared the island of Upolu and headed for the island of Savaii, only twenty-five miles away. As it became darker, the sky ahead grew red, and as we approached the island we could clearly see tongues of fire issuing from the mouth of the big crater, and gradually small threads of fire running down the mountainside — threads that grew into glowing torrents as we came closer, until by midnight we were sailing up the coast of an island that seemed to be literally aflame. The crater of the volcano is twenty-five miles inland, and about ten thousand feet high, the land sloping gradually down to the sea, where it ends in an abrupt precipice, one hundred feet high. For miles and miles, red-hot sputtering lava rolled into the sea, sending up clouds of vapour. Two miles from the seashore, we could read print plainly. As we were getting into the lee of the land, where the wind was likely to drop any minute, Jack told me to start the engines; then we slid along the shore, edging in as far as possible. The air got hot and sultry, and steam was rising from the water all about us. Jack stationed the cook in the bow with a thermometer, and every few minutes he would cry the temperature, until the water was nearly at boiling-point; then we were afraid to go in farther on account of the thousand gallons of gasolene aboard.

Henry, our new Kanaka sailor, knew this coast well, and was to take us to a certain village where he was known, but at nearly two o'clock in the morning we were still skirting the rivers of lava, and the village was not in sight. By the light of the boiling lava we could see ruined villages and hundreds of thousands of naked cocoanut trees, stripped of their foliage and standing straight and threadbare in the fiery glow, like trimmed poles. Henry finally managed to distinguish the village he was taking us to, but it was dead and deserted. The lava was all-destructive. We could get no closer than a mile to the shore, and then steamed on up the coast, hoping to find some place that had not been seared by the fires. We would get nearly to the shore, only to see a reeking stream of lava, further back and creeping down to the sea. Then on we would go again. Everyone else in the boat was awestruck by such wholesale destruction; they were leaning over the rail in wonder, without any idea of the possibility of the engine's stopping, but my heart was in my mouth all the time, for the wind had dropped, and had the engines ever stopped, it would have been all up with us — nothing could have kept us away from those cascades of lava. But luck was certainly with us. The engine ran smoothly, and as the first streaks of day lighted the east, we sighted a village that was unharmed and showing signs of human occupation. Henry pronounced this place to be Matautu, and we decided to anchor. After things were safely stowed, everyone went to sleep on deck, after a hard night's work.

It was late in the afternoon before anyone awoke. As we felt like going ashore after our rest, Jack and Mrs. London and myself set out in the launch. We came to a deserted beach. There were no natives in sight, although we could hear the hum of voices back in the village. As the beach ran out so far in a gradual slope, we were forced to anchor the launch out several hundred yards, and wade ashore. We walked up the beach to the village, whence we had heard the voices, and found several hundred natives before a small church, all praying that the lava would not come down and destroy their village. Two young girls in the centre of the group were dressed in gala array of feathers and tapa cloths of gay colours, and each was carrying an ornamental club. They simply stood in the centre, taking no part in the ceremonies. They were the first to see us, and quietly motioning to the assembly, spoke a few words. The crowd dispersed, all going away talking in quiet tones, but even if we could not understand, it was easy to guess that they were still supplicating for the eruption to cease; and their quiet manner left no doubt that they had supreme confidence in the potency of prayer.

The two girls who had first sighted us were called,

in the Samoan language, *taupou* girls. Each village in Samoa has its *taupou* girl, only one to the village, who upholds the honour of that village, entertains the guests, and otherwise makes herself agreeable. She controls the feasts and functions, and in fact has more power than anyone, excepting the chief. As she is really the most virtuous woman in the village, she is made the highest dignitary at all religious gatherings, although taking no part in them.

All the villages for twenty miles up the coast had been destroyed and the people had fled to Matautu. There were about twenty *taupou* girls gathered here. As Jack said, they looked like girls out of a job, for when they leave their own village, they lose power. Certainly they had not shown much power in letting the lava destroy their homes. Only the Matautu *taupou* girls seemed to be still in favour. These girls attached themselves to Mrs. London and showed us over the village. But such a woe-begone village! On all sides the red-hot lava was creeping down, though they had managed to divert the flow by building stone walls; but they knew that unless the volcano twenty-five miles away quieted down, their homes were doomed. It was dark when we prepared to go back to the *Snark*. We were stopped just as we got to the launch by a white man, calling to us on the beach. We went back and found a big, jolly Irishman, waiting for us in company with a tall German.

The Irishman was Dick Williams, the governor of

At Otivi Village, Santa Cruz Group

The Samoan Group

the island, and the German was the agent of an Apia trading concern. We went back with the governor to his house, and learned that he had been away all day helping the volcano sufferers. He invited us to stay ashore all night, promising to show us a better view of the eruption the next day. So, after a crowd of Kanakas had carried the launch up on the beach, we went to nicely furnished grass houses that the governor owned, and next morning, after a bath on the beach, we started for the lava flows with the two white men as guides. We walked miles between two flows of lava — hot lava that scorched our hair. At one place, we passed the frame of a grass house set between the walls of an old church. The owner had thought that on account of its being near a church of God it would not be ruined, and his goods would be safe. We walked over beds of lava that had cooled for several days and that, encrusted, would bear our weight; but we knew what lay beneath, for here and there, where there were fissures in the cooled crust, spits of steam and bubbling jets of lava flowed outward into the air. At one place, we found a remarkable thing — a small churchyard that had been unmolested by the flow. It looked as if the stream had parted and gone around the graveyard and joined into one stream after the place had been passed. We went on farther to a fresh lava stream that had just broken out. Close by was a large frame house, the home of the former governor of Savaii, now deserted. Here a mass of lava, about three feet in thickness and several hundred yards wide, was slowly coming toward the house; red and glowing, it was advancing about an inch a minute. With long sticks we gathered the lava and pressed coins into it, to keep for souvenirs. As we returned by way of the church graveyard, we stood in the plot marvelling at such a miracle — that the molten destruction had parted at this burial place! — and we ceased to look upon the Kanaka who had built his house inside the churchyard as a joke: he had sufficient reason, after seeing the graveyard saved, to believe that his own home would be preserved.

As we came to the edge of the village, we skirted a fresh flow of lava, creeping up on a church. Inside the place were crowds of natives, all praying at once that the church be saved. They were coughing and wiping their eyes from the effects of the sulphur fumes that were enveloping them. We stood and watched this sad sight. Soon the people filed out, slowly, forlornly, and we stood by to see the end. In half an hour the first of the lava struck the building, and soon was running in the doors, setting fire to everything inflammable. Next morning when I looked for the church I found only a mass of ruins.

We lived ashore five days, and on the last day I rode nearly twenty-five miles, trying to reach the leeward side of the crater, but the barefoot native guide turned back after it grew too hot for his unprotected flesh, and I got only to within half a mile of the crater, but near enough to see the awful yawning hole, nearly a mile across, emitting thousands and thousands of tons of liquid death every minute. I sat on the charred log of a cocoanut tree and wondered where it all came from. Certainly, wherever it was formed, there was no dearth of material. I afterward saw many volcanoes, but none of them had the impressive magnificence of this.

We left the harbour in the afternoon of the fifth day; our two *taupou*-girl friends came aboard to say good-bye, and as we looked over to their village and asked them to tell good-bye to our friends ashore whom we had not been able to see, they turned their eyes shoreward and burst into tears, for already a narrow stream of lava had broken through their village, and it would be only a matter of a few days when they would be living in another village, shorn of power, and their own pretty homes would be in ashes under the lava.

So it was that we up-anchored and set out for the Fijis, where we were to lose our last and final captain.

CHAPTER XI

LOST IN THE FIJI ISLANDS

FROM the Samoan Islands to the Fijis, the distance is nine hundred miles. After we had cleared the Samoan Islands, we ran along under power for several hours; then the sails were set, and by sun-down we were speeding along under an eight-knot wind, which grew stronger and stronger, until by midnight all hands were on deck taking in the headsails and reefing the mainsails. By morning we were in the grip of a summer gale, but luckily for us it was in the right direction, and with only a double-reefed staysail and a triple-reefed mizzen, we plunged along at about twelve knots an hour. Big waves, looking as large as a courthouse, would come roaring up to us, and the little *Snark* would rise on the side and hover over the dizzy depths of watery valleys — then down we would go with that queer sensation that one experiences in riding on a swift elevator, feeling as if we were falling out from under ourselves; and sometimes two waves would come so close together that the second one would break against the side of the *Snark* with such force as to throw everyone off his feet, and whoever was steering could only save himself by hugging the wheel. At such times as this, it was difficult to steer. For it is not just a matter of pointing a ship the way you want to go and then keeping the wheel geared that way, but it is a matter of watching a big wave and then easing up into it to keep from being broken into splinters; and the sails must be watched every second, for should the wind ever get behind them, they would swing across deck with such force as to drag the masts out of the ship, and everything on deck would be carried away. It looks easy enough to steer a ship, but it takes a person six months to get experience enough in it to be trusted alone at the wheel.

For three days we ran along in the teeth of the gale. Everything on deck that had not been made fast was carried away. The small boats had been taken in from the davits and lashed upside down on the deck. No fire could be made in the galley, so we lived mostly on hardtack. Everything above and below was saturated with salt water. In the afternoon of the third day, the squall broke as quickly as it had formed, leaving us rolling on a glassy-smooth sea. The wind dropped nearly calm and the mists cleared away, so that we could see the horizon. It is well known how clear the air gets after a storm. Well, we were so tired that we were for turning into our bunks, until Henry cried, "Reef ahead!" and on going into the rigging, I saw reef on all sides of us. Immediately, the sails were backed, and we hove-to. I started the engines; then, for the rest of the day, we went round and round the inside of the lagoon, trying to find the place we had gotten in at. It looked as if we were lost. Each effort puzzled us only the more. All night we kept up the attempt to find the passage, but it was not until morning that we found it, a gap in the reef about two hundred feet wide. And there were twenty-five miles of reef we might easily have struck on! How we ever got into the place is a mystery, and remains a mystery to this day.

There was not an island in sight. It was nearly sun-down when we did sight several small islands, and after threading in and out of countless reefs, we managed to get penned up in another lagoon, where we lay-to for the night. Next day was a repetition of the one before. So also was the next. For several days we dodged in and out of reefs and around small islands, charted as the Ringgold Islands. At times we were in despair. To find the concealed openings in the reef was like looking for the proverbial needle in the haystack. On the eighth day we sighted clear water ahead, and slipping out between two of the largest islands, Vanua Levu and Taviuni, we slid into the Koro Sea, which is the name of the two hundred miles of water that is made into a lagoon by hundreds of small islands circling around it. Only one small island is inside this sea, and Jack had decided to go up along the shores of this island and have a look at the villages. We were perhaps five miles off the land when a small cutter put out, and heading toward us, would have passed our bow, but the helmsman swerved around and passed close enough to speak. He was a woolly-headed

Fiji-Islander. His shouting awoke a white man who was asleep below. On coming on deck, the white man rubbed his eyes and sleepily asked: "What ship is that?" We replied: "*Snark*, San Francisco." Then he yelled: "Is that Jack London's boat?" We told him it was. "Heave-to, I'm coming aboard," he cried; and as we were in no hurry to get anywhere, we hove-to, and he came about and also hove-to. Then, in a little dingy, he was rowed to the *Snark*, and he just fell all over himself with joy. "And to think that I should ever see Jack London, and on his own boat, too! Why, I have every one of your books aboard my ship, and all your magazine articles. But, pshaw! the boys won't believe I ever saw Jack London." And he nearly cried, he was so happy.

Frank Whitcomb had been trading nearly all his life in the Fiji Islands, and Jack London's books had been about all he had read. I believe that in his eyes Jack was the greatest man that ever lived.

He loaded us down with fresh fruits and onions and potatoes. In return, we gave him several bottles of wine. And the last thing that long, lanky Frank Whitcomb said as he was rowed away from the *Snark* was: "And to think that I should live to shake hands with Jack London, and on his own boat, too!" Whitcomb was the only man who ever boarded the *Snark* at sea.

As we sailed past the solitary island in the Koro Sea, several boats tried to put off to us, but we were in a hurry, and so did not wait for them to get over the reef, but sailed on until by night we were again among small islands and were forced to heave-to until morning.

From the time we had left Samoan waters, it was Jack who always located our true position on the chart. Jack told me that if he must do the navigating, he could and would do it and would not be bothered with anyone else. So everyone on board suspected that Captain Y—— was to be discharged at Suva, Fiji. The captain had gotten angry at Wada and had broken his nose, and had it not been for Mrs. London, I think he would have laid Nakata out, so no one was sorry that we were to be rid of him.

The next morning after our meeting with Frank Whitcomb, we set sail, after being hove-to all night, and passed all sorts of queer crafts, most of them of bamboo, and soon were threading in and out of countless little green islands, going so close sometimes that we could plainly make out villages. Now and then canoes would put off to us. At one place, we went close enough to shore to see people plainly; they ran down to the beach, shouting at us. We passed many strange raft-like crafts, made of split bamboo. On some of the crafts we could see whole families, who stared at us in wonder as we slid past. These vessels were in some cases loaded with fruits and sandalwood and copra. I saw several of the same crafts come into Suva Harbor again after a week's journey at sea. The

THE LANDING PLACE AT NAMU, SANTA CRUZ GROUP

Lost in the Fiji Islands

natives have no fear, and will sometimes live for months on their queer floats without stepping ashore.

Henry was not slow in taking advantage of the smooth water, and supplied our table with different kinds of fish every day; in fact, we always fished in preference to everything else. While calmed or anchored, he caught many a shark without hook or line, by the old Kanaka method of spearing them while they lie asleep on the bottom in shallow water.

It was nearly ten days after we had been tangled up in the Fiji Islands when we sighted the large island of Viti Levu, and turned the *Snark's* bow into another of the South Seas' famous ports. Suva, Fiji, looms up from the sea, quite like a modern city, and is really the most modern in this part of the world. Nearly half of its eight thousand persons are of white blood; and Suva is also chief station of the Pacific commercial cables. Several modern hotels and large headquarters for the trading concerns are to be found here.

Fiji is also the headquarters for the British commissioners of the whole of the South Sea possessions, and here is located the British penal settlement. Prisoners are sent here from all the English possessions in the South Seas.

We dropped anchor under supervision of Captain Wooley, the harbour inspector, and by nightfall Jack and Mrs. London were installed at Mrs. McDonald's hotel, the most famous hotel in Oceania.

Directly we had dropped anchor, Captain Y—— went ashore, and walking up and down the streets of Suva, he *would* have everyone know that Captain Y—— of the *Snark* was in town. His boasting led him from saloon to saloon; and soon he was so drunk that he could hardly walk. I left him telling of his sea-experiences to a bunch of bar-flies, and went to the hotel and had late dinner with the Londons. Captain Y—— did not come aboard that night. Next morning, when Jack arrived, he asked me to pack all of Y——'s possessions and take them ashore; also, he instructed us not to allow the captain to come aboard again. I had taken Captain Y——'s clothing ashore and was making the rounds of stores, buying clothes that I had had no chance to get since leaving Honolulu. In my absence, Captain Y—— had gone aboard the *Snark,* and was showing the yacht to the captain of a big six-masted schooner. He ordered Nakata to bring drinks on deck, but Nakata refused, telling him that Mr. London had said he was discharged. Poor Captain Y—— must have felt very cheap in company with his old captain-friend, but he left the *Snark* without making a fuss, and a few days later sailed away on the six-master as an ordinary seaman — quite a come-down, from skipper of a smart yacht to the lowest position on a windjammer.

While Suva was very modern for a South Sea city, one had only to go a few miles into the interior of the island to find primitive life. I was lucky enough to get in with a party on an excursion trip across the bay and up several small streams, and spent several days among the mango swamps, seeing strange people. We had a party of Fiji prisoners to row our boat, and we went miles and miles through a dense forest of tropical trees. Every now and then, some native in his little canoe would stop to look at us in wonder.

Once a native reporter on the *Fiji Times* — his English name was George Dyer — took me over to his island to attend church. The natives all gathered in a little wooden building and squatted on a bare floor in front of the preacher, a big, bushy-haired man, who preached after the style of some of our old-fashioned exhorters. The parishioners wore nothing but loin-cloths and their wonderful mops of hair.

There was an intermission, which I misconstrued into dismissal of services and went outside to sit on a big hollow log that came handy. Pretty soon the pastor came out and tapped me on the shoulder. I could not make out what he wanted, so asked George. "He wants you," replied the boy, "to get off the log so that he can ring the bell." It developed that the preacher hammered on the log to call the congregation together, and I was unwittingly muffling the call of the Gospel.

Arriving back in Suva, I was kept busy getting the *Snark* in shape for another long voyage, doing the work that Captain Y—— had done as well as my own.

CHAPTER XII

SOUTH SEA CANNIBALS

EVERYONE has heard of the wild and savage cannibals of the South Sea islands, and to the average mind, either the whole of the South Pacific is inhabited by man-eaters, or the idea that such bloodthirsty creatures exist is simply scoffed at.

Hitherto I have told of the gentle, big, brown inhabitants of the eastern islands, known as Polynesia. But now we have come into Melanesia. Let me try to describe, as modestly yet graphically as possible, the first of the Melanesians that the *Snark* crew came in contact with.

It is hard to tell of these savages. Yet, in writing of them, I simply state facts. These people exist. There are at this time some seventy thousand of them in the New Hebrides Islands. Very few white people have ever seen them. They can scarcely be written about in language sufficiently plain to give a definite idea of them. The hundred or more pictures I made of these cannibals cannot be printed in a volume intended for popular circulation.

Probably it is best to describe these people as one would describe animals. For they are only one degree removed from the animals. I wish I might speak plainly. But a great deal of the modesty in our ultra-civilised state is a false modesty, inasmuch as it is not based upon necessity. It is this fact that constitutes the difficulty when one attempts to describe a race living in absolute savagery, unwitting of those rules of conduct we have laid down for our guidance, a race whose social relations are vastly different from ours. This much, however, I must say. Our so-called " proper " clothing is in many cases designed solely for purposes of suggestion. Men and women who go stark naked every day of their lives are oftentimes more moral and have stronger natural modesty than certain of those who bedizen themselves with fashionable silks and satins.

In my studies of various peoples as I have journeyed round this earth, I have found many queer customs and fashions. In some countries, they squeeze the foot to make it small, and a woman with a large foot is a social outcast. In other countries they cover parts of the face. An Arabian woman would expose her entire body in order to keep the lower part of her face hidden. The Chinese men, as a sign of rank and distinction, develop long finger-nails, and we can well remember when our own women wore ridiculously large bustles that looked very funny on the street. By the way, speaking of bustles, I wish to say that the habit of wearing them did not originate in any of the fashion-centres. Bustles have always been and now are the only article of apparel worn by the women of the New Hebrides. And funny as these women look with only large plaited grass bustles on them, we must not consider them foolish, for they have just as much right to their fashions as the women of America, England, France, Germany, or any other civilised country, have to theirs.

Having seen all these fashions, I am willing to grant to men or women the perfect liberty to dress or adorn themselves, or go undressed, as they see fit. Having, as I believe, seen the origin of the bustle among these primitive folk, I fully expect to see some day the prettiest ladies of our land wearing enormous nose-rings, as there are places in the world where such nose-rings constitute the entire wardrobe.

Ignorance is not virtue. Virtue is knowledge coupled with self-restraint. And so let me call attention to a people who are as directly opposed to us in their views of morality as could be imagined. These people are sex worshippers, and their ideas of right and wrong lead them to call attention to the very subjects we seek to hide and dismiss from our minds.

To go back to Suva, Fiji. Captain Warren was no longer a member of the *Snark's* crew. As we lay alongside the wharf at Suva, the crew painted and scraped masts, decks and booms, and after loading with water and provisions, we were again ready for sea. Tehei was dressed in his first suit of clothes, of which he was as proud as a peacock. Our compasses were swung and adjusted by an expert. Our chronometer was taken aboard an Australian steamer

South Sea Cannibals

and corrected, and we were ready to try our luck with Captain Jack London. And when I think of the crew of the *Snark,* I always think of the crew that sailed out of Fiji, and the same crew that stuck to the trip to the end. Up to this time, I had seen come and go three captains, two engineers, several sailors and a cabin-boy. The crew that sailed from Suva included Mr. and Mrs. London, myself, and four dark-skinned persons: Nakata, the Jap cabin-boy, Wada San, the Jap cook, and the two Tahitians, Tehei and Henry.

We cleared Suva Harbor at 12:30 on the afternoon of Saturday, June 6, 1908. The harbour master, with his crew of Fiji convicts, was the last to leave; then we just slid out of the bay with a strong beam wind, and in an hour had left Suva out of sight. We passed a small cutter, and her crew of bushy-haired Fijians cried good-bye in their own language, and dipped their flag. About four o'clock we got to the entrance of a very narrow channel and between two small islands. I took the wheel, and Jack sang out the course from the bow. By six o'clock we were through and headed for the open sea, at which everyone was glad, for reefs and small islands cause much worry.

The next day I cleaned up the engine room and did small carpentering jobs about the ship. The sea was quite rough, and we had the skylights battened down; but because of the clearness of the sky we did not expect very nasty weather. We were speeding at about seven knots. All day, Jack studied navigation. For the first several days out of Fiji he had no time to write. He navigated by every method known to captains, and then proved his navigating as we used to prove our arithmetic problems at school. On Wednesday morning, I took the time while he got the sight; then we corrected the two compasses, he watching one compass and I the other. Jack figured that day that we had done ten thousand miles in the *Snark* since leaving San Francisco.

That evening, Jack announced that at a certain point on the compass, at sunrise next morning, would be the first island in the New Hebrides, called Futuna, and next morning at five o'clock there was a call for all hands on deck. I hurried up, expecting to see a storm closing in on us, but instead the sky was clear and Jack was excitedly pointing to a rocky island at the exact place he had told us of the night before. Jack said: "I told you so," and for the rest of that day he went around with his head up in the air, with the bearing of a person who knew much more than any others on board, and we all looked at him in awe and told him he was a great navigator.

Futuna was a high, flat rock, as seen from the sea. We did not go close enough to examine it. We had a good breeze, and all that day we passed small uninhabited islands, and that night slowed down, for the island of Tanna was directly ahead, and we were afraid to go into the bay at night; but early next morning we dropped anchor opposite a mission station in a long, narrow bay.

The third cylinder igniters blew out when I tried to use the engine to help us into this bay, and we had trouble in finding an entrance, for the place seemed reef-locked, but we took a chance, and finally got in. We anchored one hundred yards off a high bluff, on the top of which was a little white church, almost hidden by the dense jungle. We saw clumsy canoes coming toward us, and soon two hundred of the puniest, dirtiest, most unhealthy little thieving natives came aboard. All afternoon they kept arriving in canoe-loads. All wore remnants of white men's clothing, filthy beyond description. Some had only an undershirt; some, old trousers; and there were old hats of all kinds. One carried an umbrella. Others, again, wore red singlets, so full of holes they would scarcely hang on their backs. Their ears were pierced with holes I could have stuck my thumb through. They were all missionaries from the mission school on the top of the hill — and great missionaries they were! In the afternoon, when we three whites started ashore, we cleared the deck of the natives, and they cleared the deck of any spare ropes or marlin they could find loose. We missed nearly everything that was small enough for the natives to get away with. We went ashore and had dinner with the only missionary on the island, Rev. Watt. He had been for twenty-eight years at this station, and had managed to convert the coast natives only, but in the interior the natives were as savage and primitive as the day God had made them — he sighed when he told us of the interior natives. We asked him to take us on an excursion to see these natives, but he flung up his hands in horror. "No! It was no place for a woman," and we could not persuade him to alter his decision. He told us of a lawless trader living on the island, and for us to be careful of him, he was a very bad man; he was friendly with the bush natives. And right then Jack whispered to me that we must find that bad, wicked trader and get him to take us to visit the savages that we had sailed thousands and thousands of miles to see. On going aboard that night, we found the wicked trader sitting on our deck, smoking Jack's cigarettes. He was a big, jolly-looking Scotchman. He was overjoyed to see us, for it is mighty few white people that Trader Wiley ever sees in Tanna. He had been trading here for over seven years. In order to trade among the different tribes, he had learned their languages, and to gain their friendship had doctored the sick and set broken bones. He had been the means of bringing peace between several of the tribes that before his advent had been continually at war. But the missionary considered him a bad man because he had gained such a hold on the natives, and, doctoring their ills and injuries, refused to doctor their souls.

Mr. Wiley stayed for supper, and told us some interesting yarns of the island. Up to one year ago, the different tribes were at war with each other. No tribe dared go outside its own boundaries, unless it wished to precipitate a rumpus. But the English warship *Cambrian* came and threw bombs in some of the villages, and now the natives were quiet through fear of having their homes destroyed. It had been three years, Mr. Wiley said, since a cannibalistic feast took place, and he had been there to see it. Having the confidence of the natives because he smuggled old-fashioned "Springfield" rifles in to them, he was allowed to go and come as he pleased. He had gone up into the bush after copra one day, after one tribe had been defeated by the tribe he was visiting, and was asked to stay and watch the feast that night, which he did — he found four bodies cooked and ready to eat, with the heads off and the bowels removed.

Of course he would show us the bush people; but he warned us that they were not the kind of people that we had been used to. It was agreed that on Sunday, June 22, he was to take us up to the village where he had seen the cannibal feast. On Saturday, Jack and Mrs. London went to see one of the most noted volcanoes in the New Hebrides, which is located on this island. I wandered up and down the bay, looking in the village huts and trying to find curios, but the natives seemed to have none. One little four-foot grass hut and a few dirty mats is all the average man here possesses.

I gossiped with Mr. Wiley and his partner, Mr. Stanton, in their little 10-x-15 store, where they ate, slept and traded. Very little money was in circulation; they traded out of their stock for copra. One stick of cheap tobacco bought ten cocoanuts; and three sticks would hire a man for one day to take the meat from the nut and dry it into copra; so it will be seen that the remuneration of labour in the New Hebrides is nothing magnificent. One stick of tobacco is worth a cent.

Saturday night, Jack, Mrs. London and I took supper with Rev. Watt. The missionary was a fairly decent sort of man, but I don't approve of his methods. In the evening, I developed film in his dark-room.

Early Sunday morning, Tehei landed us on the beach, where we found Frank Stanton waiting for us. He explained that Mr. Wiley was sick and could not go. We four started off, and for several hours tramped over hills and through valleys, penetrating a jungle of trees and vines and ferns so dense that in places we walked through pitch-dark recesses, into which the sun had never shone. Sometimes we rested under a big banyan tree, with its hundreds of roots and its branches turning and growing back into the ground until the single tree might cover as much as a half acre. We passed several of Mr. Stanton's copra houses, where he came on certain days each week to buy cocoanuts; then we struck off through a deep ravine, the walls forty and fifty feet high, with just enough room for us to walk single-file. All the time, we were gradually rising higher and higher above the sea-level. Often we had to pull Mrs. London up after us, but she was game and never lagged a bit. About one o'clock we emerged without warning into a clearing set on the side of a mountain, a clearing about a half-mile across. Many grass houses were set in a circle around this clearing. In the centre of the circle squatted about fifty men, as many children, and a few women. They were the most savage, heathenish looking folk I have ever looked upon. I had heard of and seen pictures of such savages, but I had hardly been able to convince myself that such animals existed: but here was ocular demonstration. They were smeared over their bodies with coloured juices from berries, and several of the younger men had queer white designs painted on their faces. The men wore belts around their waists — that was all; around their ankles were anklets of porpoise shell or cocoanut shell, and there were some that were carved of stone. Many wore strings of white shells around their necks. Through their enormously distended ear-lobes were thrust pieces of wood as big as one's wrist, or ear-rings of porpoise shell. But the crowning beauty was their heads. The hair, dyed red, was about a foot long. Locks of about one hundred hairs were wrapped from the roots to within one inch of the end with cocoanut fibre; and the whole head was one cluster of these bunches. And every man carried a large knife. As for the women, they wore a dried palm-leaf hung on in front by a string around the waist; except for a miscellaneous collection of anklets, bracelets, and necklets, this was all they wore.

Most of these savages broke for the bush when they sighted us; all but fifteen or twenty who knew Mr. Stanton well. Stanton spoke to them; they advanced with hands outstretched; and we shook hands all around.

"How can I describe these people in my diary?" Mrs. London asked.

"'Worse than naked,' and let it go at that," Jack replied.

And so, in turn, I can describe these people at no greater length and no better than to say, as Jack said, that they were worse than naked. For several hours we sat with them in the clearing, and showed how Mrs. London's Winchester could shoot eleven times in the twinkling of an eye. I made dozens of photographs, and tried to photograph the women; but they were very shy. I got only one, as she was diving into her house.

The men who had run for the bush we could see on all sides of us, peeping around trees and through the dense brush at the edges of the jungle. They were armed with spears, so we kept our hands on our guns all the time, but Stanton assured us they were not danger-

MRS. GODDEN AND HER SCHOOL PEOPLE, NEW HEBRIDES ISLANDS. MR. GODDEN, THE MELANESIAN MISSIONARY, WAS MURDERED A WEEK PREVIOUS TO THE GROUP BEING PHOTOGRAPHED

ous. Nevertheless, we were not going to take any risks.

Late that afternoon, we started back for the bush. For some time we could see painted faces peeking at us through the jungle. When we arrived on board the *Snark* late that night, I gave a big sigh of relief. I had been far from comfortable among these ferocious-looking bush people.

I desired very much to develop my film that night, but Rev. Watt refused to let me use his dark-room. "Christians should do nothing at all on the Sabbath!" he told me; and I gathered from his tones that he knew of our expedition inland, and that he was far from approving of it.

The New Hebrides are entirely of volcanic origin. There are about thirty active volcanoes in the group, of which the greatest is on the island of Tanna. At night the sky is fiery red from the reflection of the red-hot lava in its crater, and about every half hour the air is rent with a terrific explosion, and from the direction of the volcano the sky seems afire.

On the morning after we had visited the bush people, Henry, Tehei, Nakata and myself secured guides and went to the volcano, walking for miles through barren desert land, hundreds of hot springs and geysers on all sides of us. As we drew closer, the ground under our feet would tremble with each explosion. At noon we reached the edge of the crater. Just as we got there, there came a tremendous explosion, and away we ran, guides and all. When we recovered our courage, we crept up to the edge, and looked down nearly half a mile into what looked like hell. Out of the bowels of the earth were thrown huge boulders, which spent their force and fell back with hideous reverberations into the pits whence they came; and away at the bottom, the farthest down I have ever seen — and I believe it is the bottom-most point to which one can see — were two boiling lakes of lava, and when an explosion came, the lava would be thrown spattering against the encrusted crater sides, nearly to the top, and then run in thousands of rivers of liquid fire back to the bottom. The rumblings and explosions were deafening. I had to leave the edge of the crater, for there was stealing over me the overwhelming desire to jump off and to the bottom of the twin lakes of molten death — a desire that everyone has experienced when looking down from a vast elevation.

We got back to the bay about two o'clock that afternoon, where we found that a whole village of bush-boys had come down to buy tobacco. There were about fifty of them, all naked, and they had brought bows and arrows and spears. I gave a shilling, a brass ring, and a red handkerchief for a bow and two arrows, then invited the crowd aboard, for I knew Jack would want some of their bows and spears, and I myself wanted to get some good photographs of these natives. I took a few of them over in the launch, and the rest came in canoes, until we could scarcely move around on deck. Jack snapped twenty good exposures of them, and I, too, got busy with my cameras. Then began the trading, which lasted for over an hour. Many a bow, spear, and pack of arrows shifted hands that afternoon, in exchange for tobacco, cheap jewellery, candy and red cloth. Jack boxed up his things and sent them back to California, while I boxed mine and sent them to Independence.

We lay at Tanna a week. Then, at four o'clock on a fine Tuesday afternoon, we motored out of the harbour and slid twenty miles up the coast, until we got out from under the lee of the land and caught a light breeze. All the next day we sailed to windward of Erromango, heaving-to at night for fear of running into land in the dark, and early the next morning putting on sail and heading for land twenty miles away.

As we were cruising in a general westerly direction through the New Hebrides, a little incident occurred which throws a side-light on the man, Jack London. One day, when weather conditions were perfect and everyone was on deck enjoying himself, an animated ball of variegated colours dropped slowly down into the cockpit at the feet of Mrs. London, who was at the wheel. She eagerly picked it up, calling out, " Lookie, lookie, what I've got! " It proved to be the prettiest little bird we had ever seen. Jack got out his book on ornithology, and proceeded to study book and bird, but nowhere was such a bird described.

It was evidently a land-bird that had gotten too far

from shore and had fallen exhausted on the deck of the *Snark*. We all stood around looking at it as it lay in Mrs. London's hand, while she chirped and tried to talk bird-talk to it. At last Jack said: "If it's a land-bird you are, to the land you go," and changing the course, we sailed for the island Mallicollo, just barely visible ten miles out of our way. We sailed as close to the shore as possible, and the little multi-coloured, pigeon-like bird, having regained its strength, flew in among the cocoanut trees. Then we headed out and continued our cruise up through the score of small islands composing the Western New Hebrides.

Critics of the man, Jack London, may call him an infidel. Colonel Roosevelt may call him a "nature faker." Others have not agreed with his ideas of life, but I have little doubt that this is the only time a captain ever went twenty miles out of his way when his fuel was low (our gasolene tanks were fast empty-ing), just to put a poor little bird ashore to go back to its mate and its young.

On our way through these islands we lived entirely on deck, so as to miss none of the beautiful scenery. The weather continued equable. We rode the water as silently as a canoe. The islands around us shel-tered the sea from any disturbances, leaving the sur-face of these island straits perfectly calm. We sailed a day and a night past a score of active volcanoes. One towering cone of land protruded from the water like an enormous ant-hill, smoke wreathing the top in the day, and the fiery red craters acting as lighthouses by night. Once we put into Vila, anchoring between two small schooners in the bay. Vila has only a few white people, traders and some governmental officials. And here is a queer government. These islands are owned jointly by France and England; one governor will make a law, then the other governor will make a law directly opposed. It is all a joke among the traders. The schooners we saw were *blackbirders,* which made a practice of going to other islands and capturing natives, to be sold in the labour markets of Fiji and Samoa. When I think of this practice, I do not really wonder that the natives are so savage against the whites. As we came into this port, the French flags were at half-mast for a captain that had been killed in another island while trying to get labour.

It was now decided that the *Snark* must be getting on faster, in order that we might pass through the Indian Ocean before the typhoon season. We went by the last of the New Hebrides and next day cruised past the Banks Islands, but did not linger. For another day we sailed past the Santa Cruz Islands. Then for three days we slid through an open sea.

In my diary, kept during this part of the trip, I find some interesting entries.

Monday, June 22, 1908.— To-day we are about five miles off the last of the New Hebrides. It is a big volcanic island, five thousand five hundred feet high. We have only a three-knot breeze and the sea is as smooth as I ever saw it. We have the awning under the mizzensail amidships, where Jack and Mrs. London are lying on their cots reading. Also, the awning is set over the cockpit. The sun is shining brightly, without a cloud in the sky. Henry, Wada and Nakata are asleep in the life-boat; and Tehei is at the wheel — nearly asleep, too. I've been reading nearly all day, and as soon as my work is through I'm going to crawl into the launch and go to sleep.

Tuesday, June 23, 1908. — Last night late we sighted an island of the Banks group. The stars shone so brightly that it was very plain twenty miles away. To-day the breeze has freshened, and the sea is pretty rough — so rough that one big wave came over the deck and down my open skylight, drenching me as I was painting my big engine, so that I have had to batten down and quit work in the engine room. Tehei caught several large bonita on his pearl-hook, so that we have plenty of fish on our table. No one will eat cooked fish now, for we have at last learned to eat it raw. The fish is cut in strips, soaked one hour in salt water and lime-juice, then eaten in a sauce of lime-juice and olive oil. For a long time I could not stomach this delicacy, but now I find it very good. The Kanakas do not even wait for the salt water, but cut strips off the fish while it is still struggling on deck.

Wednesday, June 24, 1908. — Every day, Jack gives me a lesson in navigation, and I in turn give Henry a lesson. Last night, as we three were playing cards,

Jack gave a yell and pointed to Mrs. London's bunk, from which a centipede six inches long was crawling. And Henry says he has seen several on deck. Not very pleasant companions! But our worst enemies are the cockroaches — millions of them. When I am in my bunk and they crawl over me I don't even bother to brush them off; but, of course, we have to skim them from our coffee and chase them out of the food.

Friday, June 26, 1908.— A wild and woolly night. Lightning and thunder everywhere. We are hove-to, for Jack says that land is not more than twenty-five miles off in some direction, but we don't know which, for it has been hazy all day. It's dark as pitch, except when a flash of lightning shows several serious faces on deck. Wonder what next! Last night we hove-to, but it was fine weather and we three played cards during my watch. To-night we tried it, but we could not keep our minds on the game with such a furious sky overhead. In Kansas, I would say a cyclone was nearly on us, but here in the South Seas I don't think it can be less than a hurricane. I am in the cockpit watching the wheel, although we are not moving; but should a current start us west, I must set the sails to put us in another direction, and that very slow!

Saturday, June 27, 1908.— This has been an awful day for me, and I'm dead tired but not sleepy. Again we are hove-to, in about the same position as last night, only we now know where we are. About fifteen miles ahead is a low wooded island, and away back of it the lofty peaks of several islands of the Solomons — the darkest and least-known islands in the world.

They were discovered by Henry at daybreak this morning; and immediately Jack told me to start the engines, for it was dead calm. I did so, and No. 1 insulation plug on the igniters blew out, and I stopped to repair it; then, as soon as I had her going, No. 4 blew out; I repaired it, then started again, when the pump broke; I repaired it, and then found my cylinders were not getting oil; and so on, all day until to-night. I find my magneto "going bad"— and Lord only knows how I can repair it! and the batteries are weak, and we are just in a position to need the engines badly. With the five-horse-power out of order and the seventy-horse-power trying to get out of order, I feel pretty blue, but Jack takes it all right. I'm going to call Tehei now and go to bed in the finest bed I've had for a long time — the spinnaker sail folded up aft the cockpit. I am wearing only a *lava-lava,* and this faint sea-breeze blowing over me almost makes me forget the engines and their troubles. I have a good lantern and a good book, so I'll get a little reading before I go to sleep.

Sunday, June 28, 1908.— Jack called all hands on deck to make sail at six this morning, after which I went to the engine room just to look at the engine and see if I could find some way to make it run. I just turned the wheel over in order to test the spark, when she started off as nice as could be. I turned on the propeller and stuck my head out of the hatch to see everyone on board jumping for the steering-wheel, for we had been in a dead calm, and no one was in the cockpit. Ahead was a little blue patch of land, miles and miles away, which we started for. Well, from six-thirty this morning to one-thirty this afternoon that engine ran without a kick. In an hour we picked up another island ahead, then another, two little patches of land lying just off the mainland. The passage between was about a mile and a quarter. Up this we steamed. We could see the natives on both beaches running to their canoes, but we were going too fast for them. We went in Port Mary on Santa Anna island. Hundreds of natives ran down the beaches, and tumbling into canoes, darted after us, all the time screaming at the top of their voices. After edging through the small lagoon and dropping anchor, we were surrounded in an incredibly short time by a hundred canoe-loads of savages — people who in looks and actions fully justified my expectations of what South Sea Islanders should be like. They started aboard, but with guns we kept them back; and they circled round the *Snark,* waving spears and clubs and shouting at the top of their voices. And their looks certainly made necessary the precautions we took, for they were a most savage-looking lot.

They had big heads of bushy hair. Half of them wore large nose-rings of tortoise shell and of wild-boar tusks. All of them were adorned with ear-rings.

Some ears were plugged with small logs of wood, two inches in diameter. One had the handle of an old teacup in his ear. The men of the New Hebrides looked truly civilised beside these fierce and grotesque figures. One of the islanders had the tin-wire sardine-can openers in his ears; but the strangest of all was the one who had the shell of a clock depending from the cartilage of his nose. All had anklets and armlets, and wore short *lava-lavas* of native cloth. And all were armed with spears, bows and arrows, and clubs. Some had immense bamboo combs in their hair; and through the noses of fully half our visitors were thrust long bamboo needles — clear through, so that the ends stuck out far beyond the cheeks; and on these ends were, in some cases, hung little rings, or pieces of shell. Their cheeks were tattooed in monstrous designs: little boys ornamented and tattooed just as fantastically as were the elders. Their teeth were filed to points, and were dead black; their lips, large and negroid, were ruby red.

Their canoes were the prettiest and most graceful of any we have yet seen. They are not mere dugouts with an outrigger, but long double-ended light-shell boats, the bows making a graceful curve several feet in the air. There is no outrigger. The canoes are paddled with long, slim, strangely carved paddles. Each boat is painted a different design, like a fine piece of tapa cloth. They glided round the *Snark* in the twinkling of an eye. It was all we could do to keep the savages from boarding us. Not that they acted hostile, but they looked it.

Soon other canoes arrived from the other island, and there is no use denying that we were getting pretty well frightened, until, along about the middle of the afternoon, a canoe with only one occupant came alongside, and a big, naked savage, uglier than the rest, paddled round and round the *Snark,* trying to attract our attention. He smiled an ugly, ghastly smile that made us shudder, and finally, when he had our attention, he stood upright in his canoe, and with a bow that was meant to be graceful, said: "How-de-do," and then, losing his balance, fell into the water, his canoe turned over, and those three or four hundred cannibals laughed until their sides ached. It turned the tide for us, for the native swam to the side of the *Snark* and we could not refuse to let him aboard. Then he started talking English to us, real genuine English, and so far as I can remember, this is what he said:

"What name he belong you? Peter he name belong me. You no fright along people along Santa Anna, every people he stop along shore. He good people. You come along shore along me, me make 'm good time along you too much."

Being questioned, Peter told us that he had worked on a plantation for a missionary, and that the missionary had taught him English. He said that his people were good people, and asked us to go ashore with him.

Only one white man is on this island, a trader named Tom Butler. He had been to the other side of the island, but hearing of our arrival, he came aboard from his cutter, which, loaded with cocoanuts, was on the way home. Butler is nearly in his grave. He could scarcely get aboard, for he seems to be nearly paralysed. He was a sailor on a trading schooner until his mate was killed and *kai-kai'd* (eaten). He killed seven of the natives and could not get aboard again, so made his way here, and has been trading ever since. As he came over the rail, he whispered to Jack to watch out for Peter, the native who speaks English. He said he had tried to spear the manager of a big island trading concern who came here in his own schooner six months ago. These natives are all head-hunters. This village and the one across the bay are continually at war with each other, and each tribe collects the heads of the other tribe. Jack and Mrs. London went ashore with him, and brought back news that it is the most heathenish place they ever saw. The women, they say, are naked. Large carved totem poles in the centre of the village are covered with obscene figures. The natives are all armed with clubs, spears and bows. To-morrow I shall go ashore, and see for myself. In the morning the natives are coming out with weapons and other curios for us to buy. I'm very much frightened about my right foot. On the shin a large sore, big as a dollar, has started, and it is eating right into my leg. It seems that no medicine aboard will cure it, and there is no doctor within thousands of miles that we know of. My ankle and leg has swollen to twice its natural size. Jack, I'm afraid, has one of these eating ulcers, too. If no doctor is on Florida Island, and if we are no better when we get there, I think we will sail for Sydney, Australia, for treatment, and that without delay.

Monday, June 29, 1908.—I meant to do some work to-day on the engines, but early this morning the natives started coming with things for us to buy. Jack and Mrs. London sat on their couch on deck with a few hundred sticks of tobacco and a satchelful of beads and red handkerchiefs, coloured calico and cheap jewellery, and started buying. And here ended my attempt to work on the engines. Jack asked me to let him buy anything I wanted, as he wished to keep a uniform price. All morning he traded, then knocked off for dinner, and started again in the afternoon. By night he had about two hundred different curios. For me he got seven spears, all different, two dancing-sticks, two war-clubs, two fine hair-ornaments, two ear-plugs out of the same man's head, one sennit ear-stick, ten anklets and armlets, one calabash (which has been used to drain human blood), two hand-clubs, two fine big shells, and scores of other little trinkets. The whole thing cost fifty sticks of tobacco and one handkerchief. On our deck is a pile of fruit and yams and pumpkins three feet high. Bunches of bananas are hanging to the mainmast, along with eleven pigeons as big as chickens. One sucking pig, cleaned and ready to cook, was sent out by the trader. About one dozen large shell-fish, fine raw, lie aft.

All day canoes have come and gone, long, graceful, light, and strangely painted. Sometimes there would be fifty naked men on deck at one time, fierce-looking fellows, their ears full of rings and plugs and sticks. Some carry their pipes there. Some wore great shell nose-rings; others had porpoise teeth stuck in the ends of their noses. Their faces were tattooed and cut in strange designs. In their big bushy heads were feathers and bamboo combs. Of anklets and armlets we bought nearly all they had — two yards of calico would easily make breech-clouts for fifty of these men, so they effected rapid exchanges.

Tuesday, June 30, 1908.— Again this morning we traded with the natives until we are wondering where we will put the things. About one hundred spears alone are hard to pack away. After lunch, Jack, Mrs. London, and I went ashore in the launch. As we could not get clear up to the beach, Tehei had to carry us out of the boat. We had our guns strapped on, and carried four kodaks. We went up to the trader's house. Imagine our surprise to find a whole beachful of naked girls. Absolutely naked. Jack looked at me and then at Mrs. London, and I looked back at them. Each was anxious to see how the others would act. But these people did not appear sensual

CANNIBAL VILLAGE, FOATE, SOLOMON GROUP

or unnatural at all. They were just like animals. We each turned our eyes shoreward and tried to look unconcerned and as if we had been used to such things all our lives. We sat on the porch and talked with the trader, while the girls got us cocoanuts. These girls, from ten to twenty years of age, had a few strings of beads around their waists, some had a single string hanging in front, and there were anklets and armlets and necklaces; but of garments to hide their nakedness there was nothing at all. Some of them were not bad looking, save for the black, pointed teeth and the hideously red lips. I was told that the teeth were coloured by chewing the betel-nut. With Peter guiding us, we tramped about a quarter of a mile to the village, a hundred natives in the path ahead and a hundred behind. And we kept our hands on our guns all the time, for this would be a fine place for the islanders to get some *kai-kai* (food) for a cannibal banquet. And I have little doubt that our heads are vastly coveted.

At length, we came to a log bridge, over a shallow stream of water. Mrs. London was not allowed to go over — she must wade through, as this bridge is taboo to women. Jack could not resist chaffing Mrs. London, for up to this time she has been treated like a lady by the natives we have come in contact with, but here a woman is only a woman, and has none of the rights of men. Poor Mrs. London was humiliated, but Jack enjoyed it. We came into the village. Men and women too old and feeble to walk would peep at us through their grass houses. We came upon a mammoth grass house, facing the sea. This place was as large as a good-sized store-room. From the front protruded the ends of war canoes. We wanted to see them better; but Mrs. London was again stopped, and in company with Peter, Jack and I went inside and inspected two canoes large enough to hold fifty men each, and a dozen smaller ones. These were the war canoes, used only for the fighting. At the rear of the house was a large coffin-shaped grass box. We looked in, then stepped back in horror; and holding our noses, Jack and I beat a hasty retreat, for inside the box was the body of a man, looking like a pin-cushion, so full was he with sharp barbs. Peter told us that he was the best king that ever ruled them, that he had been dead a week, and that the points in his body were the arrow-points used in their envenomed arrows. Everyone knows that a dead body contains the most virulent poison in the world. By steeping their arrow-points in a chief's body, they think that the poison will be more effective. I bought one hundred and fifty of these arrows. But I shall have to be careful how I touch them.

As we passed out, we saw several old men squatted in front of the house, making hollow wooden fishes by the use of stone axes. We were told by Peter that these men were chiefs, and that after they die their bodies will be allowed to putrify. Then, after the arrow-points have been poisoned in their decaying flesh, their bones will be put in one of the hollow fishes and set on a shelf in the canoe-house, where we saw about a hundred such fishes. The old men were making their own coffins.

We went through the village, which is closed in by a fence of small sticks woven together. The houses touch one another, so that the whole village covers only a few acres, with streets about ten feet wide. In a small square at the centre stand tall carved images. At the foot of the village, in a small enclosure about twenty feet square, they showed us the graveyard. Every body goes into the same hole. The pit is simply opened up, the body tossed in, and then it is covered over again. Scores of naked women and children followed us about, and large men with clubs and spears. I really did not feel any too safe. They showed us another boat house in which rested a big log-fish, filled with the bones of chiefs. I made photographs of the women and men. Jack made head studies. Then, walking back through the streets, I took pictures of houses. For Jack I made a picture of two men whom the sharks had bitten. One had his leg bitten clear off; the other had all the flesh stripped from the bone.

We then went back to the clearing in the centre of the village, where the men gave a dance for us, while half a dozen old rascals sat in the centre making dance music on hollow logs. We gave the dancers tobacco and each a handful of cheap candy; and then Peter took us to see his wives — two of them, and fine looking ladies they were. They were not naked, but each wore a short fringe of grass, the smallest dresses I have ever seen, and, I believe, the smallest dresses in the world. I bought one of them from Peter's elder wife.

We went back to the trader's house, where five young girls danced a very pretty dance, making a hissing sound for music. Mrs. London gave them a string of beads each. We came back to the boat and ate supper; then for several hours on deck the Japanese boys danced, and Wada acted out some pantomime. Tehei danced the Tahitian *hula-hula* and Henry did the Samoan *seva-seva*. Nakata is a fine dancer. All the while, Mrs. London played Hawaiian *hulas* on her *ukelele*. We had a good time until so late that I did not have to stand my watch, and Tehei stood only part of his. We have to keep " anchor watch," for a little wind from the west might make us swing on the reef — and then, we can't trust the natives.

Wednesday, July 1, 1908.—Again all morning Jack bought curios, until we have just cleaned out the village. I got a few more things, among them an arrow with a special poison tip. Jack made the chief several presents to get up a dance for us in the afternoon, so right after lunch we were taken ashore in the launch by Henry, and were escorted to the village by a young chief. There we found more men making the hollow fish-coffins. It took some time to get the dance started, but finally fourteen young men lined up in two rows and eight squatted in a circle with a flat board for a drum — one man striking it with a stick, the rest chanting. I can't describe the dance. It was similar to an Indian war-dance, and yet not the same. They jumped around, yelled, alternately squatted and stood, keeping up much the same thing for an hour and a half. Then Jack and I gave out more candy and sticks of tobacco. The naked girls stood around in the circle, curiously watching us. One old man with only a stump of an arm asked for a stick of tobacco. We found out that he had lost the arm while dynamiting fish — the explosive went off too soon. On the way back, he stopped us at his hut, and made Mrs. London a present of a sennit armlet. This was the only present given us by the natives here. At length we got back to the *Snark*, where we found that the trader had sent us a big string of fish. A native got us a dozen pigeons to-day. We found several young breadfruit, and with plenty of *kai-kai* we sail out of here in the morning.

. . . .

That night, Peter, the native came aboard, and told us that if we wanted to get our washing done, his wife would do it for us; so it was settled that early next morning Nakata was to go ashore and help with it. Next morning, almost before sun-up, Nakata went ashore. A little later we white people followed; but we found no washing done. The Japanese are great practical jokers in their quiet way. We found Nakata trying to show the naked women how to wear Mrs. London's clothes. He succeeded very well, until he accidentally tickled one of them, and immediately they all jumped a good arm's length away from him; and as those on whom he had succeeded in getting dresses did not know how to get them off, and for fear of being tickled would not allow him to touch them, there was no washing done.

Next morning, Jack called all hands and they heaved anchor, while I started the engine and we steamed out of the harbour. We went about two miles before I shut down; then we flew along with an eight-knot breeze up the coast of the big island of San Christoval (or Bauro), an island seventy-two miles long by twenty-five wide. A missionary lived on one end of San Christoval, and a trader on the other end, and the people were killing and eating each other right along.

At three o'clock, Jack told me to start the engine, as the breeze was dying out, and he was afraid of being caught on a bad coast with no moon to steer by and reefs all about. We decided to stop at a small island six miles off San Christoval — Ugi is its name, and it has a good harbour. When we were about five miles off, a whale-boat with a white man and half a dozen black boys came alongside, and I stopped the engine until he got aboard; then we pushed on again with his boat towing behind. He was a Mr. Drew, a member of the Melanesian Missionary Society, stationed on

San Christoval. He accompanied us to Ugi, and decided to go to Florida Island with us. We got in just at dark, and were met by a trader in his dingy, who piloted us to a good anchorage alongside his little ketch, a hundred yards off shore. His name was Hammond. He was an Australian who had only been here one month. The last man got frightened and left, for the natives of Malaita, a very savage island, had come down in canoes and killed nearly every trader that ever set up in business here; and he had got word from one of his boys that they were coming again. Hammond had been in the Solomons for eleven years, however, and spoke the language well. He told us that two years before he had landed at Port Mary — our last anchorage — just as the natives were coming back from San Christoval, victorious in a fight with one of the hostile tribes; and these Port Mary natives were heavily laden with war trophies, such as heads, arms and legs.

The two men stayed for supper, and we held long and interesting conversations with them, in the course of which we learned many new things of the dark islands into which we had poked the *Snark's* nose.

The next morning, July 3, we had the best treat we had had for ages — milk, sweet, fresh cow's milk! One glass apiece! Mr. Hammond had sent it over before we were up. I had almost forgotten that milk grew in anything except cans. Mr. and Mrs. London went ashore to see the natives, while I stayed aboard to give my clothing a good overhauling, and to sew for myself some *lava-lavas*. Several natives came out to trade curios, but they had the same things we had gotten in Port Mary, so I did not buy.

The next day, Saturday, was the Fourth of July. In the morning we discharged a round of ammunition from each of our guns, and that was our celebration — quite different from the one the year before at Honolulu. At ten o'clock the trader came alongside in his whale-boat, manned by his Santa Cruz boys, and we went to the village. A crowd met us at the beach. The women here were clothed, each in a yard of calico. They were all Christians, so they said; but I confess that the heathens we had previously met were far more hospitable and were better looking. The old chief led us around the village, which, like the one at Port Mary, was enclosed by a low fence. The huts all faced a narrow street, and the rear of the huts was flush with the fence. The huts themselves were the dirtiest things I ever saw — of grass and sides and roof, very low, with a bamboo porch in front. On the inside was a dirty sleeping bunk of bamboo. Of other furniture there was little or none.

We returned late that afternoon, and went aboard the *Snark*. Jack went through the medicine chest, trying to find something that would cure the large ulcer on my shin. Every day found this growing in size and soreness; and I became seriously concerned. At Port Mary, I had asked the trader, Butler, about it,

South Sea Cannibals

and he had told me that it was a " yaw," or Solomon Island sore, to which all white men were subject. Corrosive sublimate, he further declared, was the thing to cure it. Now the result of corrosive sublimate on a large raw surface like that! It burnt like fire, but it seemed to help.

We now set out for a leisurely circuit of the larger islands. In this circuit, it was our luck to see thousands of cannibals, and also to observe the work done by the missionaries among these benighted savages. Right here, let me explain that cannibalism is not practised because of any love of human flesh, but rather because the natives believe that they acquire the fighting qualities of the men that they eat. Thus they hope to get the strength and prowess in battle of their enemies; and for his reason, they like to eat white men, whose skill and courage they admire.

We never saw a cannibal feast, but we saw plenty of evidence of the practice in the thousands of human bones on shores and reefs.

All these cannibals are head-hunters. One may see tiny mummified heads stuck up outside the huts. The more heads a man has, the stronger he imagines himself to be. A man with fifteen heads reckons himself as strong as fifteen men. The mummified heads are taken from enemies in battle. The bones are all drawn out, and then the head is dried until it is only the size of one's fist. To possess the head of a white man is a special honour. A village with a white man's head considers that it has a wonderful talisman. Naturally, we took great care not to become luck-bringers for any of the natives among whom we sojourned.

Some years ago, a party of German scientists landed at Malaita, one of the most inaccessible islands in the group, to explore. They very much wanted to take back some of these heads as relics, and offered fifteen sticks of plug tobacco for each. The market was brisk for a few days, but soon all the posts outside the huts had been stripped, and the supply slackened. Then suddenly trade revived again — but it was noticed that the heads brought in were fresh! It turned out that the natives had been doing a little private killing in order to keep up the supply. One native had sacrificed several relatives in his desire to please the Germans and get their tobacco.

And then the missionaries. There are so many different kinds of missionaries in the South Seas that I must divide them into their classes and try to tell of these different classes as they appeared to me. Probably another person going among them would see them in a different light from what I did. Of course, I cannot pretend to know all about what the missionaries are doing in the South Seas, but I do know what some of them were doing. Some of them were engaged in excellent work — the noblest work in the world. And some were doing absolutely no work. Let me tell of both kinds, at the same time explaining that if some of the missionaries are not doing what they ought.

it is no reason why we should shut our eyes to the fact that there are others who toil eternally and well in their allotted paths. For that matter, it is the frauds who make it so hard for the missionary who works in good faith for the regeneration of the savages.

Missionaries in Polynesia I have never considered in these pages. For the eastern Pacific has reached such a stage of civilisation that the missionaries are now called preachers, and have their regular congregations, just as in civilised countries.

The first missionary I had met was Rev. Watt, at Tanna, New Hebrides. After twenty-eight years at this same station, he had managed to convert about two hundred mean, thieving little beggars. He made the natives, as a sign of conversion, wear the ragged and dirty clothing I have described, which clothes, once put on, were probably never removed. As I have said, these missionary boys stole everything they could get their hands on, but of the scores of bush natives that came aboard, we never caught one taking a thing; and the heathen natives had offered to give us a feast and to guide us to see their island, but the missionary boys we had not been able to hire to guide us, and for the fruit they brought aboard, they asked many times its value. For my part, I can see no actual good Rev. Watt has accomplished in all his twenty-eight years. Trader Wiley, the big, genial Scotchman, has done more towards civilising than has the missionary. Wiley brought about peace between many of the tribes that before his advent were continually at war. He also adjusts their quarrels; and the natives come to him for advice and medicine, and for surgical operations.

Dr. Drew, the missionary we met at Ugi, is stationed on San Christoval. Dr. Drew, when he first landed, started learning the native language, and it was over a year before he began teaching the word of God to the natives, but in that year he won the natives' confidence. He worked on their pride by offering prizes for the best-built house and the cleanest house. He helped them lay out streets, and the dirty village, with its houses stuck anywhere they could find ground to put them, gradually took on a healthful, systematic look, and natives from other villages came in and built neat grass houses. Then Dr. Drew gave away as prizes one yard of blue calico, only the one colour, and soon the whole four hundred natives were wearing *lava-lavas* just alike in shape and colour. Dr. Drew went no further toward dressing them, for he realised that as soon as a native puts on white man's clothes he begins to imitate the white man, and to imitate the white man in that part of the world is bad policy. Dr. Drew did not attempt to become a native, but maintained his dignity all the time he was learning the language.

After he had mastered the language, Dr. Drew taught them to read in their own tongue, and then translated the Bible for them. When we of the *Snark* went among his four hundred Christian natives, we were treated better than any natives in the South Seas had ever before treated us. And Dr. Drew caused this great revival by setting an example, and not by trying to beat religion into them. I doubt if any of the natives knew what was happening, so gradual was their uplifting, until they finally found themselves full-fledged Christians — and that kind of Christian will never backslide. If there were more such missionaries in the South Seas, cannibalism and heathenism would soon be a thing of the past. These natives now have their cricket and football teams, and Dr. Drew teaches them English, and cooking, and even boat-building and sailing.

Another missionary, Mr. Whittier, came up from Australia with a scheme to adopt the simple life. He lived in a grass house, ate native goods, wore no other clothing than the native *lava-lava*. His idea was to live like the natives and become one of them, thinking by this method that they would trust him better. But it was no use, for when the white man lowered himself to their level, they had no more respect for him.

As the little *Snark* poked her nose in and out of savage ports, the first thing we looked to see was the kind of *lava-lavas* the women wore. If they wore cloth *lava-lavas*, they were invariably Christians, but if they wore grass *lava-lavas*, or were naked, they were heathens. But we could never be sure of the men by this method, for they received the cloth *lava-lavas* from the traders in exchange for cocoanuts. Of course, they kept all the traders gave them, and left the women to hustle for themselves. As may be imagined, it doesn't cost much to dress a woman in this part of the world.

The principal good done by the missionaries — the sincere missionaries — is that they take the natives out of their horrible, dirty state and teach them self-respect; and surely this is a big step toward civilisation.

The greatest good is being done by Church of England missionaries, who own the finest mission ship in the world, the *Southern Cross*. This ship, in its cruising among the islands, persuades the best and most intelligent natives to go with them to Norfolk Island. Here they are put in a mission school, and later returned to their homes to start schools of their own. A white missionary is left with the new convert until he has his church built and things are running smoothly; then the native is left to shift for himself. Some of the native missionaries have maintained good clean villages, but the *Southern Cross* is needed about twice a year to untangle the mismanaged affairs of most of the stations, for however sincere the native teacher may be, he seldom has any executive ability.

The native churches are generally the neatest buildings in the village, and are used for schools as well as for churches. The natives squat on the ground, and use rough log benches for desks. Their church-bell is a hollow log, and their contribution-box is always of cocoanut or shell. Their singing is wonderfully pleasing, especially if a missionary has trained them.

The Christian natives and the heathen natives always seemed to be the best of friends. As a consequence, the most incongruous things sometimes occur. In one place, I saw a coffin-shaped box with a body sticking full of barbs, and within a few hundred feet stood a mission-house in charge of a native teacher. Native missionaries are always called teachers. Why it is, I do not know, but I have never heard a native Christian worker called a missionary.

The French traders ten years ago traded off about five hundred old Snyder rifles to the savages, and as soon as a white man is known to be about, these old rifles are gotten out for show. But they have no cartridges, and if they had, I don't believe the guns would shoot, for the muzzles of those I saw were stopped up with rust.

On the island of Florida, in the Solomons, a missionary made a whole village of converts by playing on their childlike love for display. This missionary had no influence with them for several months, until one day a government schooner anchored and half a dozen black police boys paraded the village, marching in time and carrying guns. As soon as the government vessel had departed, the boys of the villages were trying to imitate the drilling of the police boys, using their old Snyder rifles. The missionary was quick to take advantage of this opportunity to get into their confidence, and, by drilling the boys, he was soon in their good graces; and gradually he turned their love of pomp and display into more useful channels. And now he has a well-founded mission-station and his chief asset is his teams of drilled, athletic boys. Other teachers, encouraged by his success, have taken up athletic work among their followers.

One great difficulty to be overcome by these wilderness apostles is the lack of concentration in savage minds. It is difficult to keep a native's attention long enough to teach him a lesson or to instill moral precepts.

I have noticed that doctors always make the best missionaries. Their medical treatment will give them a hold and win them confidence where nothing else could. Also, a man is a better missionary than a woman, among these savages. For a woman is not respected. A big, strong, athletic man, who can do things that the natives see with their own eyes are better than what they can do, will always have a following, but the man who relies solely upon preaching will never do any good. But to be perfectly fair, I must say that most of the missionaries whom I saw were putting skill and enthusiasm into their work, toiling by day and by night, and in most cases these simple teachers were not putting forth their time and toil in vain.

CHAPTER XIII

OCEANIC CRUISING

The Solomon group is divided into German and British Solomons, but the British section, about twenty-five large and small islands, being the more interesting, we did not bother to look much into the German section.

The large islands of Guadalcanar, Malaita, San Christoval, and Ysabel are as yet entirely unexplored in the interior. In none of these islands has anyone been back more than a few miles from the coast.

On the island of Guadalcanar, an island eighty miles long and forty miles wide, are half a dozen plantations and a trading and mission station, in which probably twenty-five persons live. Their homes are well guarded and stockaded, but even with the most rigid precautions, a white man is set down as missing at frequent intervals. Only a few months ago, I received a letter from a friend in the Solomons, telling of the massacre of a trader at a station where the *Snark* once anchored.

After our cruise in the western islands, the *Snark* dropped anchor at the largest plantation in the Solomons, called Penduffryn, on the island of Guadalcanar, owned and managed by two Englishmen, George Darbishire and Thomas Harding.

As Mrs. London was not feeling well when we anchored here, she was left at the plantation, while Jack and I and the two Kanakas and two Japs took the *Snark* over to the island of Tulagi, twenty-five miles away. The engine ran all the way. We made the twenty-five miles in three hours, dropping anchor at Tulagi late in the evening. Jack and I went up the side of an old extinct volcano to the house of the Governor of the British Solomons. The Governor was away, but the Assistant Governor received us, and promptly fined Jack £5 for not getting pratique papers here first. Otherwise we were treated hospitably. Late that night Jack set out in a whale-boat for Penduffryn, leaving the rest of us to get the boat cleaned with the help of the Governor's native recruits. For one week, twenty native divers scraped the *Snark's* keel with cocoanut husks, and in company with a government engineer, I took the *Snark* on short cruises, testing the engines, and after everything had been thoroughly overhauled, I took the *Snark* back across the straits of Penduffryn, and went ashore to find a regular reunion of white men.

There were traders old and young, *beche-de-mer* fishermen, old beach-combers and blackbirders. All were delighted to hear that visitors were at Penduffryn. For one week, this largest group of white men that ever gathered on the island of Guadalcanar made things hum with good time. Everyone was so happy — and we acted like children. We had big card games and even a masquerade ball. Darbishire, who was always the life of the plantation, dressed as an English lady, and I was his partner to the dance. The music did not amount to much, but Mrs. London's Hawaiian *ukelele* made enough for us to dance by. The merrymaking lasted several days, until it ended by all present agreeing to take the Oriental dope called *hashish*.

Darbishire was the first to partake. After he had passed under the influence, we decorated him with parts of Mrs. London's clothes, and I did a little artistic work with water-colours. For several days he went around the house in a half-dazed state, and would at times drop dead asleep while standing on his feet. One after another took this *hashish*, until the night Jack took it. He went clear off his head, acted so wild that Mrs. London was frightened; and no one else would take it. Next night was to have been my turn.

At Penduffryn they have seven native boys trained to cook and do the housework, so it was very little that the white people had to do. During the day I usually worked aboard the *Snark*, rowing ashore at night for late dinner. And then I was busy a good deal of the time with my photographic work.

I seldom moved about at night, alone. The natives were pretty restless just then at Lunga, a station fourteen miles below here: eight blacks from Malaita working at the station ran away to the bush, and threatened to get some white heads, then, stealing a boat, to go back to Malaita. One day, at Penduffryn, a lot of powder and cartridges was found in a hut belonging to a native. The man was taken to the house and handcuffed, and all the recruits were called in from work. Then Mr. Harding told them that the man was going to be sent to the Governor, who would sentence him to three years hard, unpaid labour. Until a boat left, no one was to speak to him. But the next morning, when his handcuffs were taken off, the culprit bolted, and thereafter made his appearance among the other natives at night, inciting them to kill every white man at Penduffryn.

After the loot was found, a search was made of all the houses, and two fellows were found to have spears. Again all the men were called from work, and before them all these two fellows were forced to strip their *lava-lavas;* and Mr. Darbishire, with a big boor-hide whip, gave them the worst licking I ever saw anyone get. He made deep cuts in their hide, from which the blood spurted. It nearly made me sick, but I knew the whipping was necessary; for it is solely by intimidation that the white man rules in the Solomons.

Meanwhile, things were going badly with the *Snark* crew.

Henry and Tehei were down with island fever. Nakata had caught *ngari-ngari,* or scratch-scratch. Jack had terrible yaws, and I had equally terrible yaws. We, too, took occasional spells of fever. Dosings of

ARTIFICIAL ISLAND, OFF MALAITA, SOLOMON GROUP

quinine and applications of corrosive sublimate and blue vitriol were daily occurrences. The blue vitriol drove me nearly crazy — Jack called it horse doctoring; but it was the best that I could do. Henry developed *bukua* on his face; Tehei fainted several times, and wept and prayed; all this made us the most invalided crew ever seen in the South Seas. This much I learned, however, from our tribulations: anyone coming to the Solomons should first purchase a barrel of quinine for the fever and a barrel of corrosive sublimate for the yaws, and leave an order for more to follow.

I was looking forward to getting out of this particular part of the world. It was too wild and raw, too full of sickness and sudden death. How I longed for a real bed, with sheets, in a place where it was not too hot to sleep! The rain pretty near drove us out of the *Snark*. We had awning all over the deck, and side curtains, but the tropical showers that blew up in a minute and swept away the next were fast and furious while they lasted. No matter how well the canvas was set, the rain got through and pushed below to our bunks. But I determined that in Australia I would get two large ventilators for my room. Then no rain could bother me, for the hatch would be shut. Also, I was thinking seriously of fitting up my bunk with sheets. If the *Snark* was to be home to me for several years to come, I might as well arrange for comfort.

Because of Henry's and Tehei's sickness, Jack thought it best to get a white man to look after things, so he hired a German named Harry Jacobsen; a man who had been mate of the *Minota,* a recruiting schooner that had gone ashore on Malaita and been looted by the savage islanders. The *Minota* had been recovered, but just now was not putting out, so Jack was able to get Mr. Jacobsen without much trouble. Our machinery had gone wrong, and we had to wait at Penduffryn until fresh parts came from Sydney, Australia. It was during this wait that the *Minota* was fitted out for another recruiting trip to Malaita. Captain Jansen and Mr. Jacobsen invited Jack and Mrs. London to go along on this blackbirding cruise; so I was left in charge of the *Snark*.

Soon afterward, only twenty-five miles away, the *Minota* grounded on the Mallua Reef, close to the cannibal island of Malaita. Soon they were surrounded by scores of man-eaters in canoes. Of course, Jack and all the rest were well armed, but the savages were so numerous and so treacherous that a day-and-night watch had to be kept against a surprise and a terrible death. They sent up rockets, which, as a matter of fact, I saw; but I had no idea that it was the *Minota* which was in trouble. I thought some other vessel was on the rocks. Anyway, I was quite unable to go to their help, with my engines out of order. Their safety during the time taken to re-float the *Minota* was really owing to the efforts of a missionary

Oceanic Cruising 315

— one of the few missionaries in the Solomons who had any influence with the cannibals. He got his mission-boys to form a guard for passengers and crew, and thus averted the peril. Poor fellow! he was killed soon after.

In addition to the yaws and the fever, a new trouble came into the life of the *Snark* family. Jack's hands had begun to swell up, turn very sore, and peel skin. The nails were very hard and thick, and had to be filed. And it was the same with his feet. Nothing like it had ever been heard of before. The traders and beach-combers could diagnose yaws and fever, but not this. Both Jack and Mrs. London were considerably alarmed at this strange manifestation. "It is plain we are not wanted in the South Seas," Jack said, more than once. "California is the place for me."

"And me for Kansas," I assured him.

Wada and Nakata began to dilate upon the virtues of Japan, while Henry and Tehei were praying day and night that they might get back safely to the Society Islands.

After we had lain at Penduffryn a time, Mr. London decided that we would make a visit to the fabled Ontong Java islands that the traders were telling us so much about. They were situated about two hundred miles away from the Solomons, and their exact location was not known. The people were said to be of a queer race, and as we were out to see the unusual, we set sail from Penduffryn, and after two days' beating up the Invincible Straits, we anchored at the island of Ysabel, and lay there seventeen days, trading and hunting wild game. Here Wada, the cook, went clean out of his head, and running away, went to live in a village of coast natives; and we were compelled to sail off without him. Jack promised Nakata a new suit of clothes if he would do the cooking until we reached a port where we could get a new cook. Nakata tried to hold his own job and the cook's job, but got sick, and then Tehei and Henry and I took turn-about getting meals. When we sailed away from Ysabel, we were forced to cut loose our big eight-hundred-pound anchor, for it had gotten caught in the coral reefs so tightly that it was impossible for us to get it out.

Ontong Java is about two hundred miles to the west of Ysabel. Now and then a trading vessel comes here, and once a year a steamer collects the annual output of copra. I suppose the steamer knows the position. Certainly it is never gotten from the chart.

The first day out of Ysabel we had fine weather, but the next day the sea got rough, and for six days it rained and blew as it only can in the tropics; and to add to our discomfort, Tehei got blackwater fever and lay down on deck fully decided to die. Nakata was still sick, and to cap matters he got a second dose of ptomaine poisoning. Mrs. London and Jack came down with fever, and their yaws grew worse. Henry's *bukua* continued to bother him. And I daily writhed in the agony of alternate washes of blue vitriol and corrosive sublimate. We were so sick and miserable that very little attention was paid to the navigating, and for several days we sailed in a half-hearted way, looking for the islands. One day, Jack's observations indicated that we were inside the lagoon, and next day we had sailed clear past the islands. But one morning Henry called all hands on deck to see the cocoanut trees just visible above the horizon. We sailed up the coast of small islands, some of them only large enough for one cocoanut tree, and the greatest no larger than an ordinary city block. These thirty-nine islands circled around a lagoon ten miles wide. Not one of these islands was over two feet above the water-line, and absolutely the only vegetation was the thickly growing cocoanut trees.

While looking for an opening between the little islands, a canoe with two occupants paddled off from one of the islands and we let them aboard. It was certainly a surprise to see Polynesians again, instead of the little woolly-headed negroids of the Solomons. These men were big, brown-skinned, straight-haired fellows — that is, their hair would have been straight, had they ever combed it. As they came over the rail, Henry spoke to them in his own tongue; and what was our amazement to hear them answer him. And then Tehei decided that he wouldn't die, and started talking to them.

Our surprise will be appreciated when I say that these people's rightful home was five thousand miles to the eastward. They did not know that there were any others in this part of the world who could speak their language. They piloted us inside the lagoon, and then to our further surprise we saw a white man's frame house on the beach of the largest island. When we dropped anchor, this man came aboard, and a happy man he was that day. For it was a lonesome time he had, with a sight of white people only once a year, when the steamer came after his copra.

He was a Dutchman, and had lived here so long that he had almost forgotten how to speak English. We came ashore with him, and went directly to his home. While we were there a small boy brought up a tiny shark's jaw and presented it to Jack with the king's compliments. As we had bought these small jaws for a half-stick of tobacco, Jack was disgusted and started to throw it away, but I asked for it and he gave it to me.

Then we were taken to see the king, who was squatting on a mat in the centre of a large grass house, his half-dozen wives seated around him. We shook hands, and with the trader as interpreter Jack made the king a present of coloured calico and some tobacco, and then told the king that he must give us a hundred cocoanuts in return. The old king started to say no, until Jack made as if to take back his presents, when the king hastily ordered the cocoanuts to be sent aboard. We went on through the village and came to the graveyard, and it was the most remarkable graveyard I have ever seen. The graves lay so close together that there was scarcely room for a tombstone. The tombstones were straight slabs of granite, with no writing, but some of them had queer heads attached. There were no mounds over the graves — they sparkled with pure white sand, beaten flat; and all the graves were levelled off the same way, until they appeared like a long, paved sidewalk. At the outer edge of the graveyard were three wooden crosses that marked the graves of the former wives of the Dutch trader. He pointed to the three graves with pride, and later on he showed us his three living wives. He informed us that if one of them didn't make copra better he might find it necessary to make a cross for her — and I believe he meant it. For he was very brutal. A fine handsome young fellow had attached himself to our party wherever we went, and once the Dutchman gave him a crushing blow with his fist, apparently without reason. After that, Obi held aloof.

On going back to the trader's house, we noticed a Solomon Islander working around the place. When we asked why this native should be so far away from home, we learned that he had been recruited about five years before to work on a plantation for the trading company, and had been put at this lagoon to prevent his getting way. Those who have read Jack London's story, "Mauki," will understand, for this native was the original of that interesting character.

We lay at this lagoon for nearly a week. I got a great deal of fine coral in all colours of the rainbow, but it all faded white, except the red, which was so brittle that it broke to pieces. I saw trees of coral twenty feet high, and wonderful gardens of it, through which parrot-coloured fish swam in and out.

After piling our cockpit full of green cocoanuts that the king's subjects had selected for us, we had prepared to leave, when word came to us that across the lagoon were two missionaries, a Samoan and a Tonga Islander, who wanted to see us. The Dutchman had been careful not to tell us of them, for a very good reason.

Why the Dutchman did not want us to know of these missionaries, perhaps the most remarkable in the world, we soon learned after we had left this lagoon and stumbled on to another.

Two years before the time we were at Ontong Java, the mission-ship *Southern Cross* had steamed into this harbour with two missionaries, one of them from Samoa, the other from the Tonga Islands. These two men tried hard to land, but the natives said no, that their idols were good enough for them and they had no desire to change — if the white men wanted to land there would be no resistance, but no dark-skinned natives were going to be allowed to tell them about new gods.

The *Southern Cross* could not afford to remain long at this place, for it kept them moving to make their rounds twice a year, so the two missionaries were left with fifty days' food and water in an open boat. Then for fifty days these missionaires tried to land, but were met with spears at the beach; and when the food and water was all gone, the Dutch trader took pity on them, and told the king that he had received a message from the great white master, saying that if the men were not allowed to land they would send schooners and kill everyone on the islands.

The king then allowed the trader to take the men in his house and nurse them; and after they returned to health they built neat grass houses and tried to work among the islanders, but their work went slowly and it was not until the Dutch trader killed one of his wives and the missionaries proved it on him that they gained any hold. Then the missionaries started a crusade against the trader, but the natives did not have the courage to deport him, and it got so warm for the missionaries that they were notified to leave the largest island and never return. Then these missionaries went to live on another island, and for years they never saw any civilised people, for the trader took good care that no vessels ever anchored across the lagoon. When we of the *Snark* sailed over to them, they cried, they were so glad to see white people. We gave them potatoes and tinned goods, and promised to report them at the government station when we got back to the Solomons.

We then sailed out of the lagoon and headed west with a large crowd of natives following in canoes. We were clear of the islands by sundown, and Jack set the course for another lagoon that was reported to be some two hundred miles farther west, and the watches were set with confidence of a perfect night's rest. Just enough wind was blowing to keep the sails full, and there was scarcely a ripple on the water. Wada and Tehei kept their watch; then I was called on deck, and was lazily smoking and steering at the wheel. Everyone else was asleep on deck and I was only enough awake to keep the *Snark's* head on the course, when I heard a slight rustling on the water ahead, which increased in volume until it rose into the unmistakable roar of a reef. Hastily bringing the vessel up into the wind, I roused all hands and after a good look at the reef, Jack ordered the *Snark* about, and until morning we beat back and forth. When daylight came we were in sight of another small lagoon that looked like Ontong Java in miniature. We had no trouble getting inside the reef, and sailed five miles across the lagoon to the largest island, and dropped anchor. In no time at all our decks were crowded with big, brown Polynesians, who, while they seemed healthy fellows, appeared absolutely devoid of intellect.

We tried hard to get some spears, but the natives refused to sell, no matter what we offered. There were about fifty of them: soon they began chanting a weird kind of song. We found that this was in honour of their king, who was on his way out to us.

"PENDUFFRYN," THE LARGEST COCOANUT PLANTATION IN THE WORLD. ISLAND OF GUADALCANAR, SOLOMON ISLANDS. MRS. THOMAS HARDING AND PLANTATION LABORERS

Oceanic Cruising

Shortly a canoe finer than the rest came alongside, and the old bewhiskered king, a fine old chap with nose-rings and ear-rings, came over the rail. We received a shock, for his body was covered with tattooed designs of guns. The old fellow ordered the natives to the stern of the boat, and, advancing, made us a speech of welcome. We tried to get his King-spear, a beautifully carved weapon, designed to catch a victim going or coming, but he would not part with it. Of course, we were expected to make the king a present. It had been a joke with us about the useless things that kings and chiefs had been giving us; so more in the spirit of a jest than anything else, Mrs. London gave this king an old night-gown of hers. He seemed so vastly pleased that Mrs. London put it on him. That did the trick: he was so delighted that he at once gave us his King-spear; and for days we saw him running about the island in the night-gown, the proudest man in the world, and certainly the best-dressed native for miles around.

With the idea of showing us what a great and lordly king he was, he invited us ashore, and parading us through the village, he called all his subjects together and made a speech to them. I don't know what he said, but they were highly pleased; and that night a dance was given for us. We noticed the same people we had seen in the afternoon; and next day, on going to some of the close-by islands, we found them uninhabited, and gradually it dawned upon us that the first group of people we had seen were the sole inhabitants of the Tasman Lagoon. On counting them, we found fifty-nine men and forty-eight women, and only one baby. It was easy to see the finish of these people. They had married and intermarried until every solitary native was closely related to every other native; and should they continue to intermarry so closely, should there be no infusion of fresh blood, their race must become thoroughly idiotic, and soon go down to death.

I believe the most peculiar trait of these people was their idol or devil-devil worship. They had no good god, but believed that if they kept their devil-devil in good humour, everything would be well, and that if the devil-devil should get angry, they would have floods and diseases and everything in general would go to ruin. To keep the devil-devil in good humour, they had built large houses with fresh mats for him to sleep on; and every boat or house that was built must first be passed on by their wooden devil-devil, and by certain signs they could tell whether he was pleased or not. One of these devils I sent back to America, and I still have it.

At this island, we found another of those queer graveyards that we had seen in Ontong Java. There were hundreds and hundreds of these strange graves, which proved that the reefs comprising this lagoon had once been well inhabited.

We collected several of their peculiar grass dresses at this place. I secured one just before it was finished.

There are dozens of islands in the Solomon group where few white men have ever been seen in the interior, and there are islands where a white man has never been seen at all. We made a call at one of these places — quite an accidental call. We were caught in the tail end of a hurricane and were blown about for a time, not knowing in the least where we were. Then there came a sudden calm, and we found ourselves near a little group of islands. Presently, the natives came out in canoes to see us. They were quite naked, and had straight hair standing out in huge masses around their heads. When they saw us, they were the most amazed people in the world. They felt our white skins, and rubbed them, to see if the colour would come off. Everything was bewildering to them. Once we thought that they were getting dangerous, and I presented my revolver at one of them. The man coolly took it by the muzzle, thinking it was a toy meant as a present. As with all the other savages, they were delighted with the mechanical toys we showed them. A Jack-in-the-box would keep a huge chief happy for hours. One of them found an old file, and thought it the greatest treasure in the world.

They left us rather suddenly. It was my fault.

Thinking to amuse them, I started the dynamo with which we lighted the boat, and gave one of them a shock. He yelled, jabbered something to the others, and at once they all sprang overboard and swam ashore. They didn't stop for their canoes, which we were obliged to cut adrift.

At night, a lot of them stood on the beach looking at us. We turned the searchlight on them, and as it swept along the shore, they shrieked and fled. Nor did they stop until they had reached the other end of the island, two miles away.

That particular island was not marked on our chart, nor was it on the latest and best charts that I later consulted at Sydney. Until we went to the place, the people believed that their little speck of an island, hundreds of miles from any other land, was the whole world. They knew nothing of tobacco or gin, which are so dear to other South Sea Islanders. And I have little doubt that there are many other islands hereabouts, where the natives believe themselves the only human beings in existence.

Strangely enough, the natives were never frightened or annoyed when I took photographs. They did not understand what it was all about, and they didn't care. But when I developed the plates and showed them their own pictures, they were delighted. In many places, they had never seen a picture before. There was one old chief whose photograph I took. When I showed him a print, he at once sent messengers to all the islands round, and the people trooped in to see the wonder. I suppose they're still admiring it, if they haven't worn it out with admiration.

We made fast time back to the Solomons. We spent several days beating through the Manning Straits between the islands of Ysabel and Choiseul. The tides ran so strong here that it was all we could do to get through, and in many places we would pass clusters of little islands so slowly that the natives in canoes would surround us, and try to get aboard, but these woolly-headed people were so savage-looking that we did not care to allow them on our deck.

In this strait we passed queer little islands built upon reefs out from the main islands. These little handmade islands were inhabited as thickly as the people could stick on them, by coast natives that had been driven off the larger islands by the bush men coming down to the salt-water villages; and when the coast natives were forced to retreat, there was no place for them to go except to the reefs, so gradually there sprang up a reef-dwelling people who are never allowed to land on the mainland. As the bush boys are afraid of the water, they never attempt to make canoes, and the reef natives control the water so effectively that the bush men dare not even fish in the salt water; and as the reef natives cannot produce enough cocoanuts and fruit to keep them in a variety of foods, the two tribes compromise by allowing their women to come together on the beach, where fish are traded for fruits and nuts. Men never dare come to the market-place where this trading is effected.

During the hurricane a few years ago, several of these islands were destroyed, and for several weeks the inhabitants were paddling among the different islands looking for a safe place to land. Some landed at hostile places and were killed. Others started new villages in uninhabited places; and some were unfortunate enough to land near plantations, and were forced into service. The traders were only too glad to get new recruits without the expense of blackbirding them.

As we passed out of the Manning Straits, we sailed past part of the German Solomons. On clear days we could see patrols of war canoes paddling up and down the coasts of the different islands, and often would pass close to small canoes on fishing trips. We let some of the natives come aboard the *Snark* and traded for the fish they carried. I believe that was one of the most interesting experiences that fell to me in the South Seas — to see these different people in their canoes, and now and then to stop to trade with them or to make photographs.

We dropped anchor for two days at an island north of Guadalcanar, where we knew there was a plantation. We were treated hospitably by Mr. Nichols, the owner of the plantation. And here we discovered another interesting bit of history in regard to Henry, our Polynesian sailor. Some years before, Mr.

Nichols had managed a pearling station on Christmas Island, and Henry was his chief diver. He had found a pearl that was worth a large sum of money, and when he turned it over to Mr. Nichols, he and Nichols were attacked by the other pearl divers and the pearl was stolen. The natives took it to Papeete, Tahiti, where they sold it for half its value. Mr. Nichols asked as a favour that Henry might stay ashore a couple of days with him; and then the two got together like a couple of old soldiers talking over the war.

It was early in the morning that we slid out of the island, on the most perfect day possible. We pushed down the coast of Guadalcanar, the awnings set and the engines running smoothly. Not a bit of wind was stirring. As we three white people were now in an awful state with yaws, and Jack's mysterious sickness was growing worse all the time, it was decided that we should get back to Penduffryn by the time the steamer arrived, so that we could get our wounds doctored. The blue vitriol washes were driving us to distraction, but thus only could we keep the disease from spreading.

Finally, after being away two months, we dropped anchor again at Penduffryn. On going ashore, we found the traders organising to make a trip into the interior of the island, to make moving pictures among the real cannibals. Mr. Harding had been trying for several years to get enough persons together to make this expedition. Here, too, another surprise awaited us. It was Wada, our cook, who had deserted us at Ysabel, now miraculously returned. He seemed to have recovered his reason, so Jack put him once more into the galley of the *Snark*.

The three moving picture men had been sent from Paris by Pathé Frères, famous the world over, to make pictures of the reception of the American fleet in Sydney. Having finished the fleet pictures, it was up to them to bring back some good cinematographic records of the Solomon Islands cannibals. For the first week they were kept busy at Penduffryn, unpacking and setting up their machines. Then all three, not being used to the damp climate, had fallen sick with island fever, and so could not make their inland trip until they had recovered. Meanwhile, their chemicals, which had been thoughtlessly unpacked, rapidly deteriorated in the tropical atmosphere; and there was no place to buy chemicals short of Australia. However, the chemicals used on moving pictures are the same as those used on ordinary films, so I was able to supply sufficient material to last them until they got back to Australia. Harding and Darbishire made preparations for the trip, and were as enthusiastic as children. For when white men exist for years on a plantation without associating with others of their race, they are apt to run wild when they come in contact with a bunch of good fellows.

We went up the Balesuna River six miles to a vil-

Making Copra at "Penduffryn," Solomon Islands

lage, named Charley after a native who had once worked on the Penduffryn plantation. This was the first time a white man had ever set foot in the interior of the island of Guadalcanar. We were gone some time, and secured some very unique and interesting pictures.

By this time, our yaws and Jack's undiagnosed illness were so bad that we were anxiously waiting for the steamer. The doctors of Australia were our only hope. Henry, Tehei, and the two Japs had practically recovered from their ailments, but we white people found life in the Solomons more trying every day. The two Tahitians and Wada were to take charge of the *Snark* and lie at Aola, Guadalcanar, until we could resume the voyage, which we hoped would be before long. On Tuesday, November 3, the steamship *Makambo* dropped anchor at Penduffryn, and lay all day discharging cargo and taking on copra and ivorynuts. That evening, Jack gave a big champagne dinner to the Penduffrynites; then we went aboard, to sail next morning, but the anchor-chain got foul, and we did not get away until Wednesday noon. We went to Neil Island, where we anchored for the night, and then to Aola, where the *Snark* was lying. Thursday noon we steamed out of the Solomons.

It seemed good to be on a large vessel like the *Makambo* after being so long on the *Snark*. She seemed as steady as a house, and I couldn't understand why only a few persons came to meals. Had they been on the tiny *Snark,* doing a corkscrew twist out in the sea, I could have understood readily. The *Makambo* seemed like a very big ship to me after our own boat; but the truth is, she was one of the smallest ships in the South Sea trade. I had a deck-cabin with a fine room-mate — a doctor from New Guinea. Only one thing about him was unpleasant — his delirium tremens. He had them two days. All night he caught snakes and cockroaches; and whenever he missed a large snake, he woke me up to catch it for him. Oh, it was lovely for a sick man! Jack and Mrs. London had the captain's room on the bridge, so that they could keep up with their work.

On Tuesday, November 10, we sighted land, and for the rest of the day steamed off shore. How good it seemed to see real land again — not cocoanut trees that just lifted out of the water, but real land! I felt so good that I had to practise a new profession of mine upon some of the passengers. While at Penduffryn, I had learned much. One day Mr. Harding told us of a black boy of his that could make fire. We asked for a demonstration. The black came up with two pieces of dry driftwood, and in less than one minute had made fire, sufficient to start up a cook-stove. Well, it looked so easy that I bet Jack that I could do it inside half an hour; but when the bet was made, they all told me that it was impossible for a white man to do it. Jack said he had never seen a black do it before, and that he had always regarded it as a myth in story-books. Anyway, I set to work, and at the end of the half-hour I did not even have a smoke started; so I lost the bet. But I was not discouraged. I kept at it, and went among the blacks. They taught me the trick, and still I could not do it; but after working at it for several days, I learned to do it quicker than even the blacks could do it. After that, it was so easy! I brought two pieces of wood along, and on the day we sighted land, I made a bet with one of the passengers that I could make fire, and I won in a walk. Then I bet him ten shillings that he could not do it in half an hour — and of course, I won.

It was on Sunday, November 15, 1908, that we approached Sydney. We got off the heads at ten in the morning, and for two hours steamed up what is supposed to be the finest harbour in the world. Certainly, I saw more big steamers and large full-rigged ships at anchor and in the docks than I ever saw in the New York or the San Francisco harbours. It all seemed American, what of the great sign-boards on every side, and it got more American as we went along. I could hardly restrain my impatience to get ashore.

Australia at last! Not under the exact circumstances we had planned, but Australia at last. Our hearts were very light as the *Makambo's* anchor rumbled down in Sydney Harbor, and we found ourselves once more in civilisation.

CHAPTER XIV

THE END OF THE VOYAGE

At the dock, I got my luggage and Jack's ashore and into a van, while Jack and Mrs. London went on up to the Metropole Hotel. After the luggage had passed the customs, I left it with Nakata, and got in a cab which took me to my rooms in Elizabeth Street. As I passed through the streets of Sydney, I could almost imagine I was in Chicago, with its traffic and hurry, its bustling and crowding. The Sydney street railways seemed to give excellent service. The stores are on the American plan, not the little shops so common in England. I had expected to see a city very much English, but my sober judgment is that Sydney is much more American than otherwise. In my Kansas home, I had always supposed Australia to be a bush country; so it was an agreeable surprise to find it as civilised as the States.

Sydney has nearly three quarters of a million people, and they dress and talk like Americans. There are dozens of good theatres, wherein are often enacted American plays. (" The Girl from the Golden West," and " The Merry Widow," were on at that very time.) About the only thing I could find fault with at first glance was the excessive amount of jewellery worn

The End of the Voyage

by the women, and, as it seemed to me, very old-fashioned jewellery — the kind we had sold over our counters in Independence a dozen years before. But anyway, I had a special grudge against all jewellery, after seeing the South Sea Islanders with their shell finger-rings, their big nose- and ear-rings, and uncouth anklets and bracelets, for, after all, was it not the same instinct for barbaric adornment that actuated the rude natives and the highly decorated women of Australia? or that actuates jewellery-wearing people the world round?

The manager of the moving picture expedition at Penduffryn had given me a letter to his agents, asking that they secure these rooms in Elizabeth Street for me. It was a suite of three well-furnished rooms, cool and comfortable, and heavenly after the weary months at sea, where I had slept in a bunk some inches too short for me. It had been six months since I had slept ashore — at Vila, New Hebrides, was the last place — and it was with difficulty I could persuade the rooms to stand still. I caught myself propping things up so they wouldn't roll off the table or the dresser; and it seemed strange that my bed did not buck and try to pitch me out on the floor.

That evening I dined with the Londons, and then we went to the theatre. Mrs. London still had attacks of island fever. Jack had had the fever in its worst form. But none the less, we enjoyed this evening, which, for all we knew, might be the last we could spend together for a long time; for on the morrow, the Londons were to go into hospital.

They went to the St. Malo Hospital, in Ridge Street, North Sydney. Here the doctors found that Jack was indeed a very sick man. The fever they could subdue, but his mysterious ailment baffled them. Jack's hands grew worse every day.

I went to a doctor, who burnt out my yaws with caustic potash. He advised me to lay up for a time, but I foolishly disregarded his counsel, and walked about the streets of Sydney. As a consequence, my yaws and fever grew more troublesome, and I was forced to go to bed. It all ended by my going into the Sydney Homeopathic Hospital, in Cleveland Street. Here I received competent medical treatment, under which my yaws rapidly healed. But the island fever has a trick of recurring most unexpectedly; and so it was with me. Just as I thought myself cured, another attack of fever would prostrate me.

As I lay in that hospital, I often wondered what would be the next stage of our journey. Where next would the little *Snark* carry her anxious crew? From now on, we would find ourselves among people very much different from the men and women of the South Seas. The world was broad, I reflected; there was no knowing what further adventures might come our way, or what strange things our wanderings would show us. One thing was sure. Greater things lay before us than we had left behind. Much as we had

The End of the Voyage

seen, we still had much to see. And I lay there and planned the various things I would do when I got well to make life on the yacht more comfortable; the appliances I would buy, the ventilators needed, and a hundred and one other things.

And then everything was dashed in a minute. The matron of the hospital brought me a letter from Jack, which contained discouraging news. I learned that he was little better; and that he might be getting much worse. His fever was pretty well conquered, but his other ailment was unrelieved.

This other ailment was a puzzler. "The doctors do not know what it is," ran the letter. "The biggest specialist in Australia in skin-diseases has examined me, and his verdict is that not only in his own experience has he never seen anything like it, but that no line is to be found about it in any of the medical libraries. My hands are getting worse. They are so bad to-day that I cannot close them. What it may lead to, I do not know; but one thing I do know, and that is that I must get back to my own climate. I shall have to give up my voyage around the world. I shall have a captain . . . to bring the *Snark* down to Sydney, where I shall sell her. The steamer does not sail for between three and four weeks from now. I shall want you to go back on said steamer, and run the engines, etc., on the trip down to Sydney . . . I can assure you that I am not a bit happy over all this."

I was dazed. I experienced a sense of deep loss. For an hour I did not know what to do. To abandon the voyage! To sell the yacht! For two years the *Snark* had been home to me; and now I could hardly bear to think of quitting her.

Securing my clothes from the matron, I went to the St. Malo Hospital and enquired for Jack. I was shown up to where he was lying. Mrs. London was in bed in the same room, sick with the fever. She could scarcely speak of the *Snark,* she felt so bad. Jack's hands were certainly in terrible condition. The skin was thick and hard, so that he could hardly close them. And, of course, it was impossible for him to write. He explained to me. There were many chances to see the world, he said, and many voyages; but he had only one pair of hands. Writing was his profession. He could not give it up. Therefore, the voyage of the *Snark* must be abandoned. The doctor had told him that even if he were cured, the affliction might return should he go among the deadly Solomons again. Furthermore, a change of diet was necessary. The things we had aboard the *Snark* were not suited to the needs of a sick man. Fresh fruit and vegetables, and fresh meats — not canned foods and salted meats — were what he must have. So back he was going to California, his native state, where his health had always been perfect.

This was on December 9, 1908. The steamer *Moresby,* on which a captain and myself were to go back to the Solomons after the *Snark,* did not sail till the 31st. With good luck, we ought to be back in Sydney by February 1.

The interval I spent in sightseeing. Australia is a very interesting place, and, as I have said, reminds one very much of the States. In the business section, the streets are extremely narrow, but elsewhere they broaden out. The street-car service is excellent, as is the railway service. On the express trains they have large American engines and the broad-gauge tracks.

The people are very enterprising; but I think the heads of government must all be preachers or missionaries, judging by the strange laws they make. For instance: Unless a person is a guest at a hotel, he is not allowed in on Sunday; if he wishes to see a friend at one of the big hotels, he must stand outside until the friend is called. The street-cars stop during church hours, both in the morning and in the evening, and so do the trains — even the fast express trains stop wherever they happen to be at the time, and do not start up again until church service is over. Few restaurants are open on Sunday; and there are no Sunday papers.

Anything said about Sydney is not complete without a mention of the harbour — the largest and finest in the world. It is miles and miles around, from head to head, and the water is deep enough anywhere for the greatest vessel to float. Almost anywhere, a ship can tie up to the shore. An enormous amount of shipping goes in and out of the heads every day; about a dozen lines run to Europe by way of South Africa and the Suez canal; and there are nearly as many lines to America. A hundred steamers ply from here to the South Seas and Asia. And there are tramp steamers and independent sailing vessels.

When I went to see one ship off for the Gilbert and Ellis Islands, I was amazed to find several old friends. The first officer I had met in Vila, New Hebrides. On a nearby sailing vessel I met old David Wiley, the trader we had visited at Tanna. And Mr. Darbishire was leaving on the steamer for the Gilberts, to take up a government position at Ocean Island. The crew was composed of Gilbert Islanders, the first I had ever seen.

Near the close of December, Jack and Mrs. London came out of hospital. We went to the great Johnson-Burns prize fight; and while it was not much of a fight — too one-sided, for the negro was by far the better man — I would not have missed it for anything. The Australians are worse negro-haters even than Americans, and they hooted Johnson and cheered Burns — which was not at all fair; and I did not grieve much to see their idol beaten until he looked like a piece of raw beefsteak.

Jack wrote up the fight for the American press, and then gave me the original manuscript, which I value highly. My valuation will be justified when I say that, with one exception, I am the only person in the world to whom has been given an original manuscript of Jack London, though more than one has asked.

I had Christmas dinner with Mr. Darbishire at the Hotel Metropole. I ran the risk of arrest by going in on a holiday. Just imagine a Christmas dinner in a tropical climate. I had always associated Christmas with some amount of snow. And we had no cranberries! Christmas without cranberries! But we made up for other deficiencies with the finest of strawberries, and watermelon; which is something my friends in America never do have at this season of the year.

At last we secured our captain — an old man who seemed to know considerable of the South Seas. Jack and Mrs. London and Nakata went over to Hobart, Tasmania, where it was thought the cooler climate would be better for them. Captain Reed and I boarded the *Moresby* and left Sydney at ten o'clock on the evening of January 8. We should have left much earlier, but delayed cargo kept the ship waiting.

There were fourteen first class passengers on board. Two were French missionaries, and the rest traders; these last returning to the islands after a few weeks of drunkenness in Sydney. (They called it their "vacation.") In the morning they all looked alike — like pieces of yellow cheese-cloth. Three or four were down to breakfast, but soon left — one man with his hand rather suspiciously over his mouth.

The old captain who was to navigate the *Snark* back to Sydney seemed a queer old chap. As he read much and talked little, we got along all right. Soon I felt so good that I had to go round tantalising the seasick people. I knew most of the traders. I opened a fresh box of chocolates, and with exaggerated generosity passed them around. One fellow was so ungrateful as to throw a stick at me.

The *Moresby* was a regular old tub — not so large as the *Makambo,* that we had come down in. Built in 1879, she was condemned in 1905, as the underwriters declared the boilers were not safe; but they gave them a coat of paint, and the *Moresby* continued to run. The accommodations were not bad — electric lights, fans, and very good food. The officers and the stewardess were very jolly. While I was sorry to leave Sydney, if only for a few weeks, I found my sorrow somewhat alloyed by the very good time I had aboard the *Moresby.* We were to get into Brisbane on the 11th, and from there it is only nine or ten days to the Solomons.

We got in Brisbane on Monday morning. After finding out that we would not sail until ten o'clock that night, the most of the passengers went up to the city. I got away from the crowd, and walked around to see the place. I think, if I were going to live in Australia, I should choose Brisbane in preference to Sydney. Sydney is a livelier and busier city, and Brisbane is just the opposite: quiet and slow; but it has

A Florida Canoe, Solomons

such broad, pretty green streets, houses like the California bungalows, and such splendid car service, that Sydney is far outshadowed. It is very tropical, too, in Brisbane; the people dress in white, and only get busy toward evening.

His name was Bannerman, and he came aboard here at Brisbane. It was nearly midnight before we cast off and headed down the river. At eight o'clock Bannerman had been deposited with several trunks and suitcases on board by a crowd of noisy young fellows. They had strolled the deck arm-in-arm until we cast off, singing: " For He's a Jolly Good Fellow," and " The King of the Cannibal Islands." And after we had swung away from the wharf, they cried after him to bring them back a few human heads, and they gave him advice as to how to handle the cannibals.

In the cabin the traders had been playing cards all evening, and before turning in I stopped to watch them.

Bannerman was standing behind, telling the traders who he was and where he came from; and from his pretentious talk, he must have been a person of some importance in Brisbane and elsewhere. Now he was going to the islands to rest for awhile at a trading station. He had signed on for a two-year job; as he expressed it, he was tired of civilisation, and of people; he wanted to get to a place where he could rest and take things easy. Of course, he knew that there might be a little trouble with the natives, but that did not bother him.

He went on talking in a loud voice of what he had done and what he could do. The traders paid slight heed to him; poker, as these men played it, took all their attention. Finally, I went to my cabin and turned in. Next morning we were out of sight of land, with a rough head-sea retarding our progress, and sending spray all over the ship. We pitched and rolled as only a South Sea trading steamer can roll. The traders were at their poker game when I went below, but Bannerman was not to be seen, and for several days he failed to show up at the table, and was nearly forgotten until we were half-way to the islands.

The sea was now as smooth as a mill-pond. The after-poop-deck had been covered with an awning. We were gathered on deck one morning after breakfast, the traders telling stories of the islands, when Bannerman came up rather shaky on his legs and joined us. He had nothing to say about himself now. A trader, Swanson by name, had been among the islands for thirty years and had had some bad experiences with the savages. He was relating some trouble he had had with a new bunch of tough recruits, where all the crew on his trading schooner was killed, and he had reached a missionary's house after days without food or water.

"On what island did this happen?" enquired Bannerman.

"On Guadalcanar," replied Swanson; and turning, he seemed to see Bannerman for the first time. "Why, I believe that is where you are to be stationed, isn't it? What part do you go to?"

I could see by the way the traders looked at each other that Swanson was about to "string" this green recruit.

"Why, I will be with Collins Brothers, but —"

"What! Collins Brothers?" and turning to another trader, Swanson asked: "Wasn't that where Jack Dupretz was killed?"

"Yes," the other assured him. "Only a few months ago, too. But I hear it was the bush boys did the work, so it's safe enough there now for nearly a year — you know, they never come down, only once a year."

"But they told me this was the most peaceful place in the islands," began Bannerman.

"Well, I reckon it is 'bout as peaceful as any place in the group; but don't you think for a minute that you can go to sleep anywhere up here with both eyes shut. Of course, you are well armed and have plenty of ammunition?"

"I have a revolver and plenty of cartridges," panted Bannerman.

"That's good; but if I were you I would get several guns and a barrel of ammunition; you can never tell what will happen here."

Now that the traders were tired of poker and had found an easy mark, they started in to throw him into a state of panic.

I had scratched my foot that morning, and careful that the yaws did not get started again in the wound, I was washing the cut every half-hour with permanganate of potash and mercury.

While the traders were busy telling their narrow experiences with the cannibals and about the different fellows who had gone to the roasting pot, I had backed out of the group and was anointing my foot with the antiseptic wash. It was necessary for me to roll up my trousers, exposing the red scars of my yaws. This attracted Bannerman's attention.

"What's the matter with your legs?" he asked.

"Nothing now," I answered. "Have just recovered from a slight dose of yaws."

"What's yaws?"

"You'll know soon enough," a trader spoke up. "Wait a few weeks from now. Everybody down here gets yaws — won't be healthy if you don't. You see, it's just a slight form of leprosy."

"But a man can be careful and not catch it, can't he?" quavered the now thoroughly discomfited Bannerman.

"No use; it catches the new fellows who have not

been 'climatised;' after you have a good dose of it once, you'll be all right."

"But I was told it was such a healthy climate."

The men laughed this remonstrance down.

"Sure it's a healthy climate, and you'll enjoy it as soon as you get over your first attack of yaws or fever. Of course, the fever may hold off the yaws for awhile — depends on which comes first."

This was about the last straw to Bannerman. He drew off to himself to think over his troubles to come.

The traders let him alone for the rest of the day; but they were preparing new tales to tell him. They had intended to help things along that night at dinner, but Bannerman kept to his bunk, although the sea was as smooth as it ever gets, and it was not until lunch next day that they got a chance to make his life more miserable. This was his first appearance at the table.

"That's right; come and fill up on white man's grub while you've got the chance, for two years is a long time to live on native *kai-kai* and tinned foods."

"Well, I can stand it, if you fellows can," answered Bannerman bravely.

"Right you are! Now that's the way I like to hear a man talk. I tell you, men, he will be able to handle the black boys, all right. Don't ever let them see you are afraid of them," he cautioned the other, "or they will sure get you."

Every trader present had a tale of horror to tell. By the time the meal was over, Bannerman was in a state of collapse. The captain sat at the head of the table and said nothing during the meal. After we had finished eating, I went on the bridge with him, and we got to talking over this new trader.

"He's the easiest mark I ever saw," exclaimed the captain. "The men generally have a good time with the new traders each trip, but this fellow seems to take it more seriously than any of the others. If he don't get wise before we reach Tulagi, I'll have to set him right — wouldn't be the square thing to send him ashore in the state he's in."

We got in Tulagi just after dark, and the dozen schooners that always come after their mail and as much liquor as they can hold, were anchored in the bay. Immediately after our anchor was dropped, their passengers swarmed aboard, all heading for the bar. I knew some of them, and I told all of them of the way we had frightened Bannerman, and they determined to help the thing along. So one captain asked three of us and Bannerman to go over to his schooner. As we got alongside, thirty natives just recruited from Malaita gave a yell, and the captain told us to get our guns ready. Poor Bannerman said he had no gun. Then the captain asked him if he had come to the Solomons to commit suicide. "Why, no man ever has one hand off his gun here!" the captain declared. At this, Bannerman wanted to go back to the steamer, but the captain said he thought the blacks were in a good humour now. The blacks were a raw,

The End of the Voyage

savage lot, stark naked, and adorned, as they thought, most becomingly, with big plugs in their ears, and nose-rings, shell anklets and armlets. But it was their bleached woolly hair that made them look most terrible.

We told Bannerman stories, and the captain, innocently as could be, mentioned a big massacre up near Collins Brothers' plantation, where Bannerman was to work. Bannerman told him this identical place was to be his future home; whereupon the captain elaborated a fiction as to three white men who had lost their heads at Collins' place a few weeks before. (As a matter of fact, Collins' plantation is really one of the most peaceful spots in the Solomons.) Bannerman then and there declared that he would go back to Brisbane on the same steamer that had brought him. But by next morning, he informed us that he had decided to try a few months of it. I think the captain of the *Moresby* had seen the joke was too far advanced, and had told him that we were "stringing" him.

Governor Woodford, whose station is at Tulagi, had just bought a steamer in order to keep in touch with the other islands, and the traders were having great fun about it. It was just about the size of the *Snark,* and looked like a tug-boat. It was painted slate colour, the same as the British warships, and had several small guns mounted on deck. All the discipline of a warship was maintained. A native had been trained to blow a bugle; at eight in the morning the flag went up, and at sunset it came down, while the black bugler played his best, and all the schooners followed example in the raising and lowering of flags. At a civilised place, this would seem all right, but at Tulagi it was comical. The traders talked proudly of the "Solomon Island fleet" and were even facetiously arranging for it to follow the American fleet's example and make a trip around the world.

The next morning after our arrival, this little steamer came in from Malaita, where it had been enforcing the law. A white missionary at Ulava had had trouble with the natives, and they had threatened to kill him; so he cleared out in a whale-boat to the governor's, who sent the steamer there. As they steamed up the lagoon they were fired on by the natives, who had old Snyder rifles. When they landed fifty police natives, they were attacked with spears and arrows, several being killed. Then the steamer sent several shells into the village, and killed seven natives. Poor Bannerman's heart throbbed on hearing this — for the captain of the *Moresby* could not say that this was a joke. He left the next morning for his plantation, accompanied by six natives, and I never heard of him again. Anyway, I'll bet that he wished more than once on that trip that he were back in Brisbane.

We found the *Snark* in good condition at Aola. We put fuel and water aboard, stored provisions, and

The End of the Voyage

unfurled the sail; and then we set out on the backward trip to Sydney.

On January 27 we set out. If the weather were favourable, we ought to get into Sydney in about twenty days. That we did not do so was owing to the captain's overcarefulness. We quickly discovered that Captain Reed was a very timid skipper. But let the words I wrote at the time tell the story.

Friday, January 29, 1909.— It's nine o'clock, and Henry and Wada and Tehei are asleep on the deck for'ard. It is Henry's turn at the wheel, but I'm supposed to be on the lookout. It's such a fine night, with nearly a full moon, and so warm and cool at the same time that it seems there could be no more perfect a night than this. A four-knot breeze and an uncommonly quiet sea, and not a cloud.

I am wearing a *lava-lava* only, and feel as if I'd like to discard it — not from heat, but it seems wicked to wear anything such a night as this. Those two mystical islands we have been heading for ever since we left the Solomons are just ahead about five miles — Belonna and Rennell. In an hour we will have to go about on the other tack to keep from cutting off a few hundred feet of Rennell. If I had my way, I should heave-to until morning, then go ashore, for these people are the most primitive in the world — no stranger has ever reported setting foot ashore here, unless a man named Stephens, who, when we left Sydney, was just getting up an expedition to visit these two islands, has been here by now. I am anxious to see Stephens about it.

But what a night! I can't get over it. The sails are just drawing comfortably, and there is no sound except the swish of the water around the bow as we cut through it. It seems as if millions of stars are trying to help the moon in making things lighter; and the Southern Cross is just overhead. Henry has gone to the wheel, and sits gazing at the stars and singing South Sea songs — now of Samoa, now of Hawaii, and now of Tahiti, taking me back to the good times we had in those islands. The *Snark* really needs no steering to-night, but someone must be at the wheel.

And this is my last of the South Seas for perhaps a long time, perhaps forever. Those tall cocoanut trees on Rennell, which we can plainly see, are the last links of the islands. The next trees we see will be of the white man's country. I'm almost sorry to get back, although the last few months among the South Sea islands have played havoc with the crew of the *Snark*. My legs have scars that will never disappear — a sure sign I am not welcomed here. Yes, it is better that we are leaving.

Sunday, January 31, 1909.— Well, I'm contented now, for I've seen the wonderful natives of Rennell, and this is how it happened. Yesterday morning, when I came on deck, I found the *Snark* too close to the shore of Rennell to be comfortable, and it was not a nice shore to see, either, for the whole coast seemed

The End of the Voyage

to be jotted with rocks, and the sides of the island were nearly perpendicular. I called the captain and we went about, having decided it would be better to go around the island from the other end, for the wind was dead ahead the way we were going and we were making more leeway than anything else. So we sailed along the coast all morning, and right after dinner Henry discovered a canoe putting off to us. We backed the head-sails and waited for them. There were two natives in the first canoe, and right after them came a canoe with three natives. The canoes were well-built Polynesian outriggers, and larger than any I've seen, but the natives, big, brown-skinned, long-haired fellows, none under six feet in height, and all muscle, were the strangest yet. Each had a short spear with a long bone point — very fine pieces of work. Two of them had big iron-wood clubs. The largest, most intelligent fellow, whom we found to be the king, was seated in a curious chair, made to fit into the canoe. After they had got aboard, I collected the five spears, two clubs, and the chair together on the skylight, then took a half-tin of biscuits, a few fish-hooks, several strings of beads, four old files, a broken sheath-knife, and the hoop-iron off an old water-cask; and putting my things in a pile next to theirs, offered to trade. They jumped on my things with a whoop. I made some photographs of them. They did not object, but I know they didn't catch on to what I was doing, for they wore a look of wonder during all the time I was photographing them. One thing that particularly struck me was the fine white teeth they all had, and their hair would have made any girl proud.

All the time they were aboard, they were trying to make me understand something that excited them. They would shout and throw their hands in the air, and jump around the deck, frightening the captain nearly into fits. He would have nothing to do with them, but sat on a box with a gun in his hands throughout their stay. But they did not know what a gun was. I am always interested in this kind of people, so tried to talk to them, as did Henry, but it was the first time I've seen him unable to use the few words he knows. The natives would have nothing to do with him or with the others, for they were too near their own colour, but I was white, and therein lay a great mystery. All the time they jabbered and pointed ashore. As near as I could make out, they wanted us to go in and anchor; but I would not get in among such a crowd of savages for anything, though I should have liked to see their women.

They wore only a small loin-cloth, made from the bark of a tree, and no other ornaments. They were tattooed all over with designs that were new to me, and the king had a small ring of shell in his nose.

They finally got so excited that the captain was frightened, and to make them leave he pointed his gun at them. But they only grabbed for it, thinking

Trading Station, Langakauld-Ugi Solomons

The End of the Voyage

it was a present. The iron and brass work interested them the most. They would feel of it and try to break pieces off, and the boats they examined all over, making queer noises at everything they could not understand. Finally the captain got so aroused that he could stand it no longer; he told me to start the engines. While I was getting it ready, five excited faces watched me through the skylight, but as the first gas explosion came, those five excited faces vanished. Our visitors had jumped overboard into their canoes, leaving behind the things I had given them in exchange for their spears and the chair. Also, they had left two strings of porpoise teeth (worth about £2 in the Solomons, where they use them for money). I kept the porpoise teeth, but the other things we wrapped in an old oilskin and threw into one of the boats. I went below and threw on the clutch, and when I came up, I saw the five men fighting over the old iron I had given them. They fought and squabbled, and dropped the biscuits overboard into the water, apparently not recognising their value. One, to whom I had given a stick of tobacco, had tasted it, and finding it nauseous, had thrown it away.

We steamed ten miles into the passage between the two islands; then I stopped the engine and we slowly drifted through. At sunset a canoe followed us for an hour, but we drifted too fast for them, and they gave it up when about five miles from shore. I'll wager it was a tired canoe-load of natives that put in to land last night, for they had to paddle hard against the current.

The captain seems to have a notion in his head that we mustn't make any speed. What his reason is, I don't know.

To-day we are calmed about twenty miles off the islands, and it's hotter than sin. The tar in the deck is melting and bubbling up through the seams, so that a person feels as if walking on molasses, when compelled to walk.

Saturday, February 13, 1909.— The day after we cleared Rennell we were struck by a southeast squall, which settled down into a gale that lasted for four days — the most miserable four days I ever spent on the *Snark*. Rain, wind, and combing seas all the time! The seas were so high that it was no use trying to beat against them, so we just lay and pitched and rolled, with the seas breaking on the deck all the while, until every stitch of our clothing was wet through. Oilcloth and rubbers are useless against such weather. The salt water would get below, in spite of all we could do. We had the skylights and hatches battened down, too. Only the staysail remained set. The fourth day we tried to set a jib, but it was carried away, and the main jib-boom stay broke off, so we were in danger of having the flying-jib smashed, but we made it solid with watch tackles, and when the wind had settled a little we hoisted the mizzen double-reefed, and another jib. We soon had to lower the

The End of the Voyage

jib, and Henry, instead of taking it on deck, lashed it to the jib-boom, and in one night it was torn to threads by the constant plunging into the seas. Now we have only a small storm-jib left to take us into Sydney.

The fifth day, the wind let us, but we still had the heavy seas. On trying to make a little sail, we found the rigging on the mizzen-mast to be in bad condition, and it took all hands a day to repair it. Then the gooseneck on the staysail broke, and as we have no other, we patched it up with ropes. On raising the mainsail, the throat-halyards carried away, and when they were repaired, the peak did the same. A good stiff wind and the heavy seas continued, so we dared not put on full sail, but have been creeping along under double-reefed main and mizzen sails and have not attempted to set the other jib. This old captain is certainly afraid to make sail, for during the last few days we could easily have had reefs out of the sails and the jib set; but as the barometer is still low and he does not like the look of the leaden sky, he will not do it. He and I had a hot argument a few days ago because I wanted more sail put on, and he informed me that he was captain, and for me to tend to my own business — so that is what I am doing. But I know we could be a couple of hundred miles to the south if he would not be so careful. Henry is madder than a hornet; says if we stop anywhere south of Sydney he will go ashore, for he does not want to work for such a timid old man. But he couldn't do what he threatens, for the authorities would not allow a dark-skinned man ashore.

Henry has a fit of grouchiness, so he is snappy and growling all the time. Tehei is so homesick that he can't be cheerful. Wada is cheerful enough; but take it all in all, it is mighty unpleasant company.

Here we are only about three hundred and fifty miles from the Solomons, and we've been out eighteen days, with sixteen hundred miles yet to go, and Wada says there are only provisions enough for ten days more, by economising; and it's not the best of grub, either. Salt-horse, sea biscuit, tinned salmon, beans, rice, and about twelve pounds of tea. More of the captain's folly, for he does not know how to stock a vessel of this kind. At first, when we left the Solomons, I did not know that there was not plenty of provisions, or what poor stuff it was, for I was living on fruit and fish nearly all the time; but now the fruit is gone and the fish that we catch are the deep-water kind, dry and tasteless, and only fit for soup or for eating raw.

I hooked an enormous shark a few days ago, but it broke a large iron hook — a foot long and of $\frac{3}{8}$ inch iron. It was all of sixteen feet long. Tehei says that's the reason that we don't get fair wind — the shark is hoodooing us.

Sunday, February 14, 1909.— Last night we rolled about on the swells of a calm, and we all felt better, for surely by morning the wind would freshen, and it would be a northeast wind, for that's the wind that should be blowing at this time of the year, but up to now it's still calm, and the little wind that is blowing is from the same old direction — southeast, and it's hotter than blazes.

I'm commencing to chafe under so long a spell of hard luck. For awhile I did not care, but to-day I've been looking over old pictures of home, and home postcards. But one thing is certain — I'll be home in less than one year now, probably before another Christmas. I'll leave Australia as soon as I can get away from the *Snark*. A short time in Europe, and then home.

I don't think I've mentioned a dog Mrs. London got off the wrecked *Minota* in the Solomons — a scotch terrier, only a pup when she came aboard, but grown since to full size. All aboard liked to play with her. She would sit and cock her head to one side while a person talked to her. Even the old, grumpy captain liked to play with her. During the heavy weather last week, Peggy could not walk on deck without being thrown from one rail to the other, and I think possibly she was injured internally; and with the lack of fresh food and exercise, she died. Mrs. London will feel bad about it, for she told me to take particular care of Peggy — that she was going to take her back to California. Now it seems as if one of the crew were gone, and the naturally superstitious Kanakas are mumbling that it is a " no good " sign.

This morning I caught a small shark — six feet four inches — but threw him overboard again, for the Kanakas were too lazy to cut him up; and after cutting up one shark, I never want to tackle another. Besides, it's so hot that no one wants to exert himself. No wind, so no one is needed at the wheel. Everyone is stretched on deck, under the boats or in the cockpit.

Sunday, February 21, 1909.— To-day is like last Sunday, only more so. No wind, plenty of sun, and the pitch runs cheerfully down the deck-seams. Last week we had some pretty fair weather that would take us along at six knots for as long as half a day, then the eternal flap, flap of the sails again. One day we made a hundred miles, but from seven to forty was the run on other days. Sharks are getting thick around us — so thick that when we try for other fish, these brutes swallow our bait. Then we have to hook a tackle to them, and heave on deck to get our hook and line back again. One day we caught three while fishing for dolphin. It's interesting to find the miscellaneous assortment of fish in their stomachs. Often, the fish will be still alive. But we get other things besides sharks. Other fish are plentiful, too. Henry speared a five-foot dolphin, and Tehei catches two or three twenty and twenty-five-pound bonita every day with his pearl shell hooks. If we happen to have a little headway at night, flying fish will come aboard, and if I can find them before the Kanakas, I have a good

The End of the Voyage

breakfast. But if they see them first, they pull off their wings and head, and eat them raw. When a bonita is pulled aboard, while it's still flopping on deck, the Kanakas will slice out a few steaks and start eating — very much to the disgust of the captain.

And nearly every night we take on a few passengers — big reef-birds that have flown too far from their homes, and have come aboard to rest. They will get in the life-boat or on the stern-sail, and tuck their heads under their wings and pay no attention to us, unless we try to touch them, and then they will give a sharp peck which is not pleasant, for their long beaks have edges like a saw. In the morning they go away hunting for fish; then at night I think I sometimes recognise the same birds back again.

We are now under regular deep-sea discipline, with watches the same as on a full-rigged ship. This captain is not used to sailing a small vessel like this. Probably he would be all right on a square-rigger, but he makes entirely too much fuss here. Henry and I come on watch at six o'clock until eight; then the captain and Tehei until twelve, midnight; then Henry and I until four; then the captain and Tehei and Wada until eight. Wada goes below to prepare breakfast, and at eight Henry and I go on until noon. Then the captain and Wada until four. Wada takes the wheel from two to four every afternoon, then Henry and I the first dog-watch to six. Now, we do not need a lookout here in the open sea, where there are no steamer routes, and with such a long time on deck at night, one must get some time for sleep, so of course it must be gotten in the daytime; and the consequence is that we don't get any work done on deck, and it's precious little I can do in the engine room.

The most serious thing now is the grub. It's running pretty low. The potatoes and onions are all gone. We have enough rice and beans for about ten days longer, with eleven small tins of meat for variety. The sugar is all gone, and we have enough graham flour for a week. It's so full of weevils that I don't care how soon it goes; but we have enough sea-biscuit (also full of weevils) to last several months; five gallons of molasses, and two hundred cocoanuts, so I guess we won't starve. And then, fish are very plentiful, but I do hope it will not come down to a fish diet, for I'm sick of them already.

Tehei, Henry and Wada take turns about being sick, but the captain makes them stand watch just the same. Tehei is useless when he is the least bit sick. He will sit at the wheel in a daze and cannot possibly steer closer than a point to the course; which makes the captain furious, as he watches the wake zig-zag like a serpent astern. He will let loose a round of adjectives that I have difficulty in understanding; and of course Tehei cannot understand, but he knows he is in some way to blame, so he sits up and looks wildly about to see what is wrong. Captain often curses the weather, the wind, the *Snark,* and everything he can think of that keeps us from getting to Sydney any faster; then Tehei sits up again to see what is wrong this time, for he thinks that of course, whatever it is, it must be his fault.

We are twenty-five days out to-day, and just half-way; the kerosene is nearly finished, so we are sailing along without sidelights.

And the captain swears, the Kanakas growl, Wada feigns sick, and I keep hunting in different lockers hoping to find something to eat.

Sunday, February 28, 1909.— Thirty-three days out to-day, and the grub nearly gone. Our five-gallon can of molasses proved to be only an empty tin, so now we have only weevily hardtack, half-spoiled beans, and tea. We find that soaking the hardtack in tea for fifteen minutes will bring most of the weevils to the top so that they can be skimmed off. But the beans are hopeless. They are eatable, and that's all. The fish have deserted us, too; but as poor as eating is, it will keep us alive for a couple of weeks, if necessary. But we might go into the Clarence river to-morrow, if we do not get a fair wind. If we get the wind, we could make Sydney in three days, but it's a nasty head-wind now, and we are only pitching up and down and not going ahead. Clarence river is twenty miles away, only three hours, if I had gasolene; but what I have will only run about five miles, and that will be needed to take us through the bar.

Since last Sunday we have had a fair wind for two

days, which set us along one hundred miles a day. Then, when everyone had visions of a square meal in Sydney inside of two or three days, the wind shifted and blew a stiff gale for two days. We put double reefs in the mizzen and mainsails, and a single one in the staysail, then put on our oilskins and settled down to two days and nights on deck, with only a few hours' sleep. Everything wet, and no food. Imagine our tempers! Yesterday the sea and wind quieted down, but we still have the head-wind. The sky is clear, however, and the barometer has gone up; so we are hoping.

Tehei is quite surprised at the number of steamers in this world. Every day, from ten to twenty pass us, going all directions, and Tehei wonders where they all come from. A revolving light from a big lighthouse twenty miles ashore also makes him wonder. I'm going to have a good time with him in Sydney.

Friday, March 5, 1909.— At last we are at anchor in Sydney Harbor — thirty-six days from the Solomons. It seems mighty good to get an all night in, and something to eat. Sunday night, we got a stiff squall from the northeast, which settled down into a steady wind, taking us along over one hundred miles a day — the best we had since leaving the islands.

Wednesday evening, at five o'clock, I started the engines just outside the heads, and we steamed up the harbour faster than the harbour regulations allow, for we wanted to catch the doctor before six o'clock and be allowed to land; and we were lucky enough to catch him as he was leaving a steamer just in from China. He passed us all. Then we proceeded up the harbour and anchored in Rose Bay. The customs officers soon came aboard; then a boat-load of reporters. I did not care for reporters, for I was hungry; so Tehei, the captain, and I pulled ashore. The captain took a tram for Sydney, while I hunted up a grocery store, and loaded myself down with provisions — all I could carry. Tehei was supposed to stand by the boat, but I found him, wild-eyed, watching the trains.

Thursday morning we got a tug to take us up the harbour, for my gasolene tanks were so near empty that I was afraid of the engine's stopping before we got up, all of which would have caused us no end of trouble. We anchored at Johnson's Bay, only fifteen minutes from Sydney by ferry. Jack and Mrs. London and Nakata came out in the afternoon and were glad to see everything all right — except Peggy. Mrs. London felt very bad over her dying. I went to Sydney with them, to the Australian Hotel. I took Tehei, who had the time of his life on the ferries and trams and elevators. Nakata took him out for supper, and I ate with Mr. and Mrs. London. I was a strange spectacle, with two months' growth of hair, nearly over my ears. But Jack made me come with them; and if he could stand it, I knew I could. Everyone else was in evening dress, for the Australian is the aristocratic hotel of Australia! And the way I did eat! and Jack piled more and more in front of me. He said he knew how good fresh food tasted after a long sea-trip. Then we took Tehei to the Tivoli Theatre (vaudeville), where he amused the audience by his open appreciation of each turn. But the moving pictures were his greatest delight. On the way home, we got an immense watermelon; and after we got to the *Snark,* he woke Wada and Henry, and the last thing I heard was Tehei telling them about it — and the first thing in the morning.

Now people are coming aboard to look at the *Snark,* and she will soon be sold. I shall remain until another engineer takes hold; then I shall go to Europe and home.

From the time of our arrival in Sydney with the *Snark,* things moved swiftly to their conclusion. When a couple of weeks had gone by, and a new engineer had been secured to take charge of the boat, the day came for me to say good-bye to the genial people with whom I had journeyed for so long. It was hard, but it had to be done. One consolation, however, I had. Some day we should see each other again. The Londons and I were residents of the same country; and the Tahitians would probably be found as long as they lived somewhere in the confines of

Polynesia. And of course, Wada and Nakata I should meet at some future date in Honolulu.

Poor Jack and Mrs. London! They were quite broken-hearted at giving up the cruise. They could speak of nothing else. At the last, after having said good-bye to the *Snark* and to those aboard, I went up to take dinner with the Londons at the Australian Hotel.

We said little in parting. There was nothing to say. Our grief at the break-up of the little *Snark* family was too deep for words. For two years, through savage seas, we had fared together; comforts and discomforts, good luck and bad luck, all had been borne together. And now it was at an end. The cruise of the *Snark* was a thing of the past.

The time came for me to go. We shook hands, promising that we should meet again in America. Then I turned and walked very slowly from the room.

POSTSCRIPT

So ended the cruise of the *Snark*. Henry, the Polynesian sailor, left Sydney on March 30, 1909, for Pago-Pago, Samoa. A week before, Tehei, the Society Islander, had gone with a sailor's bag full of gaudy calico, bound for Bora Bora. Wada San, the Japanese cook, sailed on April 11th for Honolulu.

Martin Johnson left Sydney on March 31st, on the steamer *Asturias,* after an unsuccessful attempt to join the South African expedition of Theodore Roosevelt. His letter did not reach Mr. Roosevelt until after all preparations for the trip had been made, when it was of course too late to consider his application.

The *Asturias* stopped for several days in Melbourne, Adelaide, and Perth, as well as in Hobart, Tasmania. Then it proceeded up through the Indian Ocean to Ceylon; thence through the Arabian Sea to Aden; and from there up the Red Sea and through the Suez Canal to Port Said. At Port Said, Mr. Johnson made another effort to get in communication with the Roosevelt party, but found that they had left three days before. Passing through the Mediterranean to Naples, Mr. Johnson left the *Asturias,* and spent some days viewing Rome, Pompeii, and other interesting historical spots. His next objective was Paris, where he arrived in June. Here he secured a position as an electrician at Luna Park, but not long after, feeling a desire to see his home again, he crossed the channel to England. At Liverpool, early in September, he stowed away on a cattle-boat, and after a trying thirteen days arrived in Boston, the only member of the *Snark* crew to make the complete circuit of the world.

Mr. and Mrs. Jack London took Nakata, the Japanese cabin-boy, and sailed on a tramp steamer for Ecuador, South America. They arrived at their Glen Ellen, California, ranch in June. Mr. London found his native climate most healthful, and though all three were frequently brought down by attacks of fever during the ensuing six months, his mysterious ailment soon disappeared, and his hands regained their normal appearance.

RALPH D. HARRISON.